AF324371

A Mill Village Story

A MILL VILLAGE STORY

Gerald B. Andrews

NewSouth Books

Montgomery

NewSouth Books
105 S. Court Street
Montgomery, AL 36104

Library of Congress Cataloging-in-Publication Data
Names: Andrews, Gerald B., author.
Title: A mill village story : a southern boyhood joyfully remembered / Gerald B. Andrews.
Identifiers: LCCN 2019018014 (print) | LCCN 2019980291 (ebook) | ISBN 9781588383877 (cloth) | ISBN 9781588383884 (ebook)
Subjects: LCSH: Andrews, Gerald B.—Childhood and youth. | Villages—Chattahoochee River Valley. | Mills and mill-work—Chattahoochee River Valley. | Company towns—Chattahoochee River Valley. | Textile industry—Chattahoochee River Valley—History—20th century. | Chattahoochee River Valley—Biography. | Chattahoochee River Valley—History, Local.
Classification: LCC F292.C4 A53 2019 (print) | LCC F292.C4 (ebook) | DDC 976.1/56063092 [B]—dc23
LC record available at https://lccn.loc.gov/2019018014
LC ebook record available at https://lccn.loc.gov/2019980291

Design by Randall Williams

Printed in the United States of America by The Maple Press

The Black Belt, defined by its dark, rich soil, stretches across central Alabama. It was the heart of the cotton belt. It was and is a place of great beauty, of extreme wealth and grinding poverty, of pain and joy. Here we take our stand, listening to the past, looking to the future.

To my family,
which is not just a chapter,
but the whole book.

Contents

A Mill Village Story

The Cotton State—by 1839 Mobile, Alabama, annually shipped 440,000 bales, half of all cotton exports for the entire country.

1

Introduction

Sometimes in my dreams I think the past is coming back to get me, but it never does. It's ironic that, in spite of our concerns about the dangers of the world, we spend most of our lives protecting us from ourselves. However, history isn't a matter of speculation or possibility; it's a product of evidence, proof that *it* happened. No one wants to be astonished by tomorrow; we all want to be prepared when it arrives but rarely are. The border between the past and present can be very permeable, but what history has taken for its own, it will never give back. Yet we shouldn't get too far ahead of ourselves, because reality is relative to what we remember and always grades on a curve. In today's world, honesty is a welcome postcard from yesterday. Fortunately for us, life hides a lot more than it reveals. Yet I have seen too much of the world to give it my full trust. Even so, in invocation, we should praise the non-famous men and women who brought us to this place, many of whom came from small mill villages.

Now, as an introduction, my name is Gerald and I like creativity, exclamation points, children, hugs, dogs, Auburn, and honest people who make me smile. Being raised in the long shadows of a small mill village—a textile company town—in the South, back when cotton was king, was the icing on the cake for one poor little boy—me. Just being born in America was the cake, because it was a child-friendly world. It was a place where I discovered the greatest lesson a wise man will ever learn: The mouth never speaks what the mind and heart doesn't first dictate. At the same time, a mill village in its own way conjures up a rural universe in which to live, as people become immersed in their own unique worlds. We didn't need a burst of asterisks or quotation marks to define who we were—we knew. With

3

the many uncertainties we face today, we're all looking for a safe, magical journey back to the familiar. But it's hard to airbrush the real world. I have spent my life in awe of the privilege of growing up as an ordinary little kid in a hamlet in the hardscrabble back country of the Deep South, where imagination is rarely in a state of purity. A mill village was less a place in time and more a state of mind. Reality is not necessarily what happened but the memory that remains after everything else is forgotten.

So the real world is relative; sometimes it seems to reach beyond human bandwidth. Opportunity was always the Trojan horse we tried to slip through the mill village gates, and by its very nature this wasn't easy. This is the story of that little boy, some of his challenges, and a few of his experiences. A childhood forged in a little Southern backwater put me on the path to become what could perhaps best be described as a Problem Doctor. Hard circumstances presented a sense of early independence and self-reliance, which was a heavy weight to carry, but it served me well. At the same time, it's difficult to write a rough draft of one's life because there are so many nuances.

Along the way, I learned that knowledge is the true currency of life. I was lucky and had a front-row seat on the pictorial history of the iconic West Point companies—West Point Manufacturing Company, West Point Pepperell Inc., and West Point Stevens Inc.—in the extraordinary golden mill village era. One learns that the senses are not always a reliable portal to the real world, but if you lived it, you didn't require an introduction—you were already there. Risk is never a safe route; it's simply a headlong plunge into reality. We were just simple kids, wannabes, lying in wait. I have tried to tell this story in an expressive understatement, its own world in action, as a stretched mill village boy who took a long dive into deep water.

I was born in Fairfax, a small hamlet of 3,500 people, one of several unincorporated little textile towns—Riverview, Fairfax, Langdale, Shawmut, Huguley, Lanett, and West Point—strung together on Highway 29 like beads on a necklace along the winding Chattahoochee River, the border between Alabama and Georgia. Deeply embedded in the mill village fabric was an addiction, gently, comfortably closing around a longing heart like a warm, soft hand but never giving it a painful squeeze. There was a unique safe

Fairfax Mill 1962—Home of Martex Towels.

innocence about it. These tiny enclaves were a special place where we knew that every adult would recognize us, know where we lived and to whom we belonged. There was an abundance of warm hearts and wonderfully lived-in faces. I felt as if our little towns belonged to me and I belonged to them. My alter ego could not have enjoyed it more than I did. With boyish enthusiasm, I sometimes seemed to have slipped by a normal childhood altogether because our special place was a little world within itself. As a kid I woke up every morning with gusto, kissing the floor with my feet and facing the bathroom mirror with a smile.

It's hard to size up a typical mill village in a casual glance or just a few words. They were all different. Each one was as broad as the individuals that lived there, as well managed as the company that ran the mill, as deep as the distinctive tales of the people, and as varied as the many dreams of those searching for them. No one wanted to be culled from the herd; we all wanted to be part of the whole. There were no landed gentry—everyone lived in Company-owned homes, even the plant manager. Neither was it a big book town; in fact, we didn't even have a bookstore or a public library, but the wisdom and quality of the people that lived there made up for it.

Truth was never a depletable resource.

A mill village employee's life resided somewhere between an unwritten contractual clause and a guaranteed rite of passage—with each privilege closely followed by a responsibility to the Company—which in turn looked after your interests. It was a conditional two-way street of mutual respect built upon a foundation over many years of mostly unspoken social agreements. The most uncanny thing about small-town living is how simple it was, although it brims well over the edges of the expected. There was an unfathomable respect between management and employees, as well as for one's neighbors, that was hard to comprehend. In the 21st century, the real world has proven that hope is filled with retrospective expeditions, and no matter what you think you are looking at, it can change before your very eyes. Eventually, the mill villages did. One can't escape reality; it is the most consequential of all of life's lotteries, and our task is to live in it and through it—but few escape the large white spaces and scars it leaves.

No one wanted to be considered ill-mannered or contemptuous. Everyone wanted to narrate their own story of the self and their family, the individual existence in the collective whole. Parents and grandparents patiently waited for the day their children and grandchildren could have a declaration of independence and pursue a better education and life. Everyone had their place and purpose in the whole, like a well-oiled machine, and there were not many assaults on convention. One lived through one's own atmosphere of biography—held up by honesty, integrity, trust, and reputation—buffered by common sentiments of the community. There was a strong church upbringing in a mill village, causing us, for the most part, to look at the world through a moral Protestant lens. We were primarily known for our pared-down normalcy. I'm still set alight by the patiently waiting memories of those experiences.

Each day always strides a step ahead of our druthers and we keep trying to catch up and hold its hand. So it was in the little mill towns in the Chattahoochee Valley. After almost 140 years, we were finally caught on the wrong side of history, as life evolved into an upside-down world through escalating free trade and a hostile takeover. It was something that couldn't be recycled as the last norms fell. What we considered commonplace and accepted no longer conformed to the ordinary. It became hard to acknowledge the obvious until it was knocking on your own front door, bringing complexity, ambiguity, pain, and a pink slip. No one knew how to act because all the accepted rules had changed overnight—very different from the past. It reinforced the thinking that life itself always promises risk. A last-ditch effort was made to rip the Band-Aid off the deeply agonizing Company wound and apply more medication, but everyone realized it was an infecting, fatal injury that couldn't be healed.

Behind every face is a waiting story and each of these tales has an educating moral or lesson to be learned. The real world comes along and we have to separate memories into what we keep and what we throw away through the courage of our convictions. Reading those expressions simply becomes thinking through someone else's mind. This is especially true when trying to form one's thoughts and experiences from life, through the heart and head, into expressive words, sentences, and cerebration on paper. Yesterday is an unmarked page patiently pausing, waiting for interesting comments to fill its blank space. In transformation, it becomes a visual, experiential, and vicarious treatise for others to read, hopefully understand, and assimilate. It's also important to do that while those recollections are still fresh within the touching distance of one's remembrance. Such a transition is particularly significant when a unique way of life has completely disappeared from our culture.

In this effort I present the commentator as the character in his own narrative. Candidly, that's the only way I know how to tell the story: from the personal circumstances of having actually lived it. These tales, in their simplest form, are about normal people, places, and things, and unordinary occurrences. However, you can never disclaim authorship when you have left clear fingerprints. So the reader can inhale and exhale many encounters with me, as we walk through the mill villages, their counterparts, and those related times, places, and events together, discovering that we are never who we think we are. All the time, dream weavers, with shaded eyes, are focused on the world's unfairness. . . but that didn't matter. If people rarely make sense, then why should we expect the world to? Eating one's own words is rarely a nutritious diet.

This is the perspective of a kid who grew up mostly in his grandmother's boarding house in the little mill town of Fairfax in Chambers County—a special place in Alabama where you could copyright your life and many did. Male boarders shared nearly everything: meals, a common bathroom, shower, even beds, but all slept on their own pillow. Sharing a bed in hard times seemed perfectly normal back then, but it was not an ascendant trend. A boarding house probably felt a lot like a tight university dorm, but I was never able to afford to reside in one. Most of us that lived in a mill village had to work and commute to college every day.

There were both heavy challenges and limited opportunities presented. I lost count of the many important things I learned in the thin margins of the Golden Age in the Chattahoochee Valley, back in the irrepressible heart of the 20th Century (1930s—1990s). Some of these life exercises dealt with the importance of people, their close relationships, and many problems, challenges, and situational engagements that will never occur again. It made me realize that throughout my life I have been truly blessed, far beyond that which I deserved.

In our little towns, people knew all about you, where you lived, what you did, your foibles and missteps, and the family you belonged to, but they liked you anyway. One's sensitivity was encumbered by a mélange of influences. Yet we were never overweighed with burdensome instructions; instead, we were taught how to think for ourselves. In many ways, we were as coarse as the thick canvas some of the mills made and as smooth as the truth of a Sunday morning sermon. In more elite circles, we were probably considered the Southern aspirational class with few big heads or narrow minds. Yet we were never uncomfortable in our skin. We were simply the lower-middle-class prodigy of the small towns of America, with little access to the rich or famous, but we knew they were there, offering promise. Me? I was on a constant journey between vanilla milkshakes and virtual reality.

Growing up we never had to worry about the embarrassment of riches. Neither were we inheritors of money, position, power, or a bright guaranteed future. Other than the plant manager's kids, no one else was so blessed either. But we were heirs to opportunity, truth, compassion, faith, and hard work. In America, that was usually enough, and the mill village was always a melting pot of acceptance. When you have little, nothing punishes one more than a vivid imagination unless it motivates you—and for most of us it did. Of course, where character is concerned, honesty is only the tip of the iceberg. You can always overrate life, but it's much more fun when it's understated. Yet every person I ever knew in our little towns struggled in their own way, trying to solve the reaching influence of their existence that was clearly hidden in plain sight. Sometimes I think possibilities dwell more in our imagination than anywhere else, and life's music is much better than it sounds. Yet truth never inoculates us from the hurt and pain that often rides in on the coattails of affection, and I never remember any rainy-day people.

I have studied the world map intensively, but for some reason I couldn't find Utopia. However, our little hamlets were not a bad place to start. Yet, I have never known anyone rich enough to throw away a bar of soap after the raised letters had worn off. I was just ten years old and had nothing of material value when one day I began to understand how blessed I was to have nothing. One of our primary problems was that we were generally inept at self-analysis, although quite competent at most other things. No one wanted to be pilloried by oneself, in our small town way; everybody wanted to be an original.

Early on, there was a distinct, noticeable difference between the fore-runner British mill villages and the Southern version. In England and New England, a village required at least two things: a church and a pub. But in the South, a village required at least six things: five churches and no pubs. The Company was dedicated to improving employee behavior because they owned the town, homes, jobs, property, and mills outright. In the world of commerce and Protestant discipline, a failure of imagination was as bad as a failure of ambition. The Company knew that, periodically, we need to take inventory of our morality and character, because we alone are responsible for the commodification and objectivity of our thoughts, deeds, and responsibilities. They were ahead of the curve. It was an attitude hierarchy that had its own unique philosophy, usually Bible based. You just had to be aware of unwritten rules and the fine print in the unrecorded agreement.

Along the way, when cotton was king, I worked (in over thirty management positions) with every textile mill in the valley and the Company as an itinerate Problem Doctor. I have lived in fourteen different places, in our little towns, and altogether twenty-three total locations around the country. There were so many wonderful, unforgettable individuals, and many are memorialized in this book. Sadly, the vast majority have given up the ghost and departed the realm. There was just something about the unique mind-set, the feel and even smell of small mill villages, and caring, big-hearted, endearing neighbors. They became part of you, almost as if intrinsically imbedded in your DNA, presenting bounteous happy pinch-me moments. I expected nothing from so many people, yet I received everything. Life in a small town could be an irritant, intoxicant, or inspiration; it was pretty much up to you.

With a deep breath, each day we seem to slide further down life's slippery slope into the arms of whatever is waiting with its nuances. That's when we discover we never become bigger than our earned roles in life. However, by our human nature we are weighed by the many paradoxes of vanity and self.

There are two things in particular that I discovered that I will never forget. One is the importance of giving back to that which nurtured us, because the only way to keep the world in balance is for each generation to give back more than it receives. The second thing is to understand that "hope" is not a viable strategy. *A Mill Village Story* in many ways is that tale.

2

A Southern Perspective

I'm sure that the true progress of man's evolution would have distressed Darwin and appalled God, because we perceive our world not how it is, but through many different lenses. I came to believe that Satan's primary job in our little town was not to cause trouble but just keep us distracted from the more important things—and he did a good job. So stay with me as we go back to yesterday. It's getting harder to recall the halcyon days of mill villages as they slip further over the horizon. All the while, life becomes a cabinet of curiosities to be explored, examined, and enjoyed. Its lineage starts at the beginning and goes all the way to the end, wherever that may lead.

In younger days, the conversation in one's head seems to veer toward the mundane, away from the abstract, philosophical, political, and theological. That still enables it to touch a lot of bases and is how we were designed by nature, regardless of where we live. We have to learn to sort it out. So it was, growing up in our little towns. We were normal and had come to accept our prepackaged realities, fueled by the misdirection of judging others more harshly than we did ourselves. The problem was the discontinuity; the answer was the continuum. Kids, by their very nature, are impressionable and imitate what they see and come to feel. Fortunately, we came to respect our elders and were blessed by examples of honesty, hard work, education, good manners, and personal initiative. Some things just cured themselves, while we learned to wrestle with others. For those willing to put in the effort to go a few extra miles, the roads were rarely crowded and there were no traffic jams. Of course, we could each have reflected upon our own short-comings and marginality, but no one wanted to do that. We each have been given a set of crayons and must color in our own picture, but staying within the lines is optional. That is left up to you and me.

The big hearts in our small hamlets liked to warmly cocoon the struggling child and family, and they did. Love is a tale as old as time itself. Shakespeare said that "all the world's a stage," and Southern Reality tends to behave that way. Life looks like a painted backdrop awaiting everyone's personal performance. All the while, the actions of the participants in their own plays, and the natural forces that inhabit the proscenium, establish the rapid pace to be pursued. We can pretend to follow it—or not. What we want to do is value the homespun truths and character appraisals that have made America great. My family, with all its common and unique characteristics, was always very serious and tightly knit, but it was also warm and close—about the same as everyone else's. Yet, in its own way, it was open-minded and sharply drawn; there was little wasted motion (or anything else). A large empty cardboard appliance box was one of the best toys I ever received.

When we begin to squeeze and compress integrity, we start to cross the line of consent, acting as if no defined path ever existed. Mill village honesty was not complicated; it was fundamentally about coloring between the lines. In my formative years, I not only experienced what was in reality's spicy sausage but also had a ringside seat to watch how it was made. No one wants to be confined to a mind too small to hold their own choices, because we learn in the first grade that we are in trouble when our eraser is used up before our pencil. To truly be free, we must set aside our preconceptions and let the real world play loosely with our imagination. As we grew up, we tried to place our personal goals in quotations marks to indicate not only their reach but also their tentativeness. Now, for me, one of my favorite things is thoroughly self-rehearsed spontaneity, because we never wanted to be anything but significant as kids.

Yet I'm just an ordinary person, with all the inherent human weaknesses left intact. The true beauty in most of these mill village tales is that as soon as you have completed the beginning of one, you are also nearing its end. They are compressed, short enough that you don't need to take notes and you can still remember the point being made. One prays they don't have less to say than they try to profess. Of course, the ultimate goal is for the whole to deliver more than the sum of its parts, with the commentary clear enough to be easily paraphrased by the reader.

Silence is the real essence of noise. As long as I can remember, I wanted to be an architect. I had creative ideas about how to design and build uniquely constructed, low-cost homes for people who couldn't afford one of their own in America and abroad. Surprisingly, over the years no one has used my transitional building concepts. I have been asked many times, "What happened to that dream?" The answer is simple: "Life happened." When I was a mid-teen, my dad went bankrupt in business, through no fault of his own, and I had to change the direction of my future to survive. So I became an industrial engineer and Problem Doctor, turning my critical thinking and creativity toward changing industry and the community. I let architectural silence become the essence of noise in a different direction. My personal druthers had a surprisingly short-term residency in my imagination because the truth of failure was breathing hotly down my neck. However, I still miss those little boy dreams. Yet, did you realize that if you are conventional and obey all the rules, and everything goes your way, you miss most of the fun and excitement of mistakes?

When Cotton Was King is a snapshot of compressed experiences glimpsed over the shoulder. They, in turn, help us become more like the people we pretend to be and, maybe more importantly, what we truly want to be. Sometimes in small towns you hear and learn more than you really want to know, but you mostly keep it to yourself.

After coming through a devastating economic depression, our world in the early 1940s was still wobbly—spinning, as the elders of the Homo sapiens had gone crazy once again and rashly started another devastating world war. They simply called this one "Number Two," as if there would be more coming. It left everyone shaken and stirred but not yet poured. Almost every man—and most women—in the village seemed to be either off in the military fighting or working in the mill. Each person had to earn his or her own keep. There were few handouts but always handups for the elderly, sick, and truly in need. I used to wonder, as a little boy, under so many weighty circumstances, and all the world's problems, how could I ever get ahead and amount to something?

I quickly discovered that the decisions and choices I made compared to those made by everyone else would eventually determine my "something." Competition would always be the name of the game. When you are alone at fifteen, you must first cultivate the vision you want to see. It's important to be able to dream, but you must allow other people to join you in your dream. That's where creative leadership enters the picture. There would also be some risk involved. Did I have the heart and courage for that? As a mid-teenager, I had to learn the hard way how to make the right decisions; I had no one to make them for me. So I took all my burdens and carried them with me every day the best I could, as did we all. We each wanted to get ahead in hard times, and many in our tiny backwater did. Sadly, many more didn't. I was not bashful or risk averse and probably took more chances than necessary. Being human, and life being what it was at the time, had a peculiar way of dragging the heart along with it.

Through great effort, it became a lifetime of sweet songs, as I learned to harmonize my soft mill village tenor with life's earthy music. Of course, the future is not all that simple or predictable. Neither is it fair or equitable, because we try to mythologize ourselves and, in doing so, concede reality in our own minds. This is probably human nature in a promotional (if not protective) mode. Two of my favorite things about the past were that Moses didn't have to get the Ten Commandments approved by Congress and that there were not more than ten.

To describe a mill town as "middle class" might be the correct algorithmic view, but "earthy" would probably suit the actuality much better. Abundance was not a word heard very often in our habitat, but there was always enough, with a promise of more to come. My little enclave was an unpretentious place where people could make a living and have job security while educating and raising their children in a welcoming environment. People went to work in the factory when they were 16–18 years old and worked until they retired at 65 or 70. One of the biggest events of the year was the employee inductions into the 50-Year Club, which was for those that had worked for the Company continuously for five decades. They numbered in the multiple hundreds. I knew so many of them.

That was an earmarked time that is rapidly receding in the rearview mirror. In my younger days I always felt as ready as a newly sharpened No.

2 pencil in the hand of a first-grade student with a fresh Coca-Cola writing pad. They gave us that on the first day of school every year, along with a free Coke. When you have very little, it's something you remember, because that small thing was one of the beginning highlights of each school year. It still symbolizes how I felt in grammar school and what I learned there: That you are primarily responsible for three things in life—the thoughts you think, the decisions you make, and the actions you take. However, be alert. The worst thing you can do is change all the locks on the doors of your life and then lose the keys. At the same time, residing in reality without some degree of comedy is like someone traveling through each day without a soulmate: We still feel incomplete, whether we need one or not.

Growing up in a defined manufacturing environment, I never had a flicker of insecurity. We seemingly lived in high cotton. Even kindergarten was great fun, and I enjoyed being a member of the loose-front-teeth club. Honesty became all the more potent because it was completely inescapable. How can one ever be considered an upright, conscientious man if he doesn't tell the truth? In earlier generations, authentic values were known, understood, and appreciated, but at times they were unknowable and even inexplicable. Back then, we were fully under the influence of the gospels, because everyone wanted to be needed and needed to be wanted. Today, straw men of all dominions stride over the landscape, and regardless of where you shoot an arrow, it's easy to hit one.

One day, when I was about ten years old, I realized that the word "impossible" was also "I'm possible." It changed everything!

3

A&WP Railroad

West Point, Georgia, and Lanett, Alabama, eventually became home to Fort Tyler and the many West Point companies. They are nestled side by side on the banks of the beautiful Chattahoochee River, which helps define the state line. Before the white man came, it was Creek Indian territory and the home of a nearby Creek village. The towns started out in the early 1800s as trading posts in the Indian territories that were being taken over by the government and inhabited by homesteaders. Alabama was settled through land lotteries, like much of Georgia. Gradually, a few log cabins were built and crops were planted in the fertile soil. Later, like the rest of the South, Alabama and the fruitful Chattahoochee Valley became a world center for cotton production and export, shipping to textile factories in both the northern states and Europe.

We would all like to be a thinker of remarkable range and deep insight, where an honest future is always on the verge, accompanied closely by expectant and palatable reality. In the 1800s, our American values were beginning to smell like spiritual exhaustion—always on the threshold, but of exactly what was unclear. Reason gratifies a conservative mind, except when it doesn't, which is usually when greed and self get in the way. It seems to always be the unchanging bitter core hiding beneath a shallow surface of conscience in transition. So in Creek country, government and land-hungry settlers dismantled the Creek Indian way of life (and not always legally). They were only interested in making room for themselves and expanding American civilization westward in the Chattahoochee River Valley.

The Creeks and other Indian tribes may have been forcibly moved west, but they left their mark on the area in many ways, never to be forgotten.

One was through their beautiful, romanticized names that phonetically roll off the tongue. Just a few of those, representing people, places, and things in the geographical area, are Cusseta, Talladega, Chattahoochee, Tallapoosa, Loachapoka, Opelika, Osanippa, Tallassee, Tuskegee, Chawalka, Notasulga, and Coosa.

Then, in 1866, a year after the Civil War, one of the earliest Southern textile centers was founded in what became Langdale and Riverview. Over the ensuing years, the communities of Lanett, Shawmut, Fairfax, and Huguley were formed around large textile plants and offices, added to complement manufacturing in the other towns. West Point was where the corporate administrative management and major retailers eventually settled—on the river.

The rapid southward and westward expansion of America in the early to mid-1800s was as dependent on railroads as it was on the dutifully stitched and waxed covers of Conestoga wagons. So it should not be surprising to anyone that the fabrics produced by these early companies were heavy canvas for tentage, work apparel, ship sails, and coverings for those wagons heading west. Railroads had great economic power, and the life or death of little towns often depended upon the destination of the rails and the small and large cities they eventually passed through. This was also the early story of West Point and Lanett. The most expedient route between Mobile (ocean shipping, cotton exports, and the Gulf Coast) and points north and east passed through Montgomery, Alabama (the eventual capital of the Confederacy). It continued on north directly through West Point to Atlanta, the growing economic hub of the Southeast. The eastern end of the Atlanta & West Point Railroad began in the Atlanta area and the emerging town there was called East Point. The western terminus of the A&WP was at the Alabama state line and its town was called West Point.

In the early 1800s there were no basic federal laws governing interstate commerce and the standardization of rail gauges, the width between the rails. Most railroads at that time were small independent corporations, so each intentionally set a different gauge or rail width where they intersected another company's rail line. Companies didn't want anyone else to use their railroads without paying them, so every company acted accordingly. When they arrived at the end of a privately owned railroad, all the freight

Loading cotton in 1968 at Central Cotton Warehouse on A&WP in Fairfax for other West Point Manufacturing Company Mills.

had to be offloaded from one company line onto the freight cars of the other. They made sure, by design, that the intersecting set of rails would be narrower or wider than their own. Small towns gradually built up around these off-loading intersection and transition points, eventually becoming commercial centers. So this became the initiator of growth, the lifeblood of West Point and Lanett. Later, after the Civil War, to improve economics and efficiency, the Federal Government standardized the gauge of railroads as well as highways.

If you think you have heard it all before, then you weren't listening. Folklore has always been captivating—American, Southern, European, or otherwise—because you learn so much about the early thinking of one's predecessors. It was always interesting (and to me humorous) that the actual width of the railroad tracks goes all the way back to the days of antiquity. They are actually based on the width of a mule or horse's behind. The modern highway is based on the width of two horse's behinds working in tandem to pull a wagon or an Egyptian or Roman chariot. Then automobiles, trains, and trucks were designed to fit the roads and rails that existed. Things like that fascinate me because, in our contemporary perspective, we think we are more scientific, modern, and technologically innovative than our ancestors were thousands of years ago. But, in reality, most of man's progress is simply based on the width of a horse's behind. In retrospect, I think this same attitude has also carried over to the election of our self-serving politicians.

I incubated this book in my mind for many years before it hatched. I am as interested as you in how it develops through its thoughts and words, its earliest beginning. It doesn't matter how young you are, or how old you may be; it doesn't matter if you are a man or a woman, rich or poor, successful or a failure, black or white, or any other superficial distinction—this story is for you. As a boy, I often wished I had more lyric imagination to carry me through the day, but I realized back then that I was just ordinary folk imbedded in dire circumstances, wanting to get ahead, pretty much like everyone else in our little towns.

Life is actually a big deal, an expanse of luminous things, and like the early railroads, rapidly transitioning technology. Reality is quite wide but very shallow; so wide that it's hard to go from one side to the other, but so shallow you can always touch bottom. Sometimes I think Homo sapiens are careless and don't pay enough attention to what we do because we believe we will be vindicated by history. Our actual deeds injure a lot of historical sensibilities that are emotionally shaded and tightly rationed, even in a mill village. It was a special place where you felt safe in developing a warm relationship with friends and neighbors even as the railroads brought the future to our front gate.

I think we all need a more robust literary diet than we are getting to spur on our thinking; one that stretches our minds about horses, railroads, highways, people, reality, one-industry towns, and the arc of the world we live in. That actuality forms us into who and what we become, then guides us through the changing attitudes and aspirations shaping our reality. It is not easy to live such a focused and inner-directed life. As a kid, I never remember being shielded from the discomforting realities of grown-ups, and I was taught with seriousness about the moral gravity of light with an old-fashioned mien. I came to believe that children are far more sophisticated than we give them credit for; they quickly learn right from wrong and are able to generalize from their experiences. The A&WP made its contribution to the cause as it carried change, people, and cotton up and down the valley towns to the mills and distant venues.

Back in those early days, every family seemed to struggle in some way to make its path through life. Yet it was a time, by many measures, in which little happened at all. In many ways, it was just the sameness of one day following another. We were all taught that the simplicity of existence would help rob the bad moments of their sting if we would light candles rather than stand around and curse the darkness. I think most people tried and it gave us a certain illumination, brightness, and warm feeling in our shadowiness.

Today we seem to have lost much of this authenticity in our transition to the future. Perhaps part of it was what the A&WP eventually brought to our little mill villages. Some historians call it civilization; I just call it life. The day the mills closed, we lost much of that togetherness, leadership, honesty, wisdom, and authenticity. I have tried to distill the essence of some of these experiences into these pages. Each time I reach back to a particular engagement, I try to remember the more significant parts of the activities from the formative days of my youth. Even so, I'm aware that I'm referencing just a small fraction of the life that passed through our extended hamlets during those times. But how did they evolve and become what they did? As we walk back through these times together, let's see if we can find whatever it was that got away, that came home to roost on the A&WP.

4

The Civil War

Normally I don't like to look back, because that's not the direction we are headed, although to maintain sanity it's not a bad idea to benchmark your progress and remember where you came from. Truth is a distinctive particularity to both the giver and receiver. Having lived through almost unbearably hard times during the Civil War, the South learned to embrace the unknown future with fifty shades of trepidation. This was due to circumstances and havoc in the geographical region that couldn't have gotten much worse. Perhaps the hardest thing people had to do, on both sides of the Mason-Dixon Line—other than ask for forgiveness—was to pray for patience. There is one important lesson the erudite person learns: History is not always just about what happened, but how we look at what happened.

We find in exploration of our soul that the real facts and favored myths of our genealogy are connected and shared in many ways—it's called Southern Reality. Sometimes it's in kaleidoscopic shards that won't easily fit together. As we look back, the picture would not be the same without the sentimental twilight because one's life has a mood-defining preference, and its sensibility of events that occur do not carry equal weight in a traditional sense—or as we might prefer. When things happen, even in stark retrospect, the prevailing conflicts that exist do not rule each other out. This only confirms that both exist. So it was in the Civil War.

This epic conflict was a critical and consequential segment of American history, speaking loud, clearly, and memorably, weighed by the principles of pain, suffering, and uncertainty. In that difficult era, reasoning was the way we tried to think our way through the crazy world, trying to reconcile the singularity of our own vision with the chaotic heterogeneity of the whole

The official Confederate States of America seal, featuring George Washington.

landscape we faced. Simplicity and complexity were both high values, and we couldn't afford to get them mixed up. It became a confrontation of two parties of unequal equals in an insular world. If only we had embraced the magnifying lens of hindsight!

By the end of the American Great War in 1865, the Southland had endured deep devastation, with epic damage inflicted on heart, soul, home, and physical presence. It was an indelible experience never endured before or since, a vanquished land in extremis. In a post-mortem of a failed situation, it was hard to be both the corpse and the coroner. In spite of deep mourning, everyone, both white and black, was looking for traction, opportunity, and a way forward. It was not a time of concern about life optimization but one of simply survival. Fortunately, the outward performance was usually supported by an inner faith and deep wisdom that sustained their normalcy. Their character became a dependable constant. The truly important question was not what the best answer would be to make life more bearable for everyone, but who would actually step forward in leadership to decide the best answers.

There were situations in the ensuing years that Charles Dickens would instantly have recognized and grasped. It was a time when even the best days seemed ashen, and life couldn't easily be reformulated. The script had been written. There was as much complexity as one could handle, so there was no need for impersonations; no one was acting. Hard times descended on the South for real, with little flavor to enjoy—other than the bitter. I think in the end the best people for playing Southerners in that heartfelt drama were Southerners themselves, and they never forgot. History in authenticity often becomes indistinguishable from fable or fantasy, as we take liberties in writing it after the fact. But there was one thing for sure: those hard times were real.

During those trying years, the South had invested everything it had in its historical reality, and it only resulted in suffering. Everyone—black and white—had been in a tragic, painful economic free fall. In 1865 and 1866, disrupted, broken families and entire communities were treading water, trying to endure. The secret to survival, then and now, is that when life gets tough, you just have to get tougher. Southerners endured, and along the way learned to be very hardy people. They developed a learned ability to retreat into a hard, calculated counterfeit calm. It was difficult, if not impossible, to brilliantly exploit a tragedy. At best, one just tried to survive, but simply trying stirred up a lot of dust.

There are always consequences to being on the losing side of any conflict; you draw the short straw. Slaves, even when set free, were caught in the crosshairs of this volatile situation. It was an immersive existence with weighty context and a human face for an almost abstract issue that couldn't be ignored. There was still a complex shading of class and race in America to which we needed to pay more attention. The freed slaves had to live and wrestle with the underside of political power. There was a distinct need for a bridge across the human divide that never got built, and we didn't become fully self-reflective to everyone's needs. Freedom loses its glow when one is still indentured to the real world and share-crop farming. Yet, there was a deep desire and reaching need to ignore what had happened, but it wouldn't easily go away. It had to be lived out in real time, as truth was rooted in historical imbalance, and there was always a firmly-rooted sense of place. There was also the need for a tour of the togetherness writ large, which never came to pass. On the plus side, few things are ever as strong and sturdy as one's dreams.

After the Civil War, the white Southerner again had the opportunities but had a difficult time seeing them—having economic leverage and being able to use it. On the other side, the black Southerner, now being free, could see all the opportunities he had been wanting but was not able to use them for many reasons. One pain and anguish was just replaced by another.

I have great admiration for those who were confronted with a fear of the unknown, both white and black. They were only able to live life by the hardest, day by day in the given moment. The real world presented them with a long day into night, regardless of past loyalty. Struggling to survive, they could only speak to the specificity of their destination, realizing it had to be traveled together. Nostalgia became a waste of time, an indulgence they could ill afford. Transience became the way of life, and resilience was the ultimate legacy they left to their children. History in the Chattahoochee Valley didn't age well, but it did greatly improve. Telling it all would perhaps be too much like hanging out the personal laundry to dry in the front yard for everyone to see. We don't have a clue what it's like to be another person or to stand in their shoes. We can only find comfort in our own head and see things as they appear through our own eyes. There is a great strength that comes from community and a strong binding grace in gratitude. It was an experience that could scoop the ideals and confidence from a man's soul quicker than a black cat crossing one's path on Halloween.

The last fort battle of the Civil War occurred on Easter Sunday in April 1865 at Fort Tyler in West Point, Georgia, and Lanett, Alabama. That particular day, you could hear the murmur of cultural history in the making. It may sound a little commonplace, even ordinary, but it wasn't. Many were injured and died that day for no reason at all. Because of poor communications, it became an irony of war that this last battle was fought a week after Confederate General Robert E. Lee had already surrendered at Appomattox.

With the cruel conflict behind them, everyone was ready to move on.

Reenactment of last fort battle of the Civil War at Fort Tyler, which straddles Lanett, Alabama, and West Point, Georgia.

The Civil War needs no editorial comments; it was ugly enough. The home of Dr. Asa W. Griggs, the most beautiful house in the area, was directly in front of Fort Tyler and was an important part of that epic Easter Sunday battle. It was also prominent for several weeks after, as it became a temporary hospital for badly injured Confederate and Union troops. The contentious combatants were laid side by side on the floor like mixed grey and blue cordwood. The back concrete wall facing the fort still shows the pockmarks and devastation of the day-long battle. Even the rocks and railroad spike marks were left in the wall, noting when the Confederates eventually ran out of ammunition and finally surrendered.

Harsh reality was impatiently waiting on the front doorsteps that eventful day in 1865. It seemed to co-opt more of our progenitors' headspace than they had available, often causing a deficit in thinking on their road to tomorrow. Yet, we are still haunted by the revenge of history and are bound to repeat it if we don't learn from it. We should never expect life to be perfect; we must be realistic. Dr. Martin Luther King Jr. probably said it best of all: "God had only one child on Earth that never sinned, but he never had a single one that didn't suffer."

Many men on both sides of the Fort Tyler conflict were injured and killed. A large number of Union survivors required long-term care and were soon moved into various homes belonging to Southerners in the area. Some remained in these homes three, six, and nine months before they were able to travel back north. The interesting thing was that they were lovingly and compassionately cared for by the families that had lost loved ones fighting against them in that terrible war. Once those soldiers were able to go back north, they had become personally attached to the families that had taken care of them. When they returned home, a number of them packed up their own families and brought them back to the Chattahoochee Valley to live. It always amazed me that some of the prominent progenitors of families in the West Point, Lanett, Valley, Chambers, Troup, and Harris counties today were former Yankees. This is a true and almost unbelievable story that could only happen in America.

After the Civil War, with so many injuries and deaths, exhausted and broken soldiers returned to homes and families in despair. Southern women, in their earthy vitality and streaming immediacy, became the icons of strength and tenacity, holding heart and hearth together.

The on-site Fort Tyler/Georgia Historical Commission marker reads as follows:

> 125 yards northwest, at the crest of the hill, stood Fort Tyler—last Confederate fort to fall in War Between the States. Fort Tyler was of earthwork construction, 35 yards square, surrounded by a ditch 12 feet wide and 10 feet deep, and enclosed by a wooden abatis. The fort was erected to protect important railroad and wagon bridges across the Chattahoochee River east of the point.
>
> Early Easter Sunday morning, April 16, 1865, the garrison of 265 Confederates—remnants of Pointe Coupee, Louisiana, and Waties Island, South Carolina, batteries—aided by boys and convalescent Confederate soldiers (from a Confederate Military Hospital in West Point) withstood the attack of 3,500 Federals before capitulating late in the afternoon (after running out of ammunition). Confederate forces were commanded by

General R. C. Tyler; Colonel H. Fannin; Captains Gonzalez, Trepaner, and Webb; and Lieutenants Montgomery and McFarland. Units of 2nd and 4th Indiana, 7th Kentucky, and 31st Wisconsin, commanded by Colonel O.H. LaGrange, formed part of the Federal forces.

Stone house of Dr. A. W. Griggs, Confederate Surgeon, built in 1858 (remodeled in 1951) stands 40 feet N.W., although hit repeatedly by cannon fire from both forces, original walls are intact. Here Mrs. Griggs and other West Point women gave aid and shelter to wounded of both armies after battle."

At that almost untenable time of reconciliation, a small group of optimistic businessmen in West Point, Georgia, along with local planters from nearby Chambers County, Alabama, and Harris County, Georgia, were looking forward to a better future in this disheartened and depressed region. These two groups of far-sighted men, with the same basic idea, had what evolved into the same strategic plan: to harness the momentum of the Chattahoochee River to power new textile mills in Langdale and Riverview, a relatively fresh idea in the Deep South. They would use the cotton that was grown in their own backyard. Their vision was engaged in the fall of 1865, and on August 1, 1866, the new cornerstones were laid for both mills with great ceremony, fanfare, hope, and prayer.

The mills were only a few short miles apart. So these two groups of visionaries, in a rural farming area, founded the Chattahoochee Manufacturing Company and the Alabama-Georgia Manufacturing Company in what was to become the towns of Langdale and Riverview, Alabama. They were the first of seven later connected unincorporated textile mill villages in the area with multiple corporate manufacturing plants. This vision would grow to eventually reach over 42,000 employees in the late 1980s, with nearly 10,000 of those jobs located in the Greater Chattahoochee Valley. Through exceptional management, West Point Manufacturing Company became an outsized historical textile shadow cast over the region and later the nation. The textile mills were the defining narrative in the industrial development of the area.

The Lanier and Huguley families were dominating forces in the birth,

Above, Riverdale Mill (River View), and below, Langdale Mill (Langdale), the first two mills built on the Chattahoochee River, by a predecessor of West Point Manufacturing Company, in August 1866.

growth, and rapid development of the textile industry in the South. These manufacturing plants grew into an extensive corporation that became the largest publicly owned textile organization in North America: West Point (Pepperell) Stevens, Inc. (The Pepperell operation originated in 1815 in Biddeford, Maine, and Stevens was founded in 1813 in Andover, Massachusetts.)

It evolved into a special place that tens of thousands of people enjoyed and called home for many decades. For almost 140 years, it existed in several incarnations, until, for many reasons, it came to an end and disappeared. One learns that history does not always bend and yield to our desires or prayers. Nor is it a placeholder designed to maintain the status-quo while we comfortably sit on the sidelines and wait. In the fraught history after that devastating war, many Southerners paid rent to live on the same land they had once owned. They learned the hard way that history moves on with or without us. Those many small towns and cities located deep in our Southern history have become an important part of our heritage and legacy and have helped mold many of us into who we are. It is always difficult to find comforting answers in the wreckage of a way of life that has already disappeared. This is especially true in the mill villages of the historic Chattahoochee Valley. There was always a kind of ambiguity waiting in conflict for each unmoored day, until reality came home with the chickens to roost and all the mills eventually closed. So often, over the decades, our humble villages were anxiously marking time. We dreaded the unknown prospects of the everyday that were lurking on the calendar.

Although we may breathe a little easier in the twilight of our ordinariness—as we did after the Civil War—our nation has once again come down with a disturbing case of identity crisis. We are not sure who we are, nor are we certain who we want to be. Perhaps we are even less certain of where we want to go. It has become a rather different predicament from days of yore, when we were certain of our identity and direction. Wisdom has disappeared off the screen, maybe because we refuse to follow its path. Yet the future is pregnant with possibility, and we just have to help bring about its birth.

I have an inclination to stay with the truth but still like to feed the independent mythology of yesterday's South. Southerners have a tendency to navel-gaze when nobody's looking, always trying to figure out who we

The 1856 Dr. Asa W. Griggs House (Griggs, Simmons, Andrews, Slavich House) in Lanett, Alabama, was prominent in the last fort battle of the Civil War, as Fort Tyler was literally in the back yard.

really are—quite different from Yankees, who more confidently think they know who they are, even when they don't have an inkling. We each tend to scatter our bread crumbs of shadowy clues along the trail we follow and then fail to go back and pick them up. In turn, we write our own personal parable about the reality we believe. At the same time, Southern Reality is a place as well as a state of mind, and it's not always what we perceive but what it is. Perhaps some of the reasons Southerners never understood Yankees is they talk funny and have thirty-seven religions and only two good dipping sauces.

One eventful day many years later, the Dr. Asa W. Griggs house became our family residence, with all its history and sad remembrances. Life in all its many contradictions has pretty much evolved into a high-calorie junk food buffet where, without question, we accept whatever is placed on the plate in front of us. A significant point that most people overlook is that Fort Tyler is not in West Point, Georgia; it's actually in Lanett, Alabama. The Alabama/Georgia state line legally runs down the driveway of the Griggs home, making the house and Fort Tyler in Lanett and the adjacent vacant property in West Point. We lived there for a number of years.

The funny thing was that for 100 years—at least since the beginning of U.S. Postal home delivery—the West Point Post Office had historically delivered mail to the Lanett address. It was just one of the many idiosyncratic peculiarities of adjacent mill villages in small town America, where everybody knew one another. Our house was two blocks from the West Point Post Office and one and a half miles from the one in Lanett, so it was a small town convenience for all concerned. I used to get a lot of peculiar and suspicious identity questions traveling around the U.S. and (especially) in other countries. When someone saw my Alabama driver's license with an address in West Point, Georgia, the prolonged questions began. They discontinued that postal home delivery practice a few years after we moved there, and I added a new Lanett address to my Alabama driver's license, passport, and peace of mind.

When we lived in the "Fort Tyler house," directly across the street was the ten-room, 120-year-old wood frame Hudmon home that the state line split in two. The way it was positioned, nine rooms were in Alabama and one in Georgia. They had to pay tax in two states, two counties, and two cities for one house, which we also did. A person's residence was determined not by where most of your house resided but where you slept and spent most of your time. Naturally the owner's bedroom was the one room in Georgia, although ninety percent of their home was in Alabama, so they were declared Georgia residents. Sadly, one afternoon most of the people in both cities—or so it seemed—stood in my front yard as we watched one of the few remaining Civil War-era houses burn to the ground before both the West Point and Lanett fire departments could extinguish the blaze.

Life's script is one long tease that rarely delivers what you expect, and the few times it does is usually at the end of the play when it is too late to enjoy it. So it was with us when, after twelve years, we moved to a new location, our seventeenth home in the ubiquitous journey of an itinerate Problem Doctor—the 25th home since my beginning on Combs Street in Fairfax. Looking back, when I was fifteen and Dad lost his business, I was on my own and felt like a novice sculptor. I was either a block of granite or a big lump of clay but either way had to chisel or mold my future by myself. It would be completely up to me which way I shaped my life, fully believing that anything was possible if one worked hard enough. To be considerate, thoughtful, and judicious about myself, at that particular time I felt I was all that I had. But with so many obstacles, I would also have to learn how to work smart. Surprisingly, and fortuitously, growing up in Alabama there was a lot of red mud available for sculpting everywhere you looked. Truthfully, success becomes both seductive and addictive, and we all want more.

In a sweaty statement of Southern intent, we are good natured and seem to be born with bon mots tumbling out of our mouths like loaded dice. We also seem to have a special Southern way of erecting semi-permanent monuments to nothing in particular.

This book's narrative is based primarily on autobiographical experiences. However, the world has come a long way and is quite different today than it was back then. In a post-post Civil War century, America's Meghan Markle will be the next Duchess of Sussex, entering the Royal Hierarchy of Great Britain. I watch history being made with a big smile of admiration, but I'm like Pooh Bear—today is always my favorite day. Let's go back through these brief stories and see if we can still find that which we lost, whatever it was.

We have learned the hard way that dynamic is as real as gravity and time and will reshape our world faster than we can imagine or even un-remember. However, we must be careful—the Devil always gets the best lines in life's story because we give them to him.

5

In the Beginning

We have come to live in the Anthropocene Age, an era which is shorthand for a world both enhanced and diminished by the human species. It's a place where scientific miracles, unexpected performances, and real time-less characters struggle to combine and make life whole—or not. We are stretched to our limits by befuddlements, trying to live out the half-life of our teenaged inchoateness. It does little good if we master the art and ignore the science. Yet a mill village back when cotton was king will always be there in spirit even when absent. It's amazing how the vortex of the mind can be filled just by the imagination. Irony has finally become the handmaiden of reality, often laden with surprises. It quickly became clear that you can't understand things with one eye seeing, one thought thinking, and one hand clapping. As a kid, I would have been so blessed if I could have just been old enough to see things more clearly through the transparency of a simple pane of glass.

This disruptive contemporary era is an idea contradictive in all aspects with our thinking, evolving into an existence in which all bets are off as long as humans are in charge, which we are. It is a prescient time in which the Homo sapiens have "reset the Earth's Biology," which may lead to our extinction. Yet, most of us are not worried about those things over which we have little direct control. That was our case in the mill village, as kids were always motivated by something more significant than money. Believe it or not, there is something in our hierarchical thinking that's more important: opportunity and respect, and not necessarily in that order. That's especially true if you start at the bottom and are always looking up. I never heard the word "pamper" growing up, but in spite of difficult times, the tight knots of community were not easily untied. You learned to watch your mouth and manners at the same time.

Our home was in a perfect location on Interstate 85, midway between Atlanta and Montgomery, and there were no spaghetti junctions to contend with. Life growing up in our little towns was far from a movie script or something you might dream up as a fantasy on the playground; one just hoped the future would be budget-friendly. To most it depended upon one's dream and vision of tomorrow. Regardless of the outcome, you learned that everyone looked prettier and friendlier with a smile. I loved the casual style where most people moved at the high speed of warm molasses—everything except their mind, which was as sharp as a tack. Many just sat on the front porch, sighing and waiting for reality to show up for its daily visit. We enjoyed the cool breeze in the shade while we made up our minds what we were going to talk about when someone stopped by that evening, which they always did. Over the years I have heard people say that life is not about the destination but the journey. I could tell right off they had never lived in a mill village.

Sometimes truth and character become the most vexing elements of the real world because they are not artificial or embellished actuality, like many aspects of the everyday. In the same instant, Southern Reality has an instinctive attraction to our human frailties. If Mark Twain and Will Rogers were present and evaluating today, they would probably say that directed satire is a mirrored reflection of the American spirit in action. I would have to agree. They were our best intellectual sages in looking at the past and seeing the future, always prodding us on to better things in a fun way. There have been many times that I have been accused of coming up short on wit and wisdom, but never in the fruits of fun or in the spirit of prolixity. Personally, by my nature I just like "funny"; it could come from anywhere and go where it pleased. Of course, Will Rogers and I were bosom buddies and kindred thespians, since I once played his sidekick Wally Post in the *Will Rogers Follies* at the Springer Theater—Georgia's historic state theater in Columbus. Both Twain and Rogers knew that truth with a laugh can bring wisdom while being disarming and comforting all at the same time.

I have always been informal, even believing that writing should aspire to the condition of casual conversation. So it is in these snippets of life, a brief peek at daily happenings in my town and little hamlets just like it all across America when I was a kid and after. We were simply authentic people in the real world, tending to overcomplicate life when it was really quite simple. It has only a few threads of plot, but like the yarn spun and fabrics woven in our mills, they are repeated over and over in the weave of the tales, each one helping bind the strands together. To be happy in life always requires a little memory tinkering.

The respectful relationship between management and employees in the mills gave a comfortable connection to all concerned. They were non-union plants, with leadership often rising up through local ranks of production and staff jobs in the various facilities. The plants were well managed, with few peripheral problems or prickly relationships. There was a mutual respect and rapport for one's part in the greater plan. Mill employees clarified their intentions and loyalty to the Company and it did the same to them in many economic, unifying, and comforting ways. Employees were not just people who made textiles; they were "textile people" and proud of it. Everyone was together, dedicated with minimum confrontation, marking the box as 100 percent loyal hard-working Americans. No one wanted a future that would break the warm ties to the past, yet nothing will make one more tired than standing still.

There is nothing wrong with someone being universally motivated by self-interest; it's the way we are designed and a segment of our DNA. Yet mill villagers realized that we were just part of the aggregation and compromise was important for the benefit of all. I think people in our little manufacturing towns scattered around the South and the nation fully understood this fact as we transitioned over the years from hands, to back, to brain workers. Job happiness came from teamwork and being truly needed and respected by management, fellow employees, family, and neighbors.

There were trade-offs for workers, reconciling inclinations, ambitions, and opportunities with livelihood, job security, and safety—the normal rhythm of expectations. Sometimes it boiled down to biography being therapeutic, all about living and eventual conclusions with minimum drama. There is a constant "amalgam of need" that lies behind every person. No one in town lived in a fantasy world; they clearly understood the actual one and their wants depended upon personal and corporate performance. There were also the demands and joys of the job and demands and joys of life—family, friends, finances, success, and failure. Yet, with "the best laid plans of mice and men," reality continues to ooze under the front door, causing trouble and disruption. Some of the ooze is practical and other more philosophical, each bearing its own poison and reflecting the enormity of hope in just trying to survive and be happy. Introspection is waiting alongside "self" for an introduction and is not always welcome. People in their little backwaters understood that and were probably better acclimated to the real world back then than we are today. Of course, everyone put up a good front, because no one wanted their confidence to be noticeably wobbly.

Our little towns were laced with inquisitiveness, which is a natural soft focus for make-believe. The Southern parental mantra was, "My children will have a better life than I did." The vast majority of them did. One learns not to laugh at or criticize youth for their continually changing affectations. They are just trying on new faces and personas, attempting to find one that fits to their liking. There were many ranging dreams born there, and like everyone else, I had a few of them. We romance many fantasies as our thoughts blossom and grow to new dimensions. The back story is usually more interesting than the main event anyway. Since families had lived side by side for generations, romance blossomed and people married neighbors. Therefore, many were related in one way or another. I learned to never speak about someone behind their back unless it was a compliment, because you may be talking to their relative. So, for good reason, everyone was exceptionally friendly and nice to one another.

Even in the past year or two there have been a few wandering thoughts floating by in my deeply fading memory pool. They have left me with a certain nagging discomfort. For example, I find that I always keep my best lines for conversations with myself. Maybe it's because I am afraid to expose them to public thought or perhaps even ridicule. Yet personality and character can't be as easily changed as a dirty shirt. I have also found that wisdom tends to wane once one has ascended into abstraction on the way toward the personal. Experience also tells us that the arc of the moral universe seems to bend its own uncontrollable way, with the help and reaching encouragement of its inhabitants. But the more heavy-handed it gets, the less it feels like home.

J. K. Rowling is one of the world's favorite people—not because she wrote the highly successful *Harry Potter* books, but because of the way she thinks. One of the comments made by Dumbledore is, and I paraphrase, "It's not your abilities that make you what you are; it is the choices you make," and truth is one of those. Truth is the deep taproot of a tall tree that produces many strong branches. As we travel life's congested highways, we have many alter egos, but truth helps us eventually end up favoring our better selves. That becomes as natural as an honest train of thought. Reality always leaves it up to you and me to unpack its true meaning. Some are able to do that, and others are not. Another word to the wise: I have found that history is not sacrosanct because it goes through many drafts before it's offered up for public consumption. So be careful what version you buy; it's always written by the winner, which may not be the most truthful. Sometimes the best responses to the real world are found written invisibly between the lines or in the margins of the page, where our deeper thoughts and best wisdom resides.

Of course, hospitality and friendliness are not exclusive to the South, but they do comprise the region's proud trademark. As a kid, we always thought life was lived "whole cloth"—honestly, as it actually occurred. Then we discovered the subterfuge of the known world, and its true nature, proving that the actual truth can be bent and stretched even to the point of breaking. Reality is not static and will never cease evolving. Someone always comes up with something new and unexpected. We all keep searching for a creative incubator where ideas hatch and come to life, yet one must be ever cautious of the human condition. No one in their younger years ever wants to morph into their mom or dad, but it could be the best thing that ever happened to us.

For some reason, I feel much more cerebral and articulate when I have an open mind, a problem in front of me, a pen in hand, a blank page before me, and I am left alone to conjure up my memories and thoughts. The words effortlessly flow to fill the pages.

I wanted to choose my own direction, not just settle for one that was the easiest available. So, as a youth, I always paid close attention to successful people in preparation for roles I hoped to play someday. Smiling a lot was one of them and was just natural to me. Even in those early years, I had a fervent curiosity and an appetite for education. The real world brings countless opportunities and potential versions of itself to our door. We just have to select a role model and path reflecting who we want to be and hope that we make the right choice.

I always liked science because in its clear domain there were no halfway houses. There are definitive rules, and the answer is always simply *yes* or *no*. We eventually—through trial and error—become familiar with the legacy of chaos and find there are no simple solutions. Yet, one must learn to be a little daring and paddle his or her own canoe against the current, because living is all about order, mystery, and confusion. Bob Goff put it well in his book *Love Does:* "Sometimes we have to kick doors down—we can't simply wait for them to be opened." How are we expected to leave any impression on this world if we are normal and always color inside the lines? When our time is thoughtfully invested, we have the ability to direct our efforts toward actual deeds, not just pleasant thoughts and good but unfulfilled intentions. As you boil everything down to its essence, daring is all about being yourself—nothing more, nothing less.

I don't know that I was ever hardwired to be a Southerner, but an American, yes! Being born in the Deep South does require reordering one's perceptions. Yet, regardless of where we are from, we all have a fault—in varying degrees—with our inclination toward bent truth and personal enhancement. It's just part of the innate human condition. In man's evolution, we have learned how to spin anything through the process of saying stupid things with smart words, often getting louder for emphasis that produces more shadows than light. There were few superhuman dimensions blossoming in mill villages, and it was not simply the real world in first gear casually driving down an interstate. For most people, it was a constant uphill struggle, transmission grinding, usually in second or third gear.

By the time I was five, I was reading real words, going from the letters on the page to my mouth. I wasn't guessing or pretending; I was really reading, saying what the words spelled. That's probably why I skipped the third grade. As a young boy, I quickly moved away from believing in magic and fantasy because truth was already too hard to deal with. Based on my grandfather's and father's experiences, reality was completely unfair. I became attuned to a more real and curious skepticism that I found interesting and challenging. It became more so when I met the psychic Mayhayley Lancaster, who even now I still do not understand. I was not an alpha ten-year-old, but there was something waiting for my attention every day. It made me wonder: At what point are we afraid to stop raising the ante on one's future?

Dad and mother were not wealthy but were very smart, aspirational parents. He was intelligent from an engineering perspective and was always serious. He thought he was the original rough draft and I was the copy, a new improved version. He was different in many ways, a character true to his own self, enough to carry the prohibited modifier "unique." In the late 1940s, he loved to ride his Harley-Davidson motorcycle, with me on board, until—thank goodness—mother made him quit because there were no helmet requirements back then. Dad had worked long and hard to develop a successful Kaiser–Frazier automobile dealership, eventually with thirty-one employees, and had finally gone bankrupt. He had invested every dollar he could rake and scrape into the business. He lost everything the year of my high school graduation when Kaiser-Frazier decided they couldn't compete with Ford and General Motors. He lost our home, his business, investments, all assets, and the college funds he had set aside for me to become an Auburn Architect—the whole lot he had spent his life building. It was on the weekend when he told me, and that day I harshly walked into the backside of Saturday morning for the first time in my young existence. I even tasted it that day when the salty wet tears quietly ran down my cheeks into my mouth. My thoughts had no anchor and kept floating out of reach. I overnight became a sixteen-year-old with a man's mind and responsibility, burdened with a grave problem of economic survival. It was a clear landmark, the entry gate in my coming of age—overnight. I felt I had been sucker-punched by real-world corporate circumstances and had to wait for a standing nine-count to see if I would survive the hit. I did, but barely, and it left scars.

The future has a way of showing up whether you want it to or not. In some ways, I felt I had been kicked to the curb, through no fault or intention of my dad,—just the random hurtful side of life. As a teenager, I could change very little; now I could only piggyback on Southern Reality.

The hope of a college education became a tiny needle in a very big haystack. It would be left entirely up to me to find it—if I could. The emptiness left an almost withered orphan psychology, where I had to navigate rough waters every day for six years through the twelfth-grade and until I graduated from college, got a management job, and entered a calm and seemingly more secure harbor. The experience of those unbelievably demanding years was like an un-degreed Ph.D. in perseverance. It was always subjugating my will and desires to that of survival. I eventually ended up in a mode of habitual self-searching, a quest for a new identity that continued to elude me. Fortunately, that had changed when the creative juices pointed to not becoming an architect but to morphing into a Problem Doctor. It was a completely new beginning with a different landscape.

The primary difficulty was that I had no one but myself to write the checks for college, and my little two-digit bank account was stretched and strained beyond recognition. It only contained what I deposited. I would hesitate to guess by the time I was sixteen the number of times I wrote a check on Monday, Tuesday, or Wednesday and rushed to the bank on Thursday to deposit my mill paycheck before the one I had written earlier bounced. The bank was very kind. For six years I was always broke and just longed for the wonderful day that I would only be semi-broke. I quickly learned from that disconcerting experience that it takes great character to withstand all the rigors of failure, to get up off the ground and start over from scratch at middle age, which Dad did. For me it was the beginning of six long years of education in fat-free dining.

Without a purpose, life becomes a hard thing to parse, and it remains almost untranslatable. I had a front-row seat on hard times. If I had been Catholic, I would have prayed to St. Jude for help, because he is the saint for hopeless causes. My coat may have been worn and thin, but it was enough to keep my heart warm. For me, as well as my family, this was a tough period, but I discovered you can get through almost anything if you have no other choice. There were two things that bothered me the most: the things that happened and the things that didn't. We were taught that without character and strong values, thoughts could be nudged into oblivion, like a little paper boat launched down the swift Chattahoochee River, lost forever.

So, while in the twelfth grade, I went to work in the mill before and after school each day and on weekends. At sixteen, I was a freshman at Auburn University (A.P.I.) in the College of Engineering, flat broke and on the cusp of destitution. I had to work at least forty hours every week in the mill (sixty to eighty hours per week in the summer). This included commuting seventy-four miles round trip five days a week for five years, while taking a full engineering course load, with all the labs, plus compulsory ROTC and PE, while personally paying 100 percent of my expenses. That's a long breath just trying to say it. My school/work schedule was so hectic that I rarely went to bed the same day I got up. Eventually, with a co-op scholarship from West Point Manufacturing Company, I graduated on time (in five years) with zero debt and as a member of two national honor and service societies. If one survives such a schedule, you learn that you are resilient and can do more than you think you can, especially when there are no other alternatives.

I would never wish such an experience on anyone; nor would I want a do-over. However, it's funny how life sometimes has a way of trying to compensate for the tragedy it inflicts. That almost untenable experience laid the foundation for a successful, fulfilling career and made me appreciate the meritocracy in small-town America. I didn't have much good fortune during the tough times, but in the few episodes in which it happened, I was fearful of examining it too closely, afraid I might find it wasn't real. Life speaks to us from its thoughts, beckoning us from deep down in its better nature. We just have to learn to listen to what it has to say. I felt as if the mill was beckoning me, saying, "Come, study me, learn me, make me better, and let me be your future." And that I did. I picked it up and couldn't put it down.

I also discovered many exceptionally benevolent people. Without that difficult struggle, I would never have been a footnote in business and life. As a kid, time passes at a snail's pace. At a young age, it's difficult to be practical in the theater of realism. But as we add additional decades, coupled

with common sense, it eventually becomes more a learned act of accountability and caring for others. Inner honesty and truth usually inhabit the
same space. It also comes attached to a definitive responsibility of giving
something back to the community and that which came to nurture you
along the way. It's a sad truth that we always know so much better than we
do. I have come to believe it is just part of the inherent human condition.
If we are lucky, we get old.

Years don't tend to creep up on you; they fly by more like the 100-yard
dash, as if you were on a time binge. We slow down and our mindset may
drag a little bit, but there is no expiration date on wisdom. One would
much rather walk all alone in the right direction than be in a crowd heading down the wrong path. I was never disappointed if I came up with the
wrong answer if it had also been the right question and I learned something.
To compensate for younger years, I found I used more four letter words,
like what, when, why, and how. (I know the last two words have fewer than
four letters, but if the shoe fits, wear it.) I have found that in any valued
endeavor one should actively engage the mind, strive to produce accuracy,
and end up with exciting results that are more than expected and better than
advertised. But you must pay attention, because life has a way of spending
itself at a reckless rate, often with little return on investment.

Experience, in its complexity, is filled with interesting conversational
footnotes that are never heard, or recorded, outside our own head. So,
one's personal deficits have a convoluted way of eventually restricting our
context, reach, depth, and growth. Therefore, we should never become satisfied, because no matter how far you have come, there is always a long way
to go. I eventually found that the impossible can only be exceeded by the
unthinkable. We may not like reality, but it shouldn't be doubted, primarily
because everyone wants to fill up a bigger frame, just to prove we belong in
the picture. The future symbolizes the power of reinvention and is in the
hands of the problem solvers—the creative, innovative, and inventive. We
have a choice: we can watch or participate. It's up to us.

Life, in its own special way, is self-consciously experimental because we
learn mostly by doing. So, in a peripatetic career, my suitcase did quickly
runneth over. I also found grace rarely traveled lightly. Now living in the

25th home since a little boy, I learned that home is never about where you live; it's always about who is there waiting for you. Even the ordinary man understands this rationality because it's the process of reason, understanding that few things are more complicated than the human heart. Life by its very nature seems to perpetually be in conflict with itself. We are romantics by our inherent genes because it helps perpetuate the species, and that is a big part of where man's problem with Southern Reality really began. One can rarely make life longer than fate intended, but with a little extra effort, we can make it a lot wilder and deeper.

6

Alabama

Home is not always where you were born, but it was for me, because I was born at home, early one September morning, in a small two-room mill house on Combs Street in Fairfax, Alabama. I woke up in bed with a redhead named Sarah Jim. It was in the early fringe of fall, in the thin disappearing edge—the Southern phase of the Great Depression. Dr. Hunt had just made a house call. It was actually a four-room house separated by a long continuous hall into two dwellings. The Andrews family lived in two rooms on one side, and the Siggers in the other. The oak trees along the street were close and prolific, and on blistering days, it felt as if the limbs were stretching throughout the house, leaving everything in a cooler shade. Yet there was nothing in the world as soft as the air in April in Alabama. My favorite time—ever since that very first daybreak—is when the sun comes up early in the morn, waking up all of Mother Nature's colors to brighten my day so I could start on a new adventure. It hasn't changed.

I later spent most of two decades , starting in the late 1930s, living in my grandmother's boarding house, which was a few blocks away in the same small textile mill village. My father had started his own business and we were no longer permitted to live in a Company-owned home. My paternal grandmother prepared more than one hundred meals every day. Her customers were boarders, mill and office employees, and high school students. Most of the meals were paid for, but I could never count the number that she gave away—twenty to twenty-five a week, perhaps 1,000 to 1,200 each year. The communal boarding house, with six young male boarders that worked in the mill, was snuggled comfortably along Highway 29 in the beautiful Chattahoochee River Valley.

Growing up at the feet of those much older, and intrigued with science all my life, I always wondered why there was "something" instead of "nothing" in the universe. In fact, if there was "nothing" there wouldn't even be a universe. With our finite minds, we can't even conceptualize "nothing" without there being a counterbalance of "something." So now you know how I felt as a boy in my little hamlet trying to get my mind around Southern Reality and being in awe and wonder trying to contemplate "nothing" in an existence that was filled with "something." Then, one Sunday at Fairfax Christian Church our preacher explained it all, and it sounded pretty logical to me at the time, and still does. Until scientists come up with a more plausible explanation—and they haven't yet—I think I will stick with that one.

I was nothing special: just an ordinary kid, with simple tastes, always hankering for a vanilla milkshake. In the fourth grade, my handwriting was terrible, as if a battalion of centipedes had climbed out of a bottle of black ink and walked across a sheet of white paper without blotting their feet. Over the years, it didn't improve. I was never fast-tracked for success by the abstract muses; neither was I a little kid with an oracular accent, but one fully

First church built in Fairfax by West Point Manufacturing Company for joint use of all protestant denominations, now First Christian Church Fairfax.

weighed and tethered by my Southern curiosity and the incomprehensible. I discovered that the invisible shouldn't scare anyone. It's only the upper range of the unknown, and we will never understand all that we already know. The brain is just a blank slate to be written on, and our individual reality has already scribbled its marks upon us through genetics and human nature. Beyond that, the mind is waiting on experience and common sense to add its own scratches. Oftentimes the truth may hurt, but it cleanses the soul. We had better like who we eventually become, because we will be stuck with that person for eternity.

The palpable can be scary in its mystery, even when you are an oblivious witness. This was so one soft Southern night in the 1940s. There was an ominous feeling in the air as the Ku Klux Klan began an announced march in a torch procession through the middle of the business district in downtown West Point. I do not remember seeing a single black or brown face in the crowd on that particular evening, only unsmiling white faces and white robes. There was only silence in the crowd. I also remember the words of my father: "In America, everyone has freedom of speech—even if it is repulsive and against our personal principles." Most people in the Greater Valley, comprising seven small villages of about 25,000 souls, didn't want to hear what the Klan expounded. But, like the rest of those present that evening, Dad, Mother, and I were there out of curiosity. Plus, there wasn't much to do that evening as we watched a mostly silent march with a little human hum. They were covered from head to toe, with pointed hats, all in white, faces hidden. Each costume had KKK stenciled on the chest, back, or both in heavy red or black letters. Fear comes more in a collage than in a distillation of its parts.

I had never seen one of the fifty shades of grey that was darker than black—a color that challenged the boundaries we establish in a quick-change world—until that very night, when pink faces and hard hearts were covered with white sheets. In retrospect, I have wondered if there would have been that many people on the street if we had had television and there were more interesting things to see at home. To my family, it was a spiteful, people-hating, democracy-stomping, sheet-wearing contingent on parade. I wondered why they didn't wear black; it would have been much more in keeping with the color of their hearts. Fortunately, the Klan was never a problem in our little towns, and it was the only time I ever saw anyone in a sheet or otherwise hiding. Perhaps many of them, deep down, were ashamed to show their true identity, and the image was all about foreboding and making themselves feel significant. Plus, the Company and the city didn't like them parading through town, but it was their right. One discovers early on that politics and fear, in their various dimensions, can be a great appetite suppressant. That hasn't changed. It was an error-speckled time.

To a perceptive observer, it was impossible to find a sympathetic heart in an unfeeling mind. They were void of intellect, sentiment, or even compassion. The imagination may have enabled us to deal with a multitude of daily disappointments, randomness, and even change, but I never understood why the thoughts of some weren't burdened with guilt, or even personal disgust, by their very actions. Integrity never raises or lowers the bar; it is the bar.

Being perpetually full of curiosity and energy, I always wanted to learn to dance like nobody else was watching. I listened attentively and absorbed certain insightful books and essays with the goal of self-discovery. Like everyone else, I was just trying to find the place in the world outside the mill village reserved for me. I learned it wasn't reserved; you had to make it. A creative person is usually weighed by the perils of his or her discontent and pauses only cautiously at the possibilities within their own despair. Perhaps that's why only the rare human can turn his or her life into art; I was always trying. Looking back, sometimes I think that growing up in Fairfax was like being caught between reality and utopia, or maybe polished with a bit of both. Being brought up mostly in a boarding house of constant conversation and traditional metaphor, it was a natural route to prolixity, and a rather unique way of life. I was a bookish introvert by nature and a verbose extrovert by nurture. Early on, I was more of a watchful introvert, guarded in thought, but as I got a little older I discovered that this needed to change. Sometimes I think that becoming an extrovert was an on-stage private joke.

I was continually in the presence of three African-American ladies—maids and cooks—who helped raise me. They were special, part of our family, and I loved them dearly, especially Connie Baker. With mother working in the mill during World War II, and Dad in the navy, this was not a new storyline of growing up in the South. In fact, it was a reality that many of us experienced. Connie was always there when I needed her and had the best hugs in our family. She was not married and had no children—except for me.

There was only one Connie Baker in the whole universe, and love becomes the maker and the artifice of the irony between people; color or ethnicity is secondary, tertiary, or—truthfully—shouldn't even be on the list. The warm heart erases many differences through respect, and we are all ensnarled in a special American way that will never be disentangled. This means the wise man may never see the minute differences in people because he knows everyone's heart is the same color. Fortunately, optimism always implies a reaching belief in a better outcome for tomorrow. I guess I was just programmed as a born idealist, a dreamer that started from a very low point in the food chain, which colored much of my thinking. I didn't just *believe* that everything would get better; I *knew* it would—this was America.

People like Connie were hardwired for affection and brightness, so maybe I just fit the mold invariably inherited from my mother and her. Early on, I discovered that brevity may be the most elegant approach to life but it can also be an empty bucket. It doesn't matter where or when—we are constantly on stage in an audition of some kind, and somebody is continually watching, evaluating us, often those that love you the most. This is especially the norm in a small town where everyone knows you. Yet we should be fueled, not depleted, by our past in a fantasy of resilience. Often when one tries to open a door to a new reaching perception, we must close a few windows to minimize the downdraft. I found that the real world was not just one long running play but is filled with multiple mini-dramas that are lived out one experience at a time. Life should have come in a box with carefully written usage instructions, but it didn't. We were put out to pasture on our own. There are always competing agendas that eventually define who we are, and hopefully we will select the right one.

I think all people in a mill village wanted to be positioned in a personal or familial context. There was a lot of conversation that often made you wonder where it was going. Yet, this chatting usually had a sense of humor and a profound, satirical effect. We didn't realize we were hoi polloi—just ordinary people. To tell you the truth, we couldn't even spell it. Life and work were not by chance; they were much more pragmatic, present on a routine daily schedule. I never saw any real-life couch potatoes in our village, nor any government subsidies. Everyone I ever knew worked somewhere doing something, regardless of color, ethnicity, or gender.

We never liked for our words to be taken too literally. Conversation was more designed to properly position oneself in the situation under discussion. That way we could be located within our own emotional landscape, which always had an exotic layer of Southern ardor and melancholy. Such singularly-directed plots can be easily headed into a broader narrative if desired. It then becomes an engagement of specificity, reaching out to where one wants to take the discussion. I found it less like those in the North and New England, where discourse was clearer, more direct, and blunt. In the West, it was generally more like plain, straightforward dialogue. Of course, in recent years, with the common proliferation of American technology, we have all become more homogenized in our interactions, thinking, words, and phraseology. What a shame.

Even though language is less distinct, you can still pick out one's region of origin. I discovered this in living and working around the country. There is little difference in context between mill folks and others. We all have a certain regional narrative of specificity, hoping to generate individual attention and critical acclaim. It's ingrained in the human nature that's situated within our own personal landscape, closely tied to the human art of survival.

For most Americans, our lives are backlit by privilege, and so it was in my small Southern town. But this was privilege through the abundance of opportunity, not through material wealth. At the same time, there was a certain willpower that people admired, as we tried to copyright our breaks and chances into a meaningful future. Curiosity and hard work were just an important part of the persona, tightly gripping our collective imagination. Life just seemed to have a way of trying to buff away the history of strongly moralistic Southern opinions and values. I tried to become more principled and repackage myself as an independent thinker. Along the way, we learned to never underestimate the power of the ordinary.

Visualize, if you can, the red dirt, cotton, and pine trees of Alabama— just without the air-conditioning, where the mud had all the wet squeezed out of it, leaving only red dust. The temperature and high humidity in the summer kept you in a perpetual roast. You just learned to adapt and live with it. As a kid, I liked science, especially looking into a microscope, witnessing a fascinating world you couldn't see with the naked eye, probably because it made me feel larger and more significant than I really was. I learned quickly that my future should never be mired in formula but in pursuit of the curious, unknown, and creative—that which takes thought. In fact, I always admired people who had to think for a living. One's real existence can be infinitely more complex than standard Southern fantasy. Some situations and challenges give off a complexity that extends, far beyond the rationale of tall tales and fiction, all the way over into reality and the truth. Yet I seemed to find comfort in my mental world, where only I could determine what my thoughts were and who my friends would be. I loved the South, but the only good thing one could say about the Southern mosquito was that it made us like flies and gnats more.

I'm not too experienced at fighting, and haven't been in real fisticuffs since I was ten years old, on the day Charlie Beck beat me to a pulp in a Golden Gloves boxing match at the Fairfax Rec. I liked boxing. It reminded me of life: people trying to impose their will on me and me trying to fend them off. Charlie was like a rolling ball of butcher knives that didn't stop cutting. The fact he was twelve years old didn't matter. We were the same

1972 Fairfax Little League Team—League Champions.

size, same weight division, and he beat me fair and square. Circumstances that day altered my face a bit. Fighting me was also dangerous for Charlie. I'm sure I hurt his hands as many times as his fist hit my hard head. In the first feint to slow him down, he winced when I quickly placed my left eye against his right fist. Fortunately, the mat expediently flew up to stop my fall. He also had to be careful not to stumble over me every time he knocked me down. I learned that sometimes, when boxing, it's hard to swallow your own spit, and you have to be careful there are no teeth in it. I injured both hands that day—because the referee kept stepping on them. Charlie eventually became Alabama Golden Gloves State Champion in our weight division. My record was 4 and 0 before that match, but I opted out of the fight game two weeks later. I decided to take up something safer like sky-diving, bungee jumping, or babysitting. I found over the years—and through boxing—that about the only thing that can exceed the strength of hypocrisy is a person's strong and unsparing desire for self-preservation.

Even growing up economically challenged, I always had self-confidence and never felt intimidated by anyone. Nor did I schlep my way from the mill village to the house on the hill. That required hard, thoughtful work. Neither did I become smug or challenged about normalcy, even when I felt that I fell below the mark. The generations of the 1930s, '40s, and '50s produced some of the most honest, creative, innovative, inventive leaders, risk-takers, problem solvers, and patriots this nation has ever seen. They learned what honesty, freedom, success, and failure were all about, and they learned the cost of these things—the hard way. They repeated the Pledge of Allegiance every day in school, didn't turn their back or bend their knee to the flag, knew the Ten Commandments, went to church on Sunday, and gave their lives for America. I'm proud to be one of those people. I've tried to teach my children and grandchildren to do the same. I pray every day that we all do, and that they listen.

As I got older, what really bothered me was waking up with that "morning after" feeling when I didn't do anything the night before. We came to embrace a way of doing moderately-stupid things on a nonscheduled, semi-irregular basis just for the heck of it. So, as I have grown wiser and remember the good ole days, I have decided that what I want to be when I grow up is younger. I sometimes wonder how I survived in the mill village, drinking water from a hose and not from an expensive plastic bottle. We rode our bicycles and homemade carts and skateboards down steep hills with no brakes, wearing baseball caps or no headwear at all. We ate tuna, sardines, potted meat, and Vienna sausage from a can—and survived. We rode in the back of open pickup trucks and in cars without seat belts, car seats, or airbags. We didn't have 700 channels (690 of which are junk), PlayStations, Xboxes, cell phones, CDs, or the internet. We played with real friends—face to face. Our home telephone number was 184-M, obtained through a switchboard operator.

We all got BB guns when we were nine years old and .22 rifles at thirteen, learned to use them, and were held accountable. I grew up with guns everywhere, but I do not understand the new cultural logic that, "We need more guns in our society to protect us from the fact that we have more guns in society to protect us from the fact that we have more guns in society. . ." What are we missing here? Decisions also demand common sense and some measured degree of judgment. This was never a problem in our little mill villages. Why is it today, as killings escalate beyond reason? The problem is not the guns; it's us. I have never known of a single gun killing anyone on its own.

Doors in homes were never locked back then, maybe because everyone knew that the homeowners all had guns. I really don't think that was the reason. We spent more time with friends than at our house, alone in our room, if one had their own room back then. In fact, few had personal privacy, and we learned to share—including beds and bathrooms. We were just glad they were inside. So we were happy and disappointed, and discovered meritocracy, and didn't get trophies just for showing up. We didn't know what a temper tantrum was. If so, we would have had only one. We were also taught manners and proper social graces in school and at home. Today, almost no one teaches them, and few know what they are. Whatever your version of the good life, you were able to find seamless inspiration. Everybody I knew was disciplined and got whippings in school and at home when we misbehaved and learned to do better in the process. Almost everyone had both a mother and father at home back then. All respected the law, although we were not perfect. We just knew it was much better than the alternatives—and it was. We discovered how to stand on our own two feet, set goals, work hard to get where we wanted to go, with few handouts but lots of handups.

Looking back, I remember every detail and texture of my early Alabama childhood, both the good and bad. This was primarily because the days were filled with more good than the march of negatives that came parading by on our street. I believe those experiences would have proven that I was never fast-tracked to fame by the Parnassians. Like everyone else, I was a creature of a certain time and place in Southern history. More specifically, I was shaped by the apex and eventual decline of the small-town manufacturing environment. It was the best and worst of capitalist America in concert, presenting both the highs and lows. Sometimes it was terribly uncomfortable to be a part of both worlds because they were so directly oppositional and contradictory to one another. There was also a thirty-year period of dynamic world change from about 1980 through 2010. It was the theoretical beginning of the leveling of trade and economic viability among nations. Also, it initiated a new era when political winds wrote a suicide note to manufacturing in America, one of the shortest and saddest in national history. It was an era that helped preface the sadness of "free trade" and a sharp decline in the American middle class.

I loved the vibes of a small town where you know everyone. There were few blind spots, and I don't remember a single person ever going squiggly on me. Of course, life always adds new contemporary twists to customize the theme. We all like the nourishment of being noticed and acknowledged by others; it's in our human nature, regardless of age. In the lazy summer, you kick off your shoes, open the windows, and enjoy a cool drink on the front porch, waving and speaking as people pass by on the sidewalk. Everyone just relaxing, enjoying a no-stress day, sitting there with family and friends enjoying the primary resource we had—one another. The lake was always beckoning. It was like a Norman Rockwell painting of a good day on Southern steroids. I came to conclude that, regardless of where you were born, life has proven to be a simple big tent sheltering us—nothing more, nothing less. It was pretty clear that imagination perpetually hovers

1950 Fairfax Junior High School, undefeated Greater Valley champions. From left, front, G. Andrews, J. Moore, C. Beck, M. Hicks, and K. Pigg; back, J. Teague, A. Chase, D. May, C. Carroll, and J. Wilks.

in the neighborhood of thinking. Reality seems to evolve in the congruence of context, form, and function before it falls apart. At the same time, our decisions should always entail forethought and not be forensic-free.

In the Greater Valley culture, each manufacturing facility produced a unique product mix for different markets, so there was little fabric commonality or direct competition. The unheralded glue that joined the West Point Manufacturing Company mill villages together, in an odd sort of way, was sports. Actually, in a rather idiosyncratic manner, it held them both together and, at the same time, at arm's length.

Supervised sports programs were extensive in the little towns, ranging through many Company-sponsored recreational efforts for literally hundreds of children and adults in each community. Opportunities included competition between village junior high schools, four high schools, and Company-sponsored adult baseball, softball, and basketball programs. The Company had its own public golf course, with sand-greens, in Riverview, adjacent to the Chattahoochee River. It's where I and many other mill village kids and adults learned to play the game, because it was free. Each town had its own Company-subsidized ball fields, tennis courts, and basketball gyms, and several had swimming pools. Every mill had its own "semi-pro" baseball and basketball teams that, with great pride, competed with one another and with other Company, community, and competitive corporate teams in Alabama and Georgia. In fact, talented baseball players throughout the Southeast, and as far away as New York, would be given "good" jobs in the mill to move to the community and play on these mill teams. It was a normal part of the textile-industry culture throughout the country.

As players, some renowned coaches, school teachers, and Company employees moved to the Chattahoochee Valley and stayed. A few of those who called it home were Carlton Lewis, Mal Morgan, Fob James Sr., Doug Lockridge, and Lee Head. There was also a Class D professional baseball team—the Valley Rebels—in that era. One of the more popular players, Virgil "Fire" Trucks, became a famous Detroit Tigers pitcher. In his big-league career, Trucks won 177 games and struck out more than 1,500 batters. Of course, there was also the ever-famous and athletic Milner Family that I married into.

The "Milner Nine" was one of the more noted baseball clans in the Southeast in the 1920s and '30s. They originated in the River View community, near what was called "Stripped Nation." Richard Milner was my wife Claire's great-grandfather, and John Milner was her grandfather. They traveled throughout the Southern states and were quite good. Many worked in River View Mill, or at other Valley plants. Two went on to play professional baseball. Claire's brother, Charles Smith, was one of the better athletes to come out of Valley High School in the early 1950s—an exceptional baseball player, but perhaps an even better football prodigy. According to newspaper reports, he held an Alabama high-school scoring record when games were typically low-scoring defensive battles. As a running back, he scored six touchdowns in one game, which was unheard of in the day. As peculiarities occurred at that time, he went to Florida State University on an athletic scholarship. Charles returned to his senses and eventually came back and graduated from Auburn University.

Over the years, there have been a number of exceptional high-school athletes to come out of these small mill villages who went on to play football for Auburn, Alabama, Clemson, Georgia, Georgia Tech, and many other smaller colleges. One of them of course was Fob James Jr. from Lanett, who starred at Auburn and eventually became governor of Alabama. I was privileged to serve on his Business Advisory Committee when he was in office. There was also Fob's brother Cal, President of Diversified Products, and Ray Anderson—from West Point—founder of Interface Carpets and a leader in national conservation programs. There was Gaines Lanier, who played for Auburn and became CEO of J. Smith Lanier Insurance. Other top athletes included Larry Ruffin of West Point; David Hill, Richard Wood, and Bobby Hunt, from Lanett; and George Mason, Don May, Gary Barnes, Jimmy Addison, and Dave Thompson, of Valley. Several became quite successful in the NFL as well as in business. I was just proud to be able to say I played with them.

Many people measure worth by outward appearances such as money, power, influence, sheepskins, admiration, and material possessions. At the same time, these assets can be lost as quickly as gained—as fast as the graphite marks are removed by the eraser on a No. 2 pencil. On the whole, I discovered that you are not competing against someone else's measure of accomplishments but internalizing the objectives you establish for yourself. One day, I divined that material success is not something you gather in your comfortable storehouse to hold onto for others to admire. Instead, it is something you gather up so you will have the pleasure of giving it away to someone in greater need. Many, many such people came out of those mill villages. Let's meet a few more of them. . .

7

Junior

Earlier, in the mid-1940s, when cotton was king, fifty feet away and directly across the street from the boarding house where I lived was Howell's Grocery Store. It was very convenient when the boarding house was cooking one-hundred-plus meals a day, as were the Easterwood, Barber, and Neal Grocery Stores about two hundred feet north and south on Cusseta Road. It beat riding the "dinky" (bus) from Fairfax seven miles to West Point to shop at the larger A&P. There were many small, privately-owned stores and businesses of all kinds in our mill villages. All of these grocery stores, and most of the other retail enterprises like them, are gone. Today, you can't swing a dead cat by the tail without hitting a Wal-Mart, Dollar General, or some similar proliferating franchise of national significance; they just wiped out the mom-and-pops. The economic powers-that-be tell us that's called progress, but I'm not so sure if it's at the expense of community. Reality just seems to fit the mold of a big tent pole franchise that doesn't always do well in a small one-industry town.

In this environment, I found that an honest man always remains fundamental, in a delegated way, to becoming whole. To see daylight, you must reach around inside of you and pull all of the things hidden out of the shadows into the brightness. We will never be perfect, but I think we get extra points at the end of the game for trying. In this context, there is someone special I would like you to meet, because his example and friendship had a lot to do with me growing up in the Chattahoochee Valley and who I became. It was a special relationship between the imaginary and the real. He was a unique individual of good character and a smiling personality of understatement. He was also one of the finest people you never heard of. Time has a way of spilling out into the open, and in our case it was less about him and me and more about the place and time in which we lived. Prejudice can color one's entire life and works, and it's not a pretty picture when it exists because it's a negative quality easier to identify in someone else than oneself. There are distant thoughts and pallets from which we paint and they can be in black and white or in color; it's up to you, but more colors make a prettier picture. Yet it's hard to feel at home when lost in society's margins, especially if left out of the conversation.

We especially like those things we see through our own looking glass. Since my brain hadn't fully developed, I had no specific agenda. In fact, I hadn't even been around long enough to be compromised. Then one day I met him, and Junior Cooper, an African-American boy about seven or eight years older than I was, became my best friend for years as I was growing up. He delivered groceries at Howell's after school and on Saturdays. Off the page and on the record, he was smart, authentic, cheery, and fun to be around. Junior would take me with him on deliveries in the big-basket store bike. When he wasn't making deliveries, we were playing football and baseball in our front yard, or I was helping him dust the shelves, put up inventory, stack the Coca-Cola bottles, or sweep the floor at Howell's. We couldn't play in the big ball field behind the house because it was too far away from the grocery store. I would never have been a good athlete were it not for what he taught me. When I was twelve years old, Junior told me he was joining the army. He put in a good word for me with Mr. Howell so I could get his job—and I did.

Ours was a friendship marked by respect, in spite of an unfelt but perceived inequality. I look back now and see the full measure of our closeness. Only in remembrances do we discern the unreality of yesterday's reality. We primarily learn about painful differences from the firsthand experience that unfairness delivers. Our bill of privileges should never interfere with our "Bill of Rights." The laws of actuality are remarkably universal, regardless of where you live, but prejudice has a way of sucking the marrow right out of the bone. Racism, like bias, is in theory a political issue, but it's really more the spiritual offspring of your heart and soul. We all want to be known as a whole person but that requires a certain sobriety beyond one's beck and call.

In an ugly world, we come to fight our battles out of the depths and shallows of character that we burden ourselves with. At the same time, there is a certain quality that's hard to measure—a sense of living in Southern history—but many of those embarrassing things we like to forget. Our desire for justice, honesty, and compassion makes democracy possible, but our weakness for injustice, self, and inequality makes democracy necessary. Freedom and opportunity go hand in hand, but at that time they were usually found only in the illusion of the privileged. Too many people were left disenfranchised. Fairness could never escape the grip of the narrowness of thinking that prevailed at the time. However, we must be careful of entrapment in personal fantasy, because we each appear on the scene in our own disguises. At the same moment, life becomes minor fiction, far removed from the truth and the real world. However, truth never expresses anything but itself, and it's the best the self has to offer. Back then there was a lot to bite off but little was chewy, enjoyable, or digestible because no one wanted to feel permanently estranged from oneself. We all wanted to move ahead, and we knew it was impossible to make progress going sideways.

Most of the economic hope for minorities that existed in the 1940s–1950s, in the mill village and elsewhere, didn't have much proven room for great success. It's difficult to make progress when you are standing in a space you don't own, and you always seem to be a half-step behind. We conjure up our prospects so unsettlingly even in our best moments, almost as if on a guided tour of a bad dream. One's future first takes place in our mind, but if there is little expectation, it's a lonely journey. The time-to-come for a person of color seemed to fragilely stretch, bend, and morph through lonely generations of few favorable circumstances. No one wanted to depart the realm leaving nothing but a hole in the air. I was not far enough away from childhood for my thoughts to be fully formed, but I was quickly getting there one enlightening day at a time. Time travel has never been enjoyable for people of color, whether going forward or backwards, and we need to change that mindset. It was impossible for white audiences to fully translate the minority experience in those days. There was a deeper personal narrative that those living in the mill towns just couldn't adequately fathom. It was hard for one of color to build their own dreams and sandcastles because, in the fringes and margins, there were simply too few beaches of opportunity to find enough sand.

Not many minorities worked in the mills back then. A few were in the custodial or maintenance departments, where I would later work while in college. It was a rarity for an African-American or Latino to have one of the higher-paying, more skilled production jobs. If the separate schools were not as well-grounded academically—and they weren't—how could one expect their graduates to be adequately prepared for the better-paying, higher-demanding jobs? Plus, there was that negative word I heard from time to time called discrimination. Therefore, no blacks lived in the Company-owned white mill villages. They all resided on the fringes of town, usually in small, less-desirable rental homes. One of the saddest things in the world is to lose your dream when you have no other dreams to back it up with. As a little boy, I never understood any of that. When someone left your home or neighborhood as maids or employees, they just seemed to disappear from the village until their next day of work. It's like they were living unseen, somewhere else in obscurity, a separate and unequal world. The economic disparity was sizable and the constellations of education and cultures wide, even for a mill village.

As a little boy, when we were traveling, I never understood why Connie had to eat in the car when we stopped along the way for lunch. I could never fathom why that was until I got a little older, met Junior, and asked him. He told me. I then began to discover that the more glamorous, enjoyable parts of life and its subtleties were not the most interesting, nor necessarily the most important. In real life, evenhandedness was more lip service and a charade presented in a pose of fairness. We were looking at the world with eyes tightly shut. In America, when we discriminate against anyone, we discriminate against everyone. There is always an inarguable shallowness in our history because we remember only what we want to recall and are brave enough to record. One should never give up hope because dusk can always double for dawn.

One day, when I was about nine or ten, it clearly dawned on me that the world wasn't honest, and since the beginning of time, it never had been. I was learning what prejudice and segregation were, among other things, and

I didn't like it. Yet, it was rarely discussed in public conversation. It existed and just was. Even so, that didn't make it right. Life just seemed to circle around the theme of fairness but never made contact. The close bonds between me, Connie, Junior, and my family were always there, so what was wrong with the world? Even when Connie was sick at home, my grandmother, grandfather, and I would walk two miles to her tiny two-room house and take her food and medicine. Then we'd frequently sit with her until she was back on her feet. Southern Reality seemed to have strong bonds and was constantly present because that was just the way it was. As I got older and looked in the mirror, all I could see was me, and I didn't always like what I saw. I sometimes wondered if man was prey or predator. I later discovered to my disappointment that we were both. I thought then that maybe when I got older I would have a chance to do something about it—and I did.

Even as a little boy, I thought about other people and a situation I didn't fully understand. I decided that perhaps the greatest need of all was for everyone to feel that they belonged just as much as I did. Then they could look me in the eye, not divert their gaze, and learn to love themselves. It's no good to have a window if you have no view. We were near the crossroads of success, failure, and fairness but not quite there. Equality is always about parity, regardless of the dictionary's definition. I think deep down man is a noble, intellectual animal but politically motivated by self-interests. We are also genetically wired to pursue the good, to learn truth, and to contemplate our better nature in spite of our many human frailties. Somewhere anchored by our DNA is a wandering soul trying to find itself and do what's right. The mind has a way of training our memory on the smallest things, often at the most seemingly insignificant moments; in Junior's case, he was special for many reasons. He left an enduring presence of what once was, but now is gone forever. Maybe it had something to do with the coming of age.

Where segregation was concerned, I think people in general—liberal and conservative alike—believed in fairness and progress. Yet, we usually and perhaps subconsciously upheld traditions, culture, norms, and biases because we grew up honoring them as acceptable, even when they were wrong. No excuse, just actuality, as it existed in an unreal, unjust existence. This was a paradox in practice, because those of different ethnicities that we knew and grew up with were close like family. I will say that a lot of those experiences and community practices led to a very high tolerance in exasperation, where Bruce Baker, Sam Marshall, Dr. Freeman Burns, Junior, Connie, my extended family, and I were concerned. All are now gone, except me. In the South we were up against a knot of unlikely prejudices, but I seemed to be incapable of such opinions and ethereal considerations. Prejudice is a great time saver, because you don't have to make any effort thinking about what's right and wrong. Yet it takes only a little exertion to hear the beauty of the music in togetherness, but we must listen with our hearts rather than our ears.

Most of us, since we were toddlers, in our different ranks and stratums of society, were spoon fed various versions of history and inequitable reality. We consumed it as if it were pabulum, even true and part of our DNA, as we each tried to climb our individual economic-social ladders to the next level. We didn't want to ingrain the British class system of inherited privilege, but our progenitors brought with them the revised European-Indian version, featuring the pseudo-caste system hierarchy. We just accepted it in a different, unquestioning, unanswered way. We never looked back. Then one day we discovered that the truths that really matter are always the most uncomfortable ones. Life, in its twists and turns, has subsumed us all, but it's very clear: in America, we will survive or fail together. Fortunately, duress often becomes the motor of inspiration driving some of our finest achievements.

It was becoming clear to me that the best social program was upward mobility through a better paying job for people in the mill, regardless of ethnicity. Yet, at that time, a better job was a fragile straw to grasp for one of color. It was like everything else in life: it would also have to change, and I wanted to do something about it one day. I finally understood how hard it could be to digest life on a half-empty stomach.

Junior taught me that it never costs you to give someone a smile and it comes back to you a hundred times over. And hugs—if appropriate—are even better. I reinforced that hug truth many years later, during a capital fund drive, when I was chairman of the board at our local hospital and nursing home. Junior showed me that if you create your own bag of remembrances, filled with thanks, gifts, and blessings, you can dip into it from time to time when problems occur. It's also helpful when you have a bad day and just want a lift. It's bound to happen, when you least expect it. Junior was right, and I still carry my special bag with me and keep it handy everywhere I go. In fact, I used it recently in baking a sour-cream pound cake as a Christmas gift for one of my elderly retired neighbors, who just happens to be black. His wife is in ill health and he has to do all the cooking. Now the selection of sour-cream pound cake was an easy choice because it's my favorite of all the things I bake or cook, and years ago, it became love at first bite.

Junior was the strong healing power of unexpected friendship because we had so much in common—one another. To a little boy, he was larger than life. He was grown from the family seed of a single word: authenticity. Simple word patterns, open context, even the rhythm of the Southern vernacular, could never capture the eye or intellect as well as he could with a simple smile. Doubt has a way of cutting a statement of fact in half, leaving it floating loosely in the mind in the empty space of questioning. With Junior, there was never any doubt—he was always there; he had your back. He tried so hard to get past the reaching horizon he had been conditioned to accept.

In our own interest, we find it arduous to treat different people and encounters with the same neutrality. We keep our thoughts close and hoard our investments in reality, which always seem to bend toward individual interests. Humans have a peculiar way of returning to one's own kind of private relativism. For minorities, of any category or persuasion, the real world can infect one like a bad virus, because it's problematic to maintain equilibrium and normal rhythm while unfairly struggling. I have often thought that the analytical paradigm of fairness in the universe never fully registered on reality's calendar.

Most of us think of ourselves first, and reasoning becomes the novelistic action that tightly confirms one's truth. Junior and I, in many ways, left an indelible mark on one another, two people bending with different perspectives, challenges, and anxieties, both thinking private thoughts about ourselves. The real world has a peculiar way of haunting even the mature and stable mind, perhaps because too much self makes one's limited headspace less endurable. Life never gives you a completed, tested agenda or routine plot in advance, but instead plants clues along the way for us to find. You just have to learn to be perceptive and a good detective.

In early summer, about 1949, in the middle of the night, one of the male boarders came to my bed and said, "Someone wants to see you." It was 3:00 a.m., but I went to the door and it was Junior. He was leaving for Atlanta for army basic training. We sat on the front door steps and talked for perhaps an hour about all the fun we had over the years, laughing about the things we did together, how he taught me to fight—and when not to. We remembered playing football and baseball, the funny things that happened when delivering groceries all over the community, and especially our trips to Moccasin Creek. To hear us tell it, we caught more fish from that stream than were ever actually in it. Now he was finally leaving, hopefully not forever, on a dangerous journey into the military. The Korean War was around the corner. Then, with a handshake and a big hug, he left. Soon thereafter my family moved away. It was the last time I saw him.

From time to time over the years I would ask Junior's father and brother, who by then were working in the maintenance department in the mill, how Junior was doing, trying to stay in touch. Then I got overly busy with high school, college, and finally with work, growing up and relocating to other parts of the country. I really missed Junior because he was the older brother I never had. In the South, you learn that most real friendships are made out of trust, fun, red dirt, and pixie dust.

In the ensuing years, Junior stopped by my grandfather's house several times when he came home, but I was never there. He always left me messages, or something he had brought me. After a number of years, I heard he had left the military, moved to Atlanta, got married, and become successful in the transportation business. This didn't surprise me at all because he was smart, personable, and talented; that was his stock-in-trade. By then I was living in different parts of the country. There was no reason for the fictionalized version, because I always thought Junior was the real deal. We just grew up and went our separate ways as do many good friends in life. After the fact, we have a way of airbrushing history, if for no other reason than to give us a more comfortable piece of mind.

Years later, when I became vice president in a growing company, I thought about Junior often. I wanted to provide better opportunities for all people, not despite the fact that they didn't exist but because of it. This was especially true when I established the first Minority Management Development Program, designed specifically to help promote African-American and Hispanic college graduates into the management ranks. Two of my favorite people in that effort were Calvin Williams and Oscar Crawley. Oscar eventually became corporate manager of human resources and the mayor of Lanett, Alabama. We also introduced a new minority training program to help enhance technical skills for the better paying and more advanced supervision and production jobs. I have wondered many times if I would have initiated those things without the positive influence Junior had on that little kid growing up across the street from Howell's Grocery Store. In retrospect, I probably would have, because it was the right thing to do—and should have been done decades earlier.

The fabric of two people's common rationality is woven from universal threads of shared experiences, including awkward moments and interwoven challenges, which we all endure growing up. In our case, we were just under slightly different circumstances of inequality. I'm sure it was hard for Junior to have a settled internal peace with a conviction that what he faced was unfair. We were all looking at our own situation more than at one another. Self has a perverse way of yanking one down to a whole new level of uncertainty.

If we could just remove ourselves from the equation, we would see what we had looked at a million times before and yet had never seen. Each other is really all we have, but it's also all we will ever need—if we can understand our common humanity. But in those early days in a mill village, we were in a carnival of mirrors with blind eyes, buying and selling fictions at discount prices.

I think that when we eventually have the opportunity to be fair and help someone in need and don't, it is a sin. In the realm of fairness, the things that we do not do and should can be just as egregious as the bad things we do and shouldn't. Feeding mistakes only amplifies their appetite. Sins of omission are just as guilty in the eyes of integrity as sins of commission. For this reason, I've discovered over a long journey that you learn more about yourself when you are outside your own comfort zone. We also eventually discover that it is not easy to be disciplined in an era of Instagram, Twitter, and distraction. It takes willpower. Even with all the demands on our time, it's still never too late to do the right thing. The brain always rules. Sometimes I think the body has little value other than as the physical vehicle to transport the mind around to wherever it wants to roam.

Along the way, we have made our relationships with other people much more complicated than they need to be. We all laugh, cry, hurt, love, become successful, and many times fail. We each bleed the same way, in the same color, regardless of blood type. Maya Angelou said it best: "We are more alike than unalike." The bonds of trust are so heavy it takes two people to tie them; one alone can't do it. Junior and I never had a problem.

It's our collective responsibility to deliver the promise of the American dream equally to everyone. Whenever I see someone arguing against fair, legal immigration, I wonder what he would have said if it had been used against his family when they arrived, looking for opportunity or running away from oppression? We are an immigrant nation! Attitude always begins at the personal level. We should let the past be a mirror we gaze into, not simply a possibility we ignore. Hopefully it makes us blush from embarrassment. We may have different names and faces, but we are each in our own personal way akin to Rosa Parks nervously sitting on the seat of a bus in Montgomery.

There is no place for prejudice in the world. How can you exclude a large percentage of humanity from your life and still be considered civilized? It should be clear that in America—or in the world—no one is free until we are all free and equal. I am truly moved by people who, wanting things to be better for those less fortunate or just down on their luck, actually go out and do something about it. Sometimes it's a great surprise to undress a hard man and find a heart inside of him. But I assure you, it's there—even if he hasn't yet learned to use it. He will.

Many years later, after I had become president of one of the Company divisions, I ran into someone who had grown up with Junior, and I asked if he had heard from him recently. He said, "Oh, I'm sorry, I thought you knew. Junior died about three months ago from cancer." It was one of the saddest moments of my life, as the tears welled up in my eyes. It was a crushing weight that I still hold in my mind and heart like a heavy millstone. I was shocked because I always thought he was invincible. He was so special to a little boy, who learned so much from him, who grew up to become a man with his help.

We discussed his situation for a few minutes, and as I started to leave, he said, "By the way, did anyone ever tell you? Junior named his son after you."

8

Coca-Cola

The beginning of teen years, regardless of where you live, is a most interesting and delicate time. It's a period of deep confusion, of learning and sorting out, yet there is enough emerging insight to really begin to evaluate and examine things. A question or challenge always made my eyes glisten and my brain speed up with something I couldn't reduce to just amusement or chance. We become especially creative during that period because we start questioning anything and everything. You still have a growing, expansive, inquisitive imagination but are finally beginning to make sense of things and fit the pieces of the puzzle together. The word "abundance" became more verb than noun in a mill village. Materially, there was little there but enough to go around—and the promise of even more tomorrow. You just didn't want to get caught up in the backdraft of empty temptation.

I learned to drive in a 1939 Willis Coupe when I was 12 years old, and the first thing my Dad taught me was this: you first have to get the gearshift out of neutral. I never forgot and had a heavy foot. I remember being that age as if it were yesterday. In our Fairfax village, the textile mills employed about 1,800 people, and in the very close adjacent six towns, the Company had about 7,000 additional employees, including the West Point offices. The local Coca-Cola bottling plant was recognized for having the highest per capita consumption of Cokes in the world, primarily because all available cold soft drink machines in the sweltering, non-air-conditioned manufacturing facilities were Coca-Cola only, which resulted in a frosty Coke preference and taste "addiction" in the area.

When I replaced Junior as a delivery boy at Howell's Store, groceries were always delivered to the back door of the houses in town. I noticed fifty, one hundred, or more empty Coca-Cola bottles at every home in the village. They were mostly piled up on the ground, or lined up in wooden cases like tiny soldiers ready to march off in a parade just waiting for someone to come along, save them, and place them back in service. It was obvious there were literally thousands of empty bottles throughout the broader town of 3,500 people. It made me wonder why the bottling plant had not requested they be returned. I knew they had value, so one summer day I asked a Coca-Cola truck driver if the company would be interested in my collecting the thousands of bottles and wooden cases in town and bringing them back to the store for him to pick up. Of course, that came with the understanding there would be some kind of monetary compensation for my part. A few days later, he told me management would pay one cent per bottle and ten cents per wooden case if I would collect them.

Over the next four months, working seven days a week, I rounded up over 28,000 bottles and over 800 cases for biweekly pickups—about $380 worth. At that time, average pay for adults in the mills was about $25 to $30 a week. The home owners were also happy that I removed the bottles and cases out of their back yards and off their back porches, and I never mentioned how many I broke.

I had just completed an understanding with some of my young friends in two other nearby mill village communities for a similar arrangement with Coca-Cola. I would handle the contact and agreement with Coke if they would pay me twenty percent of their weekly proceeds. It was only a little boy hand-spit agreement, but your word and pledge meant something in those days, and a lawyer wasn't necessary. Things were looking good. Then two weeks later, before they started, the truck driver told me that a new company policy was commencing the following week. The policy would state that for each case of Coca-Colas delivered to their customers a case of empty bottles had to be returned. I wondered why that practice had not been initiated before.

Evidently, I had unintentionally brought it to management's attention. It reinforced my opinion that adults—even important Coca-Cola plant managers—didn't have all the answers, because they evidently thought that people would automatically return the empty bottles back to the store. They didn't understand that people didn't really care unless they were made to do so because it took extra effort on their part. It was something they had completely overlooked. It became rather transparent to me that the world in general, and adults in particular, were not as infallible as I had once thought. The fog was clearing and the reality was becoming apparent that everything, regardless of what it was, could certainly be done better. It was a strange but exciting feeling. At the same time, I was beginning to believe that adult critical thinking was about as outmoded as a two-legged stool.

When the Coca-Cola venture abruptly came to an end, I noticed a large number of unused wire coat hangers in closets in the boarding house, with over 300 having been accumulated. There were no easily washable poly-cotton fabrics in those days and everyone used cotton, linen, or wool clothing. All heavy clothes were dry cleaned, and most cotton shirts were laundered, starched, and ironed at the three dry cleaning and laundry establishments in town. So I checked with all three and asked if they would be interested in purchasing "new" first-quality wire hangers at a good price. We worked out an agreement and over the next several weeks I went door to door throughout the village collecting excesses, sorting out the good from the bad, and then selling over 17,000 hangers at a penny apiece—or $170 worth—before they had enough and discontinued the practice. That was over six weeks pay for an adult working in the mill. I guess, in retrospect, I was an early candidate for Problem Doctor school. I began wondering why I always thought grown-ups had all the answers. They didn't.

9

Early On

Life, in its simplest form, is all about the passage of time and what we do with it. No textual emendation would be required to make the point. The decade of the 1950s was a good time to grow up. Our roots were firmly anchored in improvisation and promise. My good friend Miriam Syler, Cobb Memorial Archives historian, had the mill village pegged. She used to say, "Use it up, wear it out, make it do, or do without." The challenge was to take the plain, simple, and ordinary and make it new. We each might have become a little more content, but we didn't have group therapy in the mill village back then; we didn't even know what it was. Of course, we all have unfulfilled aspirations that follow us, and so it was with me. We attempt to shape our stories to make sense of who we think we are. In many ways I was still just a little boy, but no longer pretending like a child. Fortunately, each day shaped by the real world had a positive way of filtering through the dilemmas and superficiality of the existence we devised.

There were several times in my biography when I thought I was possibly left over from a novel Horatio Alger or Dale Carnegie decided not to write. But it was also pretty clear that neither Harper Lee nor F. Scott Fitzgerald designed or created me. I was just trying to massage my reality into something more presentable, an irresistible and perhaps unbelievable Southern story of self-invention. It seemed to take all the running I could do to stay in the same place. I was always upbeat, and rarely heard anyone say I did something in a characteristically routine, traditional, understated, or modest way. Yet I was never bad enough as a kid to have to "wrestle with Moses." It became an interactive form of imaginative therapy, always leaning away from strident complexities toward logic and rationality. Growing up is all about discovering how to wade upstream in neck-deep water, and some learn quicker than others. All the time on my journey, the unknown was a strong disquieting presence. Love for others transcends cultural boundaries and can take up permanent residence in your heart, mind, and soul. In a place where good friends are like stars in the night, you don't notice them, but they are always there looking over you.

Although I was a compulsive reader all my life, being called a "high-brow" didn't go well in our little hamlet on Highway 29. Yet I read everything I could get my hands on, never concerned if it was an old book or outdated magazine nor even advertisement flyers and things I had been fully unable to parse. Most everyone just tried to hide a huge part of oneself in plain sight—what you see is what you get. If not, there would have been an extra layer of difficulty to the every day, and no more was needed. I liked that honesty. We all wanted to understand our relationship with the world and improve our lot in life. Pretention just didn't cut it. When we clearly see the facts and ignore them, it still doesn't change actuality. I liked to travel and learn, although as a little boy I didn't get to go very far. We did have relatives in Miami, and spent some time there, but I'm not sure that's considered the South.

I loved libraries. I looked up at the full towering shelves, and it reminded me that I was somebody that's a member of a certain whole much greater than just me. I'm part of history, knowledge, art, science, geography, different peoples, and a constantly changing culture—a very important division of the dominant species sitting at the top of the tree. For years, my number one wish every Christmas was for a set of encyclopedias, but we couldn't afford them. I glanced up at the thick shelves of books and coveted all their knowledge, realizing I'm a participant in a much greater story. The world seemed to be patiently waiting on my doorstep for me to come out and play. I was excited!

Early on I discovered that every day was an open paradox of inconsistencies and contradictions. There were so many times I looked for a silver bullet to solve my problems, but I never could find the Lone Ranger. So I had to learn (the hard way) to resolve them myself. Most of our major problems are in concept, but the solutions are in the details. So I eventually ascertained that a warm, thoughtful, intuitive style of thinking was much more productive than a cold analytical approach. Perhaps this mindset existed because I always hated routine and habit. I think it's OK to break the rules of tradition as long as you can do it with imagination and panache. I eventually determined that the ordinary and conventional gives you a benchmark for progress, but it can also be dangerous, often becoming the death knell of creativity. One reason that Southern Reality has become so pervasive is that it's equally real and unreal, with little sense of comfort or relief—it exists and just is.

Much can be made of a poor Southern mill village boy if he can be caught, tamed, and trained when he is young. As kids, one of the big problems we had was there were too many ways to spend money and not nearly enough ways to make it. The mill village was also a tough environment, and if you were a boy there were two things beyond all else that you didn't want to be: too fat to run or too cowardly to fight. Neither one was good and both a disaster. It was also considered ill-mannered for one to speak about someone behind their back, even if it were true. We were primarily interested in hearing gossip about others, because when we did, it distracted everyone else from talking about you. I never knew a person that didn't have a secret to hide; some just kept them better than others. Perhaps it's simply the human condition that makes us want to fish in someone else's pond. We Homo sapiens are an odd species: one-half of us criticize what we practice and the other half practice what we criticize. Dad always said, "Life is never truthful; it's always pretentious, so never get found in an unsavory, offbeat place you wouldn't want to be caught at in daylight."

For most of us, our character wouldn't know our reputation if they met face-to-face on the street, and no one wants to honor style over substance—even though they don't deserve equal billing. We loved our neighbors, and although we didn't lock our doors, we didn't take down our fences. Everybody was different. Some people could stop by for a front porch visit and stay longer in thirty minutes than others could in three days. There was no pleasure in having nothing to do. The fun for most everyone was having a lot to do, and not doing it. My guess is it was pretty much the same in the city. I found it took less time for me to do something right than trying to explain to my dad why I did it wrong. In fact, I discovered that water taken in baths, in moderation, never hurt anyone.

It was, however, puzzling how the young and foolish could ask so many questions that the older, intelligent, and wise couldn't answer. I was never accustomed to flattery and compliments; I was more like the little boy who loved banana pudding better than anyone else but got less of it. Of course, we didn't have a clue about what we wanted in life, but we recognized it instantly.

In those days, I had an insatiable curiosity and disturbed a lot of people with all my questions. So every afternoon when I came home from school I was always glad we had a dog, so that someone in the family was glad to see me coming. With that experience, I came to the conclusion that smiling and hugs are just about the only things left on the court docket that you can't get arrested for—and today I'm not certain about that.

One of the major questions we faced growing up in the Valley was, "What effect would the rarefied air in college have on a poor country boy?" Could we even survive being financially drained and energy depleted by work while in school? Might college even bring the highest quality of failure, or would it completely lose us in the rare ether of new thoughts far over our head? What I knew for certain was this: I wanted to grow up to be the kind of person I needed when I was a kid, someone who was kind and helped others. Frequently you must make tough decisions to place yourself in position to take the next step up, and rarely are they risk free. Sometimes you must invest more now in anticipation of what could be a much greater reward later. With this thought in mind, I never tried to get ahead of myself; I just did the best I could with the responsibility I had. But one thing was always self-evident: the more you are rational, practical, logical, and try to be routine and normal, then the less inventive you become. So I always tried to keep an open mind.

Surprisingly, I found I liked to wander and wonder in the treacherous "Kingdom of Improbability," but the collegiate and corporate "Realm of Possibility" was an even greater challenge for an active mind. It was one where the tactical engagement with inventiveness was even more fun than I had ever imagined. I wouldn't say that I was a martyr to innovation, but

The Fairfax Mill Village in early 1920s.

it was pretty clear that ingrained creativity had kept mankind out of a ditch for millennia. There was so much new to learn that I had never experienced before. Of course, for the five years—60 months sounds a lot longer—when I was in college, there was always more month than money. I had no credit card or debit card, so nothing could be carried forward. It was simply the fundamental law of cash and carry: if there was no cash, there was no carry. There was nowhere to borrow money for school, and no academic scholarships back then, certainly not compared to today. So economics were very simple: when you spent what you had, you simply did without until your next paycheck. I never once asked my parents or grandparents for money. They had their own problems and needs. I learned to plan ahead and manage meager resources—or not.

As a very young boy, I was perpetually inquisitive. The questions of "who, what, why, where, when, and how" were redundantly prevalent—especially the "how." We are all molded and shaped, to a degree (perhaps twenty-five percent by some research scientists' estimates), through the environmental effect of our experiences and nurture. The other seventy-five percent of the formula comes through nature and genetics. Because of familial nurture being part of the equation, perhaps as much as eighty-five percent of who we are is initiated by the family. That doesn't mean we can fully blame our family for all our problems and bad decisions, but it is the primary influence on our biography, good or bad. I can still clearly see that indelible imprint on my life. It was the added creative cherry on my banana split.

Now don't get me wrong; we were very serious, but we enjoyed having fun in our family and in our unincorporated little town. We would have been glad to roll back our beautiful Oriental carpets and have a Saturday night "hoe-down," or do a little buck-dancing. But most of us didn't know what a real Oriental rug was, and I doubt many people had ever seen one.

There were two phrases that were standard family issue for kids in a mill village: "Yes, Sir" and "Yes, Ma'am." Used much less frequently were "No, Sir" and "No, Ma'am." Such a response was not only respectful, but also necessary for parental survival. In polite society, there were just Southern expectations that were spoken, unspoken, and implied. Conversation below the Mason-Dixon Line requires a certain friendly protocol of what to say and what not to say, to both friend and stranger. If you are a girl, never say, "I don't know how to cook." More potential husbands are lost by that than from any comment ever made. A boy, especially from Alabama or Georgia, doesn't say, "I was never a Scout, nor played football or baseball, nor went hunting or fishing." It meant either there was something wrong with your daddy or you were a sissy. Such a comment to girls or their fathers relegates you to toast. In those days, "making out" always referred to how I did on my tests at school, while "making up" was for the days I missed at school when sick. Having a "warm, meaningful relationship" meant how you got along with your neighbors or your cousins across town. Back then a nickel would mail one letter and two postcards, and $800 would buy a new automobile—everything was relative. What's a postcard? I'll explain that to you later.

The only thing that kept us from being truly rich was money. Wealth is not everything because Southerners have great integrity. I never knew a single person who ever told a lie without a good reason. Mama always believed that someone's character was like good cornbread and vegetable soup—always homemade. The big difference between integrity and image is what we are versus what we think we are. We judge ourselves by that which we perceive our potential to be, and others judge us by what we do. I guess in life's hierarchy one's self-image is about as high as you can go. In days of our youth, people may have had tougher and dirtier hands, but they also had cleaner minds and consciences.

With friends there was a strong web of trust, developed over the years through the reciprocal exchange of care-worn favors. Back then, your handshake and word was as binding as a five-page legal contract, and our little town was a safe place to live. There was also one thing for certain: we knew there were never short cuts to anyplace worthwhile.

I have never heard a Southerner say, "Sorry, I'm in a hurry, can't talk, have to run." All Southerners are congenial and like to visit with friends. In fact, you may have to send them home, but they rarely leave early. Now food is just part of hospitality and good manners in the South, and I don't recall a single person ever saying "I'm just not hungry" either. Anyone who has never heard of the SEC is either substantially below Kindergarten age or an alien from another world.

In our little backwater, the men's barbershop was like the women's beauty parlor, and we had three. Even though my grandfather cut hair gratis for shut-ins, he had a heavy hand. He would get to talking and not know when to stop. He cut my hair *once*. So Dad let me go to the barbershop on my side of town, only one block from the boarding house. I went every three weeks to Mr. Burroughs, or "Bur-pee" as I called him, since I was two years old. He lived two houses up, across the street, in a nice brick home. His shop was the bright and smelly tonsorial trail, as the comb, scissors, and clippers quickly zipped through my thin light blondish-red hair, the color I inherited from my mother. It gave me my Opie Taylor look. I was in deep repose, on Cloud Nine, in a world of my own at the barbershop, talking, waiting, and listening to grown-up gossip and village news, true or not. I would always stay twenty to thirty minutes after he had finished with me to talk and absorb. It was the hub of all village wisdom, until I had to bid it goodbye 'til the next time. I couldn't wait to get home and tell everyone what I had heard.

When I was about seven years old, during World War II, I found a praying mantis on the corner of the front porch one morning. He or she was patiently sitting there on the cover of a book I had left on the floor. It had a cover as red as a rich man's barn. It made him stand out in sharp silent contrast, like a broken wooden stick. I wondered if he liked red or even knew what the color was. For me, it was the first bit of original thinking I had done in several days. The best I could tell it was just quietly pausing in its stick-like presence to pray.

I had never seen one up real close before and wondered if a praying mantis's supplications were ever answered, and what kind of prayers would it actually pray? Were they like mine? Would its request be just like me, asking for something I didn't really need or deserve but wanted anyway? Or would his plea be about other praying mantises, perhaps in need, sick, that had lost a loved one, their job? We must have had a lot in common, but for the life of me, I couldn't figure out what it might've been. Maybe its petitions were like normal people, asking God to strike down the Nazis and Japanese for killing millions of innocent men, women, and children in war.

I began to think that perhaps the quietly praying little stick figure just had idle prayers, less meaningful and less serious things like finding others to play with, like I did sometimes. Regardless, I always believed such entreaties were supposed to be more comforting and calming, instead of making us angry at others. Maybe the problem is not in the prayers we think and offer but in us. Often our requests are about ourselves, our wants—even our revenge. For the mantis, I wished him an indolent retirement in his rocking chair on his own front porch someday, overlooking his manicured yard. So, I didn't disturb him at the time, and left him alone in his prayers, sitting on my red book cover.

Growing up in a mill town, a few years after the Great Depression, in a boarding house, left an indelible imprint on my young mind. I was not deprived, just hard-pressed. There was always adequate food, clothing, shelter, and plenty of affection—a lot of hugs—but at the end of the day, little else was left on the table for material enjoyment. The primary thing I had to play with was called "outside." Camping out, Boy Scouts, hunting, fishing, and playing sports were all par for the course. For lunch in school, without a cafeteria, I was always ready to trade my baloney or peanut butter sandwich for honey-baked ham, but I never had any takers. Most of the things I had and enjoyed as a little boy didn't run on batteries; they ran mostly on my imagination and creativity. There was another thing we had back then that was a lot better than today: the music. It was much less offensive, more romantic, not as loud, great for dancing, and you could actually understand the words.

In those early years, no one ever received allowances; in fact, we didn't even know what that was. If you wanted anything beyond absolute necessities, you had to find some way to earn money of your own, and every kid had the same objective and options were few. I was marginally more practical than impractical, but not by much. I discovered the hard way that one should be realistic and beware the bridge too far, and that the savory looking grapes that hang the lowest on the vine can be loaded with wrath.

In the 1930s–1950s, one of the singular events each year in the mill villages and farms across America was the delivery of the Christmas edition of the Sears, Roebuck catalog in the mail. It permitted the country side of life to come in contact with the city side. It was thick and heavy with all the colorful mail order excitements imaginable and more. We measured the progress of mankind, year to year, by the glorious new things it contained: fashion edicts from New York, farming equipment, auto parts, toys, colored baby chicks, kitchen appliances, seeds for planting, even prefabricated homes—all the Earth's worldly material things.

We kids spent untold hours wandering through the catalog, week after week, daydreaming, making wish lists of Christmas toys and things that were far beyond our reach but exciting to dream about anyway. If we had invested that amount of time in our schoolbooks we would have been much better off. On second thought, maybe not, because it was an open outlet to our imagination that was hard to surpass and suppress. Perhaps the greatest benefit of all was the old catalog itself, which could now be recirculated, relegated to the "Out-House" for future recyclable use. Folks that worked in the mills or lived in the mountains or on rural farms were not backwards, just practical—even more so when the "out-house" was moved "in-house."

It was absolutely essential back then to use your imagination and create your own opportunities and entertainment. It was an era devoid of TV, internet, cell phones, electronic technologies, and the many weighed interferences of recent years. We learned to imagine and create our own bent dreams and fictive reality through the radio, and the Lone Ranger, Dick Tracy, the Green Hornet, and The Shadow. In fourth grade, storytelling and creative writing, for us, was simple to understand and so much fun. We didn't get too animated or exuberant writing sentences with "periods" and "question marks," but if the sentence ended in an "exclamation point," we thought it would always be a funny, scary, or exciting narrative. Will Rogers and Mark Twain would have enjoyed those classes as much as we did.

We roamed around the neighborhood, played Cops and Robbers, Cowboys and Indians, joined the Scouts, built forts and tree houses, and created secret clubs for "Boys Only." In hindsight, as we got older, we decided that last decision was a really big mistake, but by then it was too late. At the time we were also learning the intellectual art of people skills and how to carry on a normal conversation, especially with girls, because we were not glued to electronic screens. We didn't know what the word obese meant. We never ramped up the emotional stakes beyond reason, other than if our college football team lost. In the early days, if you broke the intractable rules of the neighborhood—which were generally church-based—the residents would boo you off stage and out of town. Surprisingly, as I look back, few people had to leave. One of our favorite things to do was go skinny-dipping. Of course, two or three of the heavier boys went "chunky-dunking." Now, to be perfectly honest, I wasn't the best kid in town, nor the sharpest thorn on the bush, but I was certainly smart enough to never go swimming in Moccasin (Osanippa) Creek. Most kids didn't know any better, except for me and Junior. The Creek Indians certainly gave it the right name.

Growing up, I didn't have a crisis of identity and never liked ready-made clichés lining up to distinguish me from someone else. I was large for my age, a good student, sang in a barbershop quartet we organized when I was 12 years old, including dyed jet-black hair (as well as my scalp for three weeks). I was also a pretty good athlete. We frequently ended up fighting or wrestling in a circle drawn in red clay simply to determine who could stay inside it the longest. Having fun was as common as dirt, although I

Fairfax Mill Manager's Home on a winter day in 1972.

preferred a bit more creative thinking to express who I was. Mother Nature was exceedingly kind, and gave me almost every disadvantage possible that was necessary for later success. It was an honest and fair life, but few people had euphoria.

There was a certain creative commonality of ordinariness present in our town. No one was far behind another economically, and we all somehow survived. Every family in the community was pretty much in different seats and levels in the same boat, except management, and even then we all rowed together to reach the same objective. Salaried management and hourly-paid production employees were like different levels of cream separated from churned milk. Whether in the first class or economy section, everyone knew that no one could arrive at the same destination without the others. The managers at the top were just a lot more affluent, better educated, and had superior, more comfortable seats getting there. They enjoyed it even more after they arrived.

Of course, the plant manager was the king of the hill, so that became every boy's objective. If one was lucky enough to hit life's mega-millions lottery, they might have one chance in 234,000,000 of becoming a plant manager, opening up all sorts of private and rewarding doors reaching up into the corporate realm of Valhalla. Success was based on performance, and all those that lived in the village had about the same opportunity for an eventual advancement up the ladder to a better-paying production job. Then, if one was smart, lucky, and went to college, maybe one day they could gravitate into an even better overseer's position. Yet, if one was academically or intellectually outgunned, they could also end up far behind the curve of opportunity. But a plant manager was on a different planet. Looking back on those days, I never forgot who I was and where I came from. Yet, at the time, I never knew that when I later left industrial engineering and finance and went into management, I was also entering the cattle business and would end up confronting many sacred cows. Some you barbecued, others you put out to pasture, and a few you sent to the soap factory. I had heard that one of the greatest sins you could commit was to become a deeply superficial person, but as best I recall, I never remember meeting one of those in a mill village.

We didn't know what real bone china or chandeliers were in our little town, and few people had probably ever seen them. We never grew self-conscious about what we didn't have or tended toward self-effacing values back then, but we were proud of work and where we began. There were no gold spoons, silver platters, crystal, or linen tablecloths, and it was up to you to carry your own plastic fork and disposable plate. You were fortunate if you had your own paper napkin. We learned that most things had to be taken hypothetically, because little of what we expect is guaranteed certainty. At the same time, perhaps in contrast to this perspective, I was taught to never place a dollar sign on my peace of mind—some of the best advice I ever received.

I didn't want to be limited and defined by history, circumstances, geography, my place in society, or even my soft Southern dialect. I was a Southerner by birth, later a Yankee by choice, an American by providence, and a Problem Doctor by fate. I knew of no one that had ever been better blessed. There was no need to be poking around in the boneyards of yesterday and today with tomorrow patiently waiting on the horizon.

As a young man, I didn't have time to try to impress anyone. It would have been a fool's errand. I didn't know a lot, but I quickly discovered that the fortune of one to be blessed with unique gifts and personal attributes, in varying values and degrees, was not to be taken for granted. It enables us to engage life as gladiators, to do combat in the shrinking arena of an urgent-care world. It also permitted one to feel the vibrations of change heading our way each day.

When wisdom and knowledge claims the upper hand over self-doubt, we eventually realize that today we are only eighteen to twenty inches away from ink and pixels in the library or on a screen. There we can explore with the wise men and women of the ancient magic kingdom: Socrates, Abraham Lincoln, Albert Einstein, Henry Ford, John D. Rockefeller, Bill Gates, Nelson Mandela, Warren Buffet, Mother Teresa, Martin Luther King Jr., all of whose thoughts and lives are written on the pages before us. Everyone, regardless of status, has the same opportunity to witness and learn. If we do not open our eyes and minds to knowledge, it's our own fault, and we may miss our waiting personal link with tomorrow.

Growing up as a mill kid, I never felt that I came up short of the peculiar gifts or accomplishments that girls liked in boys—things like intelligence, the ability to dance, sing, play football and baseball, cut up a bit in public, walk them home from the movies, or hold hands. If I was ever in doubt whether I should kiss a pretty girl or not, I went ahead and always gave her the benefit of the doubt. The interesting thing was that girls also discovered boys, since they matured earlier than we did; they just didn't want us to know. However, the problem was girls first detected the guys a year or two older than we were, in the classes ahead of us in school. That didn't sit well with many of us, although pride kept us from saying anything. But in a couple of years they gravitated back into our erratic hormonal orbit.

That's when I first discovered that Mother Nature, in her infinite wisdom, was completely unfair. My dad said it had something to do with things called hormones, whatever that was. I don't ever remember seeing any around the mill village, or if I did, I didn't recognize them, until I got older. I don't think I was actually deficit in nerves and courage, nor was I long on ineptitude. My bashfulness or backwardness was nothing to be concerned about. Yet, being one or two years younger than most in my class at school—some even more, not to mention my girlfriends—made me feel something was missing. So I just relaxed and learned a lot from excellent female teachers and friends who were far beyond my years in experience. What an eye-opening education it was for a neophyte like me. But I was surprised how quickly I caught up with the others. One thing I learned off the bat was to never walk unassumingly into a dangerous minefield by discussing women's looks with other women, because the wrong people will hear about it. Then your eyesight will be questioned, along with your black eyes, and the knots on your head will become very noticeable and embarrassing.

Saying goodbye to childhood was never a big deal for me because, growing up in a constantly mature environment, I didn't really feel like a child. I never wanted to be like background music; you know, "I'm there and you hear me, but don't pay me any attention." Always around adults, I distracted my family and the many boarders and diners with my interminable questions and curiosities. I think the only thing I ever wore out faster than Converse sneakers was my parents' patience, but never my grandmother's, Connie Baker's, or Junior's. A simple answer was rarely sufficient because it was necessary to also know "Why?" I'm sure I was a pain to be around. I would probably have been sent to my room many days, if I had had a room. The interesting thing was that even at a young age, these responses began to gradually fit together in a matrix, like a jigsaw puzzle. The big picture of actuality began to form in my mind early on, and things click into place. What was occurring was a fundamental shift in mind-think. It became evident that it was OK to grow calluses on your hands, but never on your mind, heart, or behind.

I came from a normal working-class family, and I have been working since I was nine. Of course, being a good husband and father is sometimes the hardest job of all. I discovered along the way you cannot overemphasize the importance of life experiences because there is no viable substitute. You can study swimming from a book all you want, but you don't learn to stay afloat until you are on your own in the deep end of the pool. Sometimes it's near impossible to believe that so much reality can exist so far beyond the reach of one's imagination. Yet, even with all our problems, life is such a great orchestrated play. There are really no bad seats, even when you are sitting high up in the mezzanine or far away in the back balcony. I've been there.

I learned to never be discouraged when things didn't go my way, because there always seems to be a certain amount of heat-seeking intelligence that's reaching out, searching for a cold mind and an aching heart. Most of the decisions and confrontations that we face have a bite anyway, especially if they go against the grain of popular opinion. So most of life is really all about one's expectations versus one's reality, and experiences frequently become a major inflection point in your career. Of course, truth always has the staying power of success, but it's not as simple as we make it out to be. You can accept it as an ordinary flat tale, in the honest standard format, or as the super-deluxe stretched curvilinear version, which has become disconcertingly more popular in recent years. It's up to you.

A surprising discovery was that it's not the great things that happened along the way but the little things in life, filled with remembrances, that make it so special and worthwhile. For a long time I kept wondering why I continued looking back; then one day I realized that's where today's and tomorrow's answers are found. Whatever you do, don't become self-satisfied; there will always be something that comes along in a moment to dwarf your past achievements and problems and unring your bell, unless it's something you do for someone else, especially if they are unable to return the favor. That feeling is rarely exceeded. We humans seem to enjoy acting out our thoughts, observing oneself go by in action. Sometimes it even gets amusing watching someone watch himself; we have become very good at that.

I think in later life everything speeds up, and we try to manufacture something out of nothing, to replace the song of the muses we lost from our earlier days. Yet I'm still trying to figure out why the invigorated mind, at speed of light, always seems to come in the dark of the night when I'm asleep.

10

Mayhayley

Over the years, science has explained the steady replacement of perceived psychic, paranormal, and supernatural occurrences with the ordinary, normal, and practical. Superstition has been moved to the periphery and superseded by scientific knowledge and proven life principles. It's possible, but highly improbable, that there are unknown forces on Earth that we have not yet discovered. In fact, I think we would be amazed if we knew all about the things we don't understand, situations that exist beyond the confines of our senses. Once you understand physics and the fundamental laws of science and academic rationality, you can certainly scale them up to the human level and the results encountered in nature. However, as realistic and practical as we try to be in our normalcy, we all look for some degree of refuge in the mystique and the impossible hiding just beneath the surface.

At the same time, when the experience of the known expands into the domain of the unknown, then the proportion of intellectual ignorance tends to grow. In other words, the more you learn, the more you discover that you don't know. That's what happened when Amber Mayhayley Lancaster came along to screw up everything the world thought it knew and understood through our scientific knowledge. She even set erudition, scholarship, and reasoning back decades, as she resided in the imagination, somewhere out there on the horizon between myth and prophecy. We saw it but couldn't touch it and still don't understand it. She simply blew your intellect, but was not outside the realm of a child's imagination. We could never, with wit and wisdom, read the tea leaves of the sensitive gray matter that defined her. She undid me completely.

Although I consider myself reasonably well-educated, I'm on the short end of the rationality range, where there are so many things I still can't comprehend about life and human existence. One of those many unexplainable things was Mayhayley, the self-professed "Oracle of the Ages." How does one comprehend and confront such an "oracle" if one is a nine-year-old boy? I think very cautiously, or so it was with me. Meeting her was wildly compelling but very strange territory, as if the perplexing experience was assembled from a kit of odd random parts that didn't fit. What stood between me and her was a simple failure of imagination. I just never had expertise in the unique service of her blessed nonconformity, because I liked the simpler things in life that were logical, that I could see and understand. She was not one of them. I may have been a little precocious as a boy, but I wasn't naïve or clueless.

We like to stick a tag on a person or thing that gives them or it a place, if not purpose, which isn't always fair. I think it was that way with this perplexing elderly lady of mystery. The first time I heard about Mayhayley was from my Aunt Opal. I was just a little fellow at the time, but the experience remained vividly implanted in my mind, primarily from its harshness. Opal was a widow when she married my mother's brother, Nathan, about two years after her first husband's death. She had been to see the seer of Franklin, for some purpose, and when she stood up to leave, Mayhayley made a surprising statement. She said, "There is something I need to tell you, but I don't want to because it is bad. Yet, I feel I should, because I see it, but I don't want to." My aunt said, "Please tell me." Mayhayley said, "I see your husband dying, being consumed by a terrible fire. I don't know exactly what's involved, but it is a tragedy like in war, and he will be burned to death, consumed by fire in an explosion." Opal told her husband, and he said, "Let's pray she's wrong. I can't see our home catching on fire or anything like that, and I'm not in the military." Less than six weeks later, on his way to work one morning, a commercial gas truck crossed the center line in the road and hit him head-on. There was a terrible explosion and he and the truck driver were consumed by a horrific fire. Several passengers in nearby automobiles were also badly burned.

Now, there is nothing wrong with fiction or fantasy—it just needs to remain in context, even when surrounded by cotton fields. I don't think

Mayhayley knew how the answer was found; she just "saw" in her mind's eye certain things even she couldn't explain—and no one else could. It was just part of a deeper aesthetic and finely-tuned facts, with her mind trespassing into places others' couldn't go. At the same moment, it was hard for an observer of the scene to get through the harsh unexplainable mental filter of unstaged moments in which she was held captive.

There are theories of supernatural plausibility, and patterns of evidence, but they don't hold much water. It's all about the probability of the unreal. Mayhayley didn't comply with either. She just nudged the impossible into the realm of the real. I guess in its own way, the world we inhabit is filled with fantasy—things we don't understand—that's composed of bits and pieces of reality that wander around unmoored in our mind. Our cognizance tries to tell us that you can't imagine the unimaginable, but I believe you could because that's where Mayhayley resided. Once you had met her, she left a particular vivid presence that never again left your consciousness.

Fantasy can provide some engaging leaps to an alternative universe, but we still must live on Earth. This only goes to prove that questioning and fate are always bigger components of one's progress than we fully realize or appreciate. When we attempt to engage the unexplainable, it enhances knowledge, and usually diminishes our eagerness to prejudge or condemn other people just because they are different. However, in Mayhayley's case, there was a proven density of truth that no one could ever expunge. She was radically strange, and there has been no one else like her—only poor imitators. It's hard for one's lived perspective to be detached and reportorial. It's more like the collective consciousness that emerged from the unexplainable phenomenon occurring near the small town of Franklin, Georgia.

A visit to Mayhayley's rural domain required an intrepid adventurer, a singular experience from which few returned unmarked. She was an all-purpose mind bender who would completely rearrange your thinking, taking Southern Reality to places it had never been before—and may never want to go again. Actually seeing her enhanced my believing. She threw the doors wide open to my perceptions. The plot could be as exotic and distant as you cared to make it, a point of departure on a far-reaching journey in your thoughts. Your ticket and passport was only $1.10. You didn't have to be wealthy or especially sophisticated, but you needed an open mind to sit before her. You would never forget it. I didn't, and I was just standing there a couple of times in silence, watching from a few feet away, while the hair stood up on the back of my neck.

Every ravenous curiosity must feed on something. Even fairy tales come bearing gifts and nutrition for the mind as they unleash real subdued impulses into innocent thoughts and the sprawling imagination. That which reaches out from one's thinking is always trying to find something to hold on to. We all want to look behind the mysterious veil, but you can only walk away from the unknown so many times before it abandons you—and I was exceptionally curious.

In her case, *different* was a mild, sensible, and sensitive word. No one likes an imitation, and I wondered how she could be the real deal, because she didn't have a crystal ball, read tea leaves, or use coffee grounds or cards. One must learn how to embrace the agency these insights provide, because we are clearly shaped in varying degrees by the unresolvable and that which we don't understand. I just wanted to keep my thoughts afloat and not be overwhelmed when I met her. Mayhayley didn't play games. She was straightforward and told you what she saw, right out of the box. Even if it was bad and hurtful, you got both barrels. Right or wrong, it was a performance in dedicated commitment. The experience recalibrated my thinking at a very young age.

We are held hostage by those things we do not fully grasp. So it was, and still is, between me and Mayhayley. Time and again, I have found no compatibility in comparing scientific reasoning and her proven indecipherable gift of seeing the past, present, and future. I was weighed with equal parts of skepticism, puzzlement, and sympathy. My greatest challenge was not to grow a callus on my heart, but where she was involved, that was much easier said than done. You see, I liked her!

My mind was saturated with cascading thoughts about what I had heard and things reaching far beyond youth's reasoning. Yet I envisioned those things she couldn't take away from me, and what I wanted, she couldn't give. She could only interpret what she saw and in her own incomprehensible way. She couldn't change anything she could visualize. So why should I be afraid of her? I wasn't. In fact, to the contrary, I began to have a certain compassion for the fragile, elderly lady. It seemed to me that she was probably trapped in her own mind, with a miraculous ability she would have preferred not to have and probably didn't fully understand herself. Yet we can rest assured that fate doesn't ask or give us a choice about our future. Don't get me wrong. When I met her, I didn't have bright flashy tail feathers like the bird of courage, but neither was I a frightened quail. At the same time, I couldn't escape the undermining presence of her one-eyed gaze.

Contemporary culture is based on logic that can be reconciled to known facts, but Mayhayley's peerless abilities never could. Where she was concerned, my mind was in a different time and place. How many of her psychic readings came true, out of tens of thousands, I do not know. But those I personally experienced were all fully proven and completely inexplicable. A miracle is described as being something irrational, incomprehensible, marvellous, even impossible—a reaching sensation, a phenomenon, among many other things. Regardless of our belief in inscrutable paranormal happenings, miracles still exist in our world. Perhaps she performed some, and I leave it up to you to decide—I already have.

I had never had any experience with incantations, fortune-telling, enchantments, or seers until I heard about Mayhayley. In the 1940s, the early years of my enlarging mental vernacular, there was her fable-like myth, passed through word of mouth from where she resided. It was all about imbibing in the world of the incomprehensible. Her contribution to Southern Reality was not in trying to shape anyone's prayers, promises, hopes, or even the possibilities offered. There was no opinion on her part, only the facts presented as she saw them. There were no sensibilities or aspirations, just her vision. Mystery and the inquiring mind have enticingly beckoned the Homo sapiens for eons, like Mona Lisa's curved smile; then came this fantasy of a woman.

From the time I was five or six years old, during World War II and after, I heard the name Mayhayley Lancaster everywhere in the mill village. She was so very famous, even back then when everyone—and I do mean everyone—just called her Mayhayley, or Hayley. Her daily exploits were discussed in conversations at the boarding house, in the mills, and throughout homes in the Greater Valley area. It was a very strange and rare name I had never heard anywhere else—or since—so there was no confusion. Her singular identity stood out. Regardless of where we live, you hear ghost stories, and sometimes I have found there are those puzzling mysterious people that stir our imagination. So it was with her, the renowned fortune-teller, visionary, soothsayer. You didn't have to go to Greece and Delphi, on the slope of Mount Parnassus. America had found its own "oracle" in Franklin, Georgia, a few miles from where I lived. From my research, the seer from Delphi wasn't nearly as good or accurate as the lady from Heard County.

As a little boy I called her Miss Mayhayley, out of respect. I didn't want to stir up her psychic animosity. Yet my curiosity almost overwhelmed my better judgment. She had lost an eye in an accident in younger days and had replaced it with a glass one. Some people said she had used a large marble and an eye patch. She had a black patch when I first saw her. I didn't like the one remaining scary "evil eye" staring directly at me, as she did numerous times the first dark night we met. I have always wondered what she was thinking about me; maybe nothing. Perhaps she just liked my blondish-red hair. I had read the fable about Hansel and Gretel, and it vividly came to mind. I think she just liked little boys, yet she never married or had children of her own.

Her notoriety spread even further across the United States by her exploits in the court room. She helped a county sheriff solve a complicated murder case in the infamous John Wallace trial in Coweta County. John Wallace was an extraordinarily wealthy yet cruel Meriwether County land owner. He murdered one of his tenant-farmer employees for stealing two cows. Even though he destroyed evidence and issued further threats and subterfuge, Mayhayley's psychic powers helped bring him to justice and he was executed in the electric chair in 1950.

A movie was later made about this 1947 episode featuring Johnny Cash, June Carter Cash, and Andy Griffith: *Murder in Coweta County*. It extended the uniqueness of her peerless vision. When the word circulated across the land, people began writing for advice and coming to see her from New York, Chicago, Texas, California, everywhere, for her fortune-telling prowess.

Back then her exploits were a very popular topic in the daily mill discourse. No one understood Mayhayley's fortune-telling abilities, but they went to see her for advice—even the skeptics, many of whom, like me, became believers. It's hard to get those words out of my mouth and mind without collapsing under my own scientific conscience. It gave me an uncomfortable feeling, probably like a Jehovah's Witness or Pentecostal going to a traditional service hosted by Episcopalians. Yet, it helps mark one's own critical boundaries.

I don't think there was ever a surge of inventiveness in Mayhayley's projections. It was just the image she saw, a stimulated surge of recognition in her vision—not always clearly seen, but reflected in her narrative response to the questions asked. It mirrored the reality and vulnerability of an ordinary life but was not something she mischievously concocted. I never once heard anywhere of her being misleading, irreverent, sarcastic, critical, or mocking of a single vision she had, or about the person for which she was doing the reading.

What also amazed me was that each situation was unique. She never knew what to expect or who would show up at her door. Each case was new, singular for her, straight out of the box. It was a continuous parade of normal people and oddities from the shadows. She would see dozens of individuals some days, and the short response time for a personal vision was hard for one to comprehend. I would guess that an important part of her job was to become a self-portrait of the mystery of the person in charge—herself. She had learned one thing: to be careful about the difference between the promise and the delivery. She always tried to cover both bases and be the best possible version of herself.

Today there are not too many people left above ground that ever met Mayhayley Lancaster in person, in all her inexplicableness. If alive, they would probably be in their 80s or 90s. I am one of the few remaining in this exclusive, quickly-vanishing club.

When she was born, it was said there was a caul covering her face. In those days it was believed that when this happened, that person was born "with a veil," giving them special psychic powers. From my original skeptical experience, I eventually came to believe this must be true. If not, something gave her an illogical cerebral aptitude that no one—including scientists—understood, could duplicate, or could explain, then or now. I think one of the measures of her great success was that she was able to overcome everyone's best efforts to sabotage her credibility.

Amanda Mayhayley Lancaster was born October 18, 1875, near Franklin in Heard County, Georgia, and she died November 22, 1955, just one month after her eightieth birthday. She was a lawyer, political activist, school teacher, midwife, seer, and the wealthiest woman in Heard County. She had extensive landholdings, owned and operated a number of businesses, and was the first woman to ever run for the Georgia Legislature. She lost in 1926. Many of her far-reaching ideas for progressive change included improving women's and children's rights, better schools, and economically assisting the underdog rural counties and sparsely-populated areas of Georgia. All the essential issues that she had advocated were years later approved by legislation and initiated into law; she was ahead of her time. Because of the outspoken causes of her earlier years, she became a role model for many liberal young women.

She had large quantities of cash stashed around her house and barn and accumulated hefty bags of money at home before taking it to the bank. Someone told her it might be stolen and asked why she didn't put her funds in the bank sooner. She said it wasn't necessary, since she also owned the bank. It was common knowledge that a lot of money was kept at home and she had no special protection—just she and her sister Sallie and some scrounging dogs. I guess because of her unique mysterious powers, people were superstitious and just too afraid to try to rob her. I would have been.

Yet, even with her diverse renown, she became better known as a fortune-teller, an auger, and her own self-promotional "Oracle of the Ages." She performed as if presenting an incongruous magic trick, but there was no smoke or mirrors, nor strings attached. Neither was there a Wizard of Oz standing behind the curtain.

She was insanely accurate in her pronouncements. Some say she was a big gambler and numbers runner, but I don't believe that. I think it was a reputation that rubbed off from all the gamblers that came to see her looking for advice, trying to improve their odds. This was my experience, close-up, meeting Mayhayley for the first time as a little boy. She charged $1.10 for

Above, Caney Head Methodist Church and graveyard where Mayhayley Lancaster is buried, Roosterville, Georgia. Right, headstone for Mayhayley Lancaster, 1875–1955.

her predictions, the dollar for her and ten cents to feed the many dogs she had around her house. Maybe they were there for protection, perhaps for companionship, or perchance she just had a big heart for stray dogs that hung around waiting to be fed. Of course, a dollar and a dime were worth a lot more seventy-plus years ago.

She lived in an old unpainted wood frame family home, with an aged cedar shake roof, located on a typical dark unpaved Georgia county dirt road, not near any other neighbors. Her house was about sixty feet off the road, and the continual automobile traffic had worn away the grass, with a large dirt parking area in front of the house and immediately across the road. There was always a stream of automobiles and trucks lined up to see Mayhayley, looking for answers. People just appeared at random, unannounced, that she had never seen before. There was an open front porch with a single naked light bulb on the porch at the front door. I assume it was there so her sister Sallie could see all the visitors at night and let them enter in an orderly fashion, one at a time. To the best of my knowledge, and from observation, the two of them were always alone, the only ones there after her mother died. It was normal on a busy day or night to wait an hour or more to get to see her.

Mayhayley at one time had evidently permitted a refreshment concession to be set up in her yard to serve those waiting. Although, the times I was there, I never saw one. Of course, it was easy to get thirsty on a long hot day or night. I'm sure she got her cut. It always intrigued me that she began using her "second sight" gift when she was just six years old and continued for 74 years until her death. I wondered as a kid if she ever predicted she would lose sight (through an accident) in one eye, or when she would actually die. I never heard anyone say. Knowing in advance would have been a heavy burden to bear. I have heard (though unconfirmed) that psychics can never perform readings on themselves.

We were fourth or fifth in line the night I saw her the second time, and there were two or three waiting behind us. Her sister Sallie finally came to the porch and my aunt gave her $1.10. That evening, my curiosity got the best of me and as I had done before, I strongly insisted that I also go in to see Mayhayley. My parents reluctantly agreed, and Sallie said it was OK, if

I was accompanied by my mother. Now, my mother was Scotch-Irish, red-headed, and as curious as me, or vice versa. She had a mother-like twinkle in her eyes, which also indicated mischief in her thoughts. Sallie cautioned us not to say anything or stand too close to Mayhayley and my aunt. There were no formal introductions when we entered the room; it was all business, and we were the only ones present.

Standing there, fifteen feet away, seeing her through my nine-year-old eyes, and remembering stories I had heard, she was scary looking. I carefully canvassed the dark room with my eyes to try to calm my intellect and fidgety nerves. There was a kerosene lamp turned down low, and a big hickory wood fire in the open fireplace. These two light sources were the only brightness in the dimly-defined shadows flickering in the room. As the low light of the burning logs rolled off her form in the flames, I could see that her long, tired, thin face was heavily wrinkled, weather worn. It was what I would best describe as weak and vulnerable, but still foreboding. She seemed to be instantly transfixed, dedicated to the specific task at hand, which to me was proof of a cogent mind in gear. Sallie never told her my aunt's name.

My eyes wandered as my thoughts searched for the unexplainable answers to my many open questions. I decided that the unexplainable I was looking for was not in the room, but was hidden somewhere deep in her unfathomable head. As I gazed around, I spotted a well-worn Bible on the little table on her left, next to the chair. It looked as if it had been opened a million times. Maybe it had. I was surprised, because it was so unexpected. I had never considered Mayhayley—a fortune-teller—as also being a Christian. How wrong you can be about people you don't really know.

I never once saw her smile. She was singularly directed to the task. At that time she was about 75 years old, skinny, leathery looking, with glasses and a patch over one eye. She kept looking at me with her good eye, a very uncomfortable feeling on a cold night in the near dark. As she watched me, I wondered if she had remembered me being there once before. Most certainly she didn't, with so many people passing through her portals, even with a sixth-sense. I never asked, and she never said.

As before, she was snuggled down in what appeared to be a rocking chair, in an old oversized heavy-wool Army overcoat and some kind of military cap on her head, I guess to control her thin grey hair. It was a very cold night. I couldn't tell what kind of dress she had on from across the room, but she evidently had on a large apron and oversized heavy high-topped men's shoes. Her reputation preceded her, more weighed by a halcyon image than a menacing presence. In fact, I felt empathy, sorry for her emaciated, vulnerable bearing. What seems to happen when we stop being afraid is that one ends up with feelings of affinity, compassion, and even charity. So it was with me in my little boy heart of hearts. I felt only sympathy for her inherited plight.

My aunt sat in a small straight-backed wooden chair directly in front of her hunched-over form. She placed her two hands into Mayhayley's hands, who then whispered something to my aunt that I didn't understand. She looked at her hands, held them tightly, and then closed her eyes for perhaps a long two minutes, maybe three. She then opened them and softly said something we could not hear, even as close as we were. They continued in quiet talk maybe five more minutes, and then we left. I never did find out what my aunt actually asked Mayhayley, but I do know one of her comments. She told my aunt that she was pregnant, and my aunt confidently smiled and I heard her respond, "No way, absolutely not." Going home she mentioned it in the car, laughing about it with my uncle. Eight months and three weeks from that very evening, my cousin was born.

One night, a few months later, with nothing to do on a late Saturday afternoon, my dad, mother, uncle, aunt, and I went back over to the Franklin area to see what was happening at Mayhayley's. We parked across the road and watched, while talking about her many exploits and the new village gossip going on around town at the time about her prognostications. Numerous cars came and went as people went in to see her. During the hour or so we were there, all sorts of interesting-looking people stopped by. At any given time there were five or six people waiting their turn.

In about twenty minutes, two black men about twenty-five or thirty years old pulled up in the front yard. Oddly, one waited in the car with the motor running and the other got in the short queue of one or two people to go in and get a reading from Mayhayley. After he had been inside perhaps fifteen to twenty minutes, the front door slammed open and out he ran. At first the loud slamming didn't register, but then I heard a head full of noise competing with the dogs. He didn't even touch the three steps down from the porch to the ground; he leaped completely off the porch in a dead run and jumped into the car and it sped away, tires screeching. We were surprised, because it didn't look at all like the same person who went in, although he was dressed identically. The man jumping off the porch in great desperation was almost as white as I was. We concluded that whatever it was Mayhayley told him, it frightened him so much it temporarily drained the blood and color out of his complexion and almost scared him to death. We were dumbfounded. One's emotions are never easily hidden because they have a way of rising up to declare themselves, and this was one of those times.

There is a prominent, verified story that became known throughout the South—and there were many—about the celebrated Hollywood movie actress Tallulah Bankhead. She was from Newnan, Georgia, just a short distance (perhaps 20 miles) from Franklin. Tallulah had become world famous from her days in the movies, had gotten engaged to be married in Los Angeles, and had come home for a two-week visit with her family to plan the wedding. She had been given a huge diamond engagement ring. When it was time to head back to L.A., she couldn't find her beautiful new ring. She searched everywhere and was in near panic. She thought perhaps it had even been stolen.

Someone suggested she go ask the Lady from Franklin for help. Reluctantly, not believing in soothsayers but being exasperated and at loose ends, she agreed. Holding hands, Mayhayley went into her trance. She finally said, "I can't see exactly where it is; it's dark, closed up, enclosed in something. But what I can vividly see are three colors—red, yellow, and blue. I don't know what that means but that's where your ring is. Find those three colors and you will find your ring."

Tallulah didn't know what it meant either, but she went back home and searched the entire house again. She went back up to the attic where she had been looking earlier to no avail and reopened many old dusty boxes and closed trunks she had looked in the week before when she first came home. In one trunk she found a red, yellow, and blue quilt. After carefully unfolding it, there was her ring. Don't ask me!

Back in the late 1940s, my red-headed Scotch-Irish maternal grandfather Benjamin Sanford McGraw was a farmer with a lot of acreage near LaGrange, Georgia. He had several young men that worked for him. He grew food crops, cattle, pigs, corn, cotton, and peanuts. To improve efficiency, he bought an expensive new eight-disk harrow that would plow eight rows at a time, a miracle compared to his old four-disk harrow. He called it his "Gee-Whiz." He went to the field where it had been left two weeks earlier, and it was gone. He couldn't find it anywhere, and none of his employees knew anything about it, so he reported it to the county sheriff as stolen. The sheriff suggested that he go to Mayhayley to see if she could help find it. He didn't believe in fortune-tellers, but with no other alternative, he left LaGrange for Franklin.

After he paid Sallie $1.10, Mayhayley sat and held his hands, and after a short trance she spoke. "One of your employees, whom I can see," and she physically described him, "plans to steal your harrow. He has moved it to another field, out of sight, a field that you don't use. I will describe the place where it is now located, behind a small hill, away from the road"—and she did. "Behind this little mound of earth he has placed your harrow until he can safely come back with a vehicle and pick it up. If you can find this site that I have described, you will find your harrow—but don't wait too long or it will be gone."

Through her description, my grandfather knew exactly the person she was talking about. He also searched his acreage all the next day until he found the hill she had described, and exactly as she said, there was his harrow hidden in the brush. He told the sheriff and they closely watched this employee for two days. When he came late one evening to pick it up, my grandfather, the sheriff, and a deputy were close behind and caught him with the harrow on his truck. I can't explain it, nor could he or the Sheriff, but it happened. She came through again.

There was a lot of legitimate commentary about Mayhayley, but there was even more speculation and false rumors, based on prejudices. (There is that word again.) As time has passed, the more I have learned and thought about her, even discounting her foreboding appearance in later years, I think I would have truly liked her if I had gotten to know her better. I think she was viewed through an ordinary lens as an unknown phenomenon, rather than a human being with feelings and emotions. I know she had a big heart for the underdog. With such a valuable gift, maybe it was just impossible for her to ever be normal, because she wasn't. I never once saw her smile. I admired her progressive attitude and the spirit she showed in her younger years to try and help those less fortunate and those needing fairness in an unfair, inequitable world.

In retrospect, it's hard to imagine what she must have gone through, and the burden she had to carry, with such a unique, unexplainable talent. We will never know about her personal demons, the handicaps and hardships that accompanied her singular ability. In her case there was a much greater difference between "normal" and "abnormal" than just two letters in the alphabet. I'm sure over time it never got any easier for Mayhayley, because she was unable to live an ordinary life like everyone else. She was never married or had children of her own. If I were a betting man, I would wager that if she had a do-over, she would not ask the second time around for this special "gift." It was not a life she chose, but the life she was given.

Sadly, she never got to mother her own children's menagerie, although I'm sure she would have been a great mother hen. Thoughts of her continue to follow me around and it's still a bit unsettling. This tale serves as a testimony to her unfathomable second-sight. She masterfully wove together so many difficult narratives that it often kept me up late at night wondering what she would do next. Yet, in many years of evolution and acclaim, there were never any vexing ethical questions where she was involved. She would still be a moral rarity for a public figure in today's world. It's hard to reach beyond the limits of imagination; I've never been there.

I have written these words for posterity, with a keen sensitivity to state the facts experienced firsthand—a synthesis of the legacy of a unique person beyond all comprehension, an iconic individual that was discussed daily in the mill villages. The final inscription on her gravestone at Caney Head Methodist Cemetery in rural Roosterville, Heard County, is from the New Testament. It is about Jesus, and it probably says it all from her perspective: "For neither did his brothers believe in him." Perhaps it should have read: Utinam Viveres Excepteur ("If only you were alive today"). Sometimes by its very nature, truth remains in the dark corners and deep shadows, as myths have a way of hanging tough and enduring. For this little boy, just meeting her was a decisive occasion, with a crackling sense of human detail, pivoting toward the unknown and the completely unexplainable.

In the "Oracle of Franklin's" era and after, copycats popped up out of the woodwork, and in twisted specificity. It became pretty clear that these new "fortune-tellers" were just that—copycats with no credibility. In mental review, at the end of her season, I can't think of anything she did wrong. She just told the truth as she knew it. Now most of us don't always do that, or even like to hear it. Truth is small comfort if used to dispel one's integrity. Yet, no one I ever read or heard about disproved her credibility. She scared a lot of people by what she saw in their future, but she also did a lot of good. We never appreciate the value of light until we are standing alone in darkness. Everyone knows that death is an end-game. The only thing left to make a coffin more humane is to install windows, but that still doesn't change the view.

You don't have to pay me $1.10 for telling you this unexplainable firsthand story, because I don't have any dogs. But if you decide it was still worth it, like Mayhayley, I would appreciate the offer.

11

Along the Chattahoochee

Life at times seems so unreal and exaggerated that only myth and parody can do it justice, if it is adequately weighed by contradictions of richness, story, and sensibility. Some of the early manufacturing plants in the South just after the Civil War were powered by water from the Chattahoochee River, which separated Georgia from Alabama. That river was a marvel in more ways than one.

For example, because of the unique way the Riverdale Manufacturing Plant was constructed on the river to accommodate the original water-wheel power, most of the facility was located in Alabama, but the spinning room was actually in Georgia. At that early time, Alabama and Georgia had completely different legal requirements about when couples could get married. When applying for a marriage license, Alabama had a three-day waiting period, plus a blood test. Georgia didn't require either. For those reasons, one of the more popular occasions on Sunday afternoon for many years was for young couples to get married in the Riverdale Mill's spinning room. There was no bridge nearby connecting Alabama and Georgia, so it was therefore both an expedient and practical decision. I understand the Guinness Book of World Records said this was the only manufacturing plant in the world where such a unique situation occurred.

Discounting getting married in the mill, most neophytes have the wrong opinion of mill villages and villagers. Folks that lived there were a lot like farmers, just not quite as highbrow or sophisticated. Just like me, everyone was about as vanilla as plain ice cream. During those early years, I lived in fear of chitterlings, tripe, and hog jowl. In the fall, when Papa killed the hogs, neither did pickled pig's feet, pig ears, or pig tails rank too high with my taste buds. You had to live below the Mason-Dixon Line a long time ago to appreciate those delicacies. Of course, some people—like my grandfather—loved his scrambled eggs and pork brains and extra salty Kit-Fish. For some older people, these unique dishes became the height of Southern cuisine after the War Between the States, when there was nothing else.

Pardon me for clarification: the War Between the States would be the Civil War to my Yankee friends. We must be thorough and truthful in our opinions and proclamations, even if they are wrong, because the world as seen through a first glance may not be the same as it actually is. So I still wonder why my Northern mates call it the Civil War, because there was nothing civil about it. The primary reason this peerless cuisine ranked so high is that Southerners, black and white, had little left to eat at the end of that devastating conflict. This was especially true after the mercenary Yankee carpetbaggers and politicians swarmed down on the South like locusts. They picked the land and farmers clean, taking what little was left, including their farms and property. Of course, that's the Southern version, and there must be at least a half-dozen others.

My grandmother always said I was just a Yankee at heart. I was eight years old before I knew what she meant and discovered it wasn't intended to be a compliment. I was never sure if that was the facts of the truth or the truth of the facts. Even Yankee at heart, I still enjoyed the opening edge of a Southern summer, before the sun turns the eye on its stove up to boil. Yet, there were times when just getting out of bed got the day off to a bad start.

However, I loved all the real life-and-death necessities of Southern cuisine—lard biscuits, crackling corn bread, white sausage gravy, grits floating in butter, pork sausage, fried chicken, country ham with red-eye gravy, and churned buttermilk. And for dessert? Sugar-butter bread pudding. Hunting and fishing in the Chattahoochee were big-time sports in our little towns, and it was a safe bet that your neighbors had catfish, frog legs, a skinned squirrel, or rabbit in their freezer as often as they would a sour-cream pound cake or homemade ice cream. Even now, every time I pass a can of hominy, sardines, potted-meat, or a Moon Pie at the grocery, it all comes rushing back. It was heaven on a culinary shoestring for a small boy, as well as a grown adult.

We came to revel in words and dreams, long lists of them, because they carry worlds around within their meanings. Early on we needed to root and condition our thoughts in a benevolent greenhouse before planting them in our life gardens with a minimum of drama. Experience is weighed by the lovely ode to imagination and experimentation that makes us who we are. Back then, few things seemed to bother anyone, because mill folks always had a comforting naturalness and good sense of humor. There was also an innate sensitivity, if not unique concern, for the needs of one's neighbors and they were there to help. I always admired that wonderful attribute, which is not as prevalent today. But neither are mill villages along the Chattahoochee.

Like every normal Southerner, I truly love fried food, even fully realizing the downside. When I hear the deep-fryer fat start to sizzle and pop, my taste buds go into overdrive. It's like the Devil backing up to me with a wink, telling me to ignore my doctor's edicts and just enjoy myself. Fried food is good and can be so highly spiced that it takes your breath away, and that's just the mild seasoning. It often made my eyes water when it was deep fried like we prepared it on the weekend at backwater gatherings (Chattahoochee lake outings to my Yankee friends). I think most people in our mill village realized that we had the choice to make ourselves contented or miserable. The amount of effort was about the same. You can actually live happily ever after, but only a day at a time. Fried food was just part of life's shortened ritual.

All Southerners I have ever known—other than transplants who haven't yet had enough time in-grade to be accepted—are both profuse and prolific at taking liberties with our regional tongue. If we don't have a word that will fit, we just use another one or make one up to fill the conversational void. We are good at twisting the tail of reality. Of course, there are all the handy delineations that have become words and phrases that are openly accepted in the productive American lexicon. In our little town, people were straightforward and said "guts" instead of the more delicate expression "intestinal fortitude." Some of our more frequent cryptic descriptions are for artifacts or tools to repair things, which were very popular expressions in the mill village. Words like a "whatsit," a "whigmaleerie," a "whatchamacallit," a "thingamajig," "doohickey," a "whangdoodle, and a "lollapalooza."

It's also no wonder that "goodbye" is one of the most meaningful and heavily used words in the vocabulary. It's an early contraction—salutation, meaning "God be with you," very popular in the South and all across America. Another well-used word is "geezer," usually applied in the context as "ole geezer." It's a cousin to "old coot." Our thoughts are also ingrained in clichés like, "A bird in the hand makes a mess;" "His English is worse than 10,000 of his bites;" "Beauty is in the eye of the beholder, unless your eyes are closed;" and "Close only counts in kissing cousins, hand grenades, and horseshoes." When I used to ask my Dad to give me a dime to buy a Dr. Pepper, he would always say, "Do you think I'm made out of money?" Sometimes I wonder why I had such a passion and became so addicted to those soft drinks, since I could never buy one. Maybe I just answered my own question.

Let me be perfectly clear: I'm still not an "ole geezer." That would better reflect many of my elderly friends, the ones still left from the days of Chattahoochee Valley yore. Back then, everyone walked or paid twenty-two cents a gallon for gasoline. That is, if you were lucky enough to be the one in three families in town that owned a motor-operated vehicle. It denotes the days in the South when poverty, lack of formal education, outdoor toilets, poor healthcare, few jobs, and prejudice all had equal footing. Somewhere there could have been better jobs for the ordinary guy, who was earning $25–30 a week in the mill, but I don't know where those jobs were hiding. The mill was certainly better than normal subsistence, compared to tough sharecrop farming or relocating to an impersonal, overcrowded city. This was especially true when moving to a dangerous distant place away from family and friends. Retirement was just another conversational word and didn't mean much because most people worked into their 70s, unless bad health caught up with them first—too frequently it did. Of course, few individuals had a choice, because they didn't have today's government safety net to fall into if things weren't going well.

Even so, there was a lot more gratitude, respect, and trust back then than what we find in today's subsidized culture. Government had a much less intrusive part in our everyday. Yet life and living was filled with high jinks, which was heavily outweighed by the fun and low jinks. However, since the beginning of time, we all still had to undergo the hormonal turbulence of adolescence. If we were lucky, we realized that life is the autograph of all things and how we live it becomes our own personal signature. It was in those mill villages that my preoccupations were finally grounded. There is always a price to pay for whatever we do. If one is not careful, living becomes a full-fledged act of mimicry, and you may try to imitate the wrong person or example.

Today, the GPS takes you everywhere in America you want to go and back home again. In fact, you don't even have to ask your wife or girlfriend to read a roadmap, praise the Lord. Yet, in the "good ole days," I had to take a bath on the back porch or in the back yard with a hosepipe in a round galvanized tub. I don't think hot water had been invented back then, at least not on our street. For boys, I can understand why they took a bath only once a week, especially in winter. Now, I'm not so sure morality was a lot better in those days, although we like to pretend it was. What you don't want to do is have your name changed from a noun to a verb. I have never seen a reputation become full-fledged beyond one's power to destroy it. Although, at the same time, honesty reigned supreme in our little town. Honesty is saying, "Yes, officer, I did see the thirty-five MPH speed limit sign; I just didn't see you."

I have learned my own mind well enough over the years to not completely trust it. So it is with life and reality as well. It's pretty clear that we should be careful about attesting to our own wit and intelligence when there is not enough evidence for conviction. However, there are a couple of things I still can't comprehend, even with sound logic. I must be missing something in translation. Why is it that our children can't read the Bible in their school, but then the law turns around and gives one to everybody that goes to prison? Where is the logic and rationality? Also beyond my intellectual level is why we have to swear on the Bible in court when they are so restrictive that they won't even let us display the Ten Commandments outside the courthouse building. Things were quite different in the old days.

Along the Chattahoochee, we raised a lot more in our backyard gardens, common community pastures, and pig-pens than we bought at the grocery store or market. Of course, during the Big War almost everyone used the

cost thirty cents, a milkshake was twenty-five cents—in a wide variety of flavors (vanilla, chocolate and strawberry)—a banana split was twenty-five cents, and a generous slice of apple pie fifteen cents. Even then, I didn't have two discretionary nickels to rub together. I had no money, but was still working forty-plus hours every week and going to college full time. But I had both feet firmly planted on the ground and my head was in the clouds. I learned from academic roads leading through Auburn Engineering, Harvard Business School, and other graduate book-learning high roads, that DNA and where you were born is not your final destination. In fact, it's only the beginning of your journey.

In our little Chattahoochee wayside station, we liked to pursue curiosity and imagination because it always offered the pageantry of promise. Where career is concerned, without strong emphasis on education and strategic effort, way too frequently the end of the road is close to the beginning. We found Southern Reality is where the real action takes place because we like to enter the narrow and the intimidating portal of possibility. Life just seems to be caught between a vast landscape of imagination and wishful thinking. As a kid, we pressed noses to the window, looking out and thinking of all the things we wanted to do someday. We were all searching for a future we didn't know yet, and we each pursued that adventure to the end; it's a habit we call human nature.

There were so many times I felt like the cartoon character Mr. Magoo, who wanders haphazardly around dangerous vehicle traffic and somehow never gets run over. I felt that way about childhood, growing up, wondering why I was so lucky, safe, happy, and seemingly normal when so many others were not and kept getting hit. I discovered that to have an open mind you must be able to exit from your own context. A fast-moving life consistently changes the experience of being mortal. Human nature can also be very unfair. It doesn't bless us all equally, and it ties us up with our own heartstrings. The mind has to pay a premium price for innovation, and we all had to strain to make something out of very little. Almost everyone in our little town wanted to be absent of artifice or pretense, like one of those rare individuals who is very comfortable with principles, ideals, and values. One should never try to mix biography with close, critical personal analysis;

I promise, you won't be happy with the results. We will perpetually be in need of expansion of consciousness.

Our opinions are always problematic, as we evaluate other people based upon the biases we have within our own mind—which usually comes from how we were raised. The route we often choose to travel won't soothe the nerves, fill empty stomachs, or provide a roof over one's head. Be it the world, big city, or small town, you can never find satisfying answers in the wreckage of a placid way of life. That's exactly what ultimately happened in our little mill villages. It was a monumental train wreck that eventually came to pass in the Chattahoochee Valley, affecting and demeaning everyone's livelihood and future.

Even so, today more than yesterday, education is absolutely paramount, and one must learn to grow intellectually and discover how to better express oneself while making more worthy decisions. We find that each moment, it becomes more difficult to inventory the transforming world of challenge that's pausing in entrapment, waiting for you. You need knowledge and firsthand experience to help confront the convoluted description of reality patiently lingering over the next hill in surprise. We can't escape and will forever remain in Southern Reality until either it or we are fully depleted.

12

Papa and Mama

The words special, unique, exceptional, and inspirational are tossed around too loosely in conversation, but if anyone or anything ever deserved such a label, it would be Papa. I will never reach the level in my children's or grandchildren's eyes that he did in mine. In so many ways, we like to change our forebear's portrait from sepia to living color, and in turn hope to find a little of our own reflection in the process. I'm just not so sure that's intellectually honest. It's more like borrowing from Peter to pay Paul. I guess the endgame is to showcase our heroes by placing them in their family context. My grandfather clearly fit the bill as being exceptional. He told me one day to never get in an argument with an idiot because people watching may not be able to tell the difference between us. I was there a time or two, and as usual, he was right.

My great-grandfather died in a flu epidemic in 1904, when my grandfather was thirteen years old. He was the oldest of eight children and had no choice but to drop out of school and be the father figure in his family. He had to become the poles that hold up the safety net and protect his clan in very difficult times. He went to work in his grandfather's saw-mill as a lumberjack. He cut and snaked huge trees to be sawed into timber out of the forest with teams of mules and oxen. It was a very hard, rough, danger-ous, corporally demanding job. He physically became the strongest, most powerful man I ever knew, but his heart was even bigger. In later years, many afternoons we sat together on the front porch of the boarding house, snapping beans, shucking corn, shelling peas and butterbeans for the next day. He talked; I listened. I asked questions, and he answered. He understood

Early 1880s lumberjacks sawing timber for construction of original mill villages.

that life would not be nourishing if a kid is underfed with what he needs to help him grow into a man—and it wasn't always about vegetables. Papa told me once that it's possible to have both roots and wings; I discovered he was right.

He taught me early on to always have an opinion, even if it was wrong. He said, "You will learn by making decisions—even bad ones." The biggest smile I could ever remember him having was when I was seven or eight years old. I had a very creative idea that was diametrically opposed to his opinion, and he liked it. I thought I had arrived, but was long from being a finished product. One day it dawned on me, out of the blue, that Papa never told me what I wanted to hear but what I needed to know. Age should not diminish the true spirit of curiosity and investigation. I agree with whoever it was that said, "The question mark is but a bent exclamation point for the elderly." He always told me to judge an intelligent man by his questions instead of his answers. Because nothing is easy, even *hard* is difficult in its many levels—some you hope you never reach. Just try to chalk in the details with honesty, modesty, and tact and you will be okay.

His Southern wisdom and life experiences were beyond anyone I have ever known, and somehow his compassion for other people was even more reaching, magnanimous, coming right out of the cotton fields. He told me once that the future was in business. He said, "In a gold rush, the wise man knows that the money to be made is not in finding the gold, but rather in selling the picks, shovels, and shoes." He influenced me to a greater degree than I could ever have imagined, because he was always there for consciousness-raising. For years after he was gone, I felt his absence as strongly as I had felt his presence. I have thought back many times to those special moments together, to his words and sagacity. I'm sure I can't do them justice, but I will try to reflect a little of what I can remember. These are a few gems of a lengthy collection. I will try to paraphrase what he said at one time or another:

- A person that sincerely reaches out to help others will never try to count what he has done.
- Don't stop and wait for other people to smile: be friendly, and show them how.
- It is never too soon to do something to help those in need.
- There are three things in life that are the most important to remember: First is to love others; second is to love others; and third is to love others.
- You will never get an upset stomach when admitting you are wrong and having to swallow your own words.
- If you want to stand out in a world of people who care less, you should care more.
- People don't carelessly slide downhill in life; they usually do it one step backwards at a time.
- The most important trip you will ever make is to meet others halfway.
- Love is the only thing the deaf can hear, the mute can feel, and the blind can see.
- Sometimes, the only way to make some people happy is to just leave them alone.
- If integrity is not in you, you will never be able to tell if you have reached the top or the bottom.

- Too many people spend their time, energy, and money buying a ticket to a destination that doesn't exist.
- You don't have to be rich, because if you are lucky enough to have a dollar, then you have enough to share.
- Happiness is never about what you want, but more about being grateful for what you already have.

Papa told me one day, "There are only two kinds of people in the world: Those that see an accident on the side of the road and immediately stop and try to help, and those that slow down, rubberneck, and then drive on by. You must decide which you will be. Neither your dad, nor I, can decide for you. We are each capable of various realities; we just have to decide which we want to live in."

I have been privileged to meet many famous, wealthy, and very successful people in my life, but none did I idolize. My grandfather was what I am not but always yearned to be, and I am still trying. I was raised to believe that I could never have a fulfilling day without doing something for someone who could never repay me. When young, he taught me to admire the truth, and now that I've grown old, I still admire the truth. As time passes us by, we find it's nice to be important, but the wise man knows it's much more important to be nice. Papa said to smile at everyone, because for many people it's the only kindness they will see all day. You never know what personal battles they are fighting; you only know yours. Anyway, smiling is not just a nice thing to do: it's also a birthright. As usual, he was on target. His was a singular trusting viewpoint, which was as much a part of my growing up and education as anything I learned in school. He told me one day, "Character is how a wise person can become a distinctive one and stand out in a crowd." I've never forgotten it.

Papa always had a smile, even when there wasn't anything to smile about. Just seeing him lifted my spirits and made my day. Over the years there were many times we were thousands of miles apart, but it always seemed he was only a few comfortable feet away. His gaze in conversation was so penetrating it would seem he could see my soul. Perhaps he could. He played an outsized role in shaping a little boy into a man. I guess he was there at the right time, when I was trying to figure out who I was

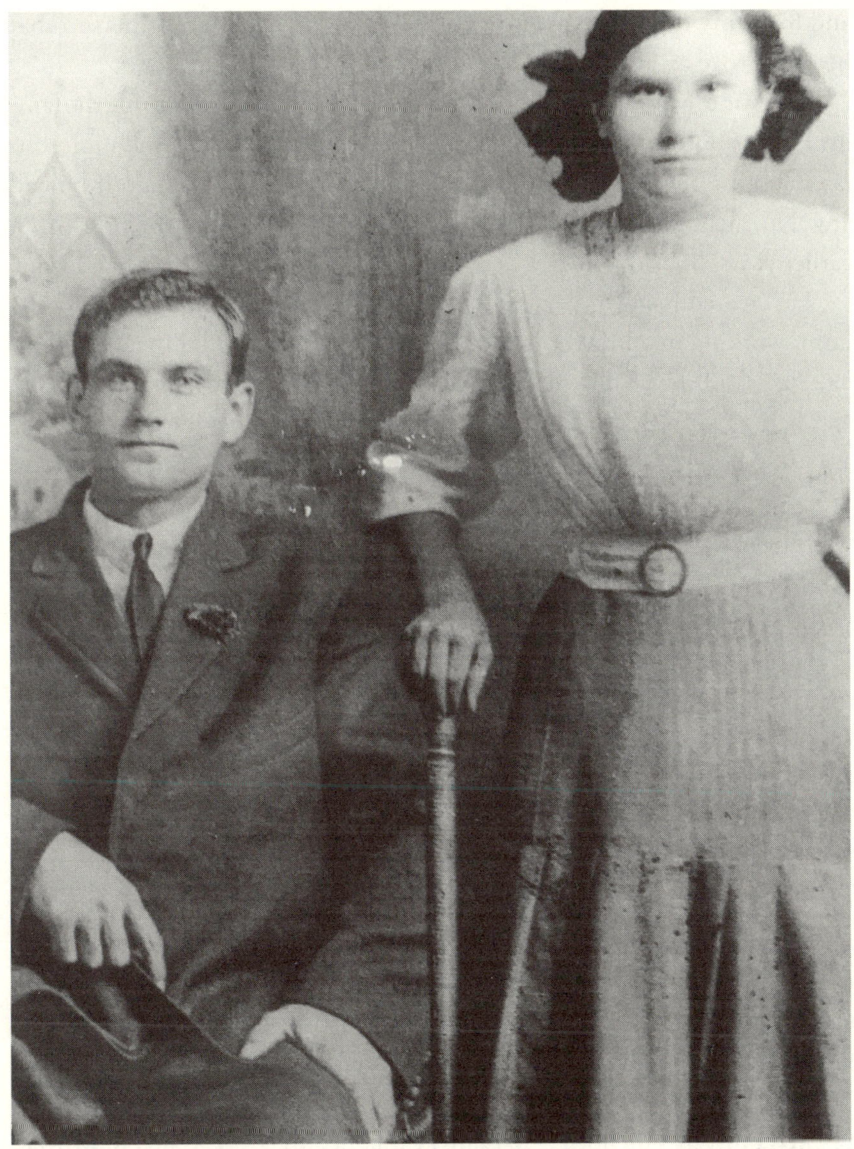

John Brown Andrews and Lula Mae Ledbetter in 1911 (Papa and Mama)—before being married.

and forge my own identity. I don't recall a single neighbor or person that he ever drove away.

Everyone loved and respected Mr. John, as he was called outside the family. He was born in 1891 and could tell a million harrowing and humorous tales about growing up, stories that would have curled his hair, if he had any. No such luck—he was bald at twenty-six. Looking at pictures from earlier years, he had a thick head of jet-black hair and was very handsome.

He created his own personal packaging, briefly in school, then on the farm, working in a lumber mill, and finally in a textile mill in a tiny hamlet. He established his own foothold in Southern Reality and authenticity. Yet, he had faith in the allure of the future and the emerging educational/scientific bouncing ball. He read the Bible every day, but there was never in his mind a conflict between science and religion. He knew that if his life was not firmly planted in faith, it could all go down the drain overnight, regardless of science and technology's contribution to the cause. He once said, "Where a man's character is not clear to you, then look closely at his friends and the company he keeps." I have done that numerous times, and it hasn't failed me yet.

I don't know that Papa ever had a plan B or plan C for his life. I think he just took one step and challenge at a time and fought off dragons each day as they came to call. He certainly wasn't dead behind his eyes. It was always so sad that he never had the opportunity for a formal education to more extensively use his wisdom and quick mind. It was always more important to him to put family first in his long list of priorities. I am thankful that he did. Because of him, I never felt immature, but always grown up, even as a little kid. I clearly remember when I was about five years old, I wondered what would happen if you planted a seed in the ground upside down. Would it grow toward China, or would it even grow at all when planted bottom-side up? He patiently explained that one to me, more than once, with notable forbearance and understanding. I just couldn't accept the logic he gave me until I was a little older and wiser. Fortunately, he understood my predicament, with great patience and endurance. In all my years, I never once saw my grandfather raise his voice to be heard. When he spoke in his deep utterance, everyone stopped whatever they were doing to listen. When things would get too easy, Papa would say, "Now nothing is as easy as pie, except pie."

One beautiful summer day, when I was about twelve years old, Papa and I were sitting in the swing on the front porch, laughing and talking. He would never say anything derogatory or negative about anyone. That particular day, I thought I had him, because slowly coming down the sidewalk, wobbling, was "Ole Horace." I said, "Papa, here comes Ole Horace. He stays drunk all the time and his wife has to work to pay all the bills. He can't keep a job in the mill. He's not good for anything." He was harmless, but a very sad case. I figured there was no way he could praise poor Ole Horace. How wrong I was.

Papa responded without missing a heartbeat. He said, "You are wrong. Of course he is good for something." I said, "What's that?" Papa said, "Well, you are right, Horace is a very sad case, but he is also one of the best 'bad examples' in the mill village. Some people end up being 'good examples' and others 'bad examples.' Horace is, by far, one of the best 'bad examples' I have ever seen. You see, in life we each have to determine which we are going to be. But without seeing bad examples first hand, we don't always know. Now I can't tell you whether you are going to be a good or bad example; neither can your parents. Only you can decide that for yourself." I determined right that minute I wanted to be one of the good examples and have been trying ever since.

I was kind of down in the dumps one day, felt a little useless, and Papa noticed. He smiled and said, "You know, everything in life has a purpose, although we don't always recognize it right off. Why, even a lowly weed. It's just a plant where its values and virtues have not yet been discovered. But it will. God doesn't make useless things, except maybe the Southern mosquito." One day he told me with a grin that "when you get to heaven, there will be only three groups of people present:

"1—Those you expect to be there

"2—Those that deserve to be there

"3—Those that are surprised to see you."

I'm sure he's patiently waiting there to see if I make it. I wonder which group he will be in?

My grandmother was an exceptional person in her own right. We all probably feel that way about our grandmothers. Her father—my maternal great-grandfather—was a Ledbetter and a Methodist minister. By the time she was 13, she had taught herself to play the organ and quickly became the regular church organist. She also taught herself to play the violin, accordion, harmonica, and banjo. This was a rather unusual group of musical instruments, and I never asked her why she selected those particular ones. She was learning the guitar when she and my grandfather were married. After that, she never had much time to practice. Yet, with all that musical talent, I never once heard her sing, but she could really play. She was also the best Southern cook I have ever seen. The closest to her perfection was my mother and Claire, whom she taught. A plethora of dishes and ingredients were bouncing around in her head, and I rarely saw her use a cookbook, even when preparing more than one hundred meals every day. Her cooking was Southern poetry in taste and enjoyment. She was also a super organizer and planner in whatever she did. As all grandmothers are, she was exceptional, with a heart bigger than all outdoors and a great life companion for my grandfather.

Mama was about five feet, one inch tall if she stood on her tiptoes. She had a head full of pretty grey curls as long as I knew her, and the deepest, darkest smiling eyes I have ever seen. Of all her varied experiences, demands, and challenges, I never once saw her bundled up in a grief-quilt. Instead, she was constantly upbeat, smiling with comfort and compassion for a little kid who became a struggling teenager and many others in need. It didn't matter if it was something to eat or a big hug; it was always there, waiting. We are fortunate that all women usually grow up to be like their mothers; perhaps the greatest downside of men is that we don't.

I was seduced early on by boarding house cuisine. Mama was such a good cook, in today's world, she would have a cult following. She made "helium biscuits" so light and tender that they would rise up off the plate and float on their own initiative. Her boarding house back door was only about sixty to seventy yards away from Highway 29. Before the Interstate Highway System in the late 1950s, Highway 29 was the New York to Florida main traffic route. Word got out to hitchhikers that Mrs. Andrews never turned down anyone who couldn't afford a meal. She always belonged to the cobwebbed tradition of compassion and common decency. A day rarely passed that three to five travelers—one or two at a time—didn't stop by for a handout. They were from everywhere: New York, Pennsylvania, New Jersey, North Carolina, Tennessee, Georgia, and other states. Mama or Connie Baker would always bring them a full plate of food and a glass of sweet tea, along with a kind word and a smile. They would sit on the tall back door steps, hungrily eating, usually waiting for seconds, which she graciously provided. I always liked people, even those I hadn't met before, and seemed to have an intuitive gift for sizing them up. I once asked my grandfather why she gave away so many free meals to people she didn't even know. He smiled at my innocence. "One should never be inhospitable to strangers; they could be gift-bearing angels in disguise." I never forgot it.

As a kid, I would go out and talk with the hitchhikers and ask about their travels, hopes, hardships, families, and dreams of success in a transitioning world. For me, it was always accompanied with a little frisson of excitement. They must have felt like they were under an intense FBI interrogation, but most just smiled, answered my questions, and kept on eating. Truth is a very effective way to raise the temperature of an otherwise chilly conversation. Being a little boy, I wasn't bashful and didn't know what to ask and not ask. Of course, no one wants to be drained of personal facade and zing. Perhaps in a better world, honesty would have been more obvious and easier to handle. When you are on the road, it's not always a good subject to discuss. So who knows if what they said was fact or fiction. With all that exposure over the years, wanderlust never did get under my skin, and maybe that was the reason why.

As Papa and Mama advised me, I always tried to be friendly, because most of those coming by for food looked like they hadn't seen a smile in a long time. They were all ages, with a lot of young adults, some teenagers, as well as a number of elderly hitchhikers. I must have asked them a million questions about why they were thumbing, where they were from, what they were going to do, their education, and their goals. The funny thing was, not a single one ever got upset at my questions. Most were open and seemed to want someone warm and friendly to talk to. The majority had been sleeping on the ground, or under a bridge, some the worse for wear, and hadn't had a bath in a week or two. Many asked to use our hose pipe in the back yard to rinse off, and it was always available, along with soap, washcloths, and towels.

Surprisingly, many of them would send Mama back a letter thanking her and would tell her what they were now doing. She would always show it to me, Connie, and the cooks. They would try to relate the letter to the individuals they could remember. A number said they hadn't had a decent meal in two or more days before they heard about my grandmother, and how blessed they had felt stopping by that day. A few even mentioned me. Astonishingly, or maybe not, some of them stopped numerous times over the years thumbing the north-south corridor of Highway 29, trying to find themselves. Some did; some didn't. It was just another part of life in a small textile mill village, and I was proud of my mill pedigree. I guess in many ways, that's a humble mill village brag. The most galvanizing voice in our head is usually our own.

Thinking back, it's just who we were that identified us as mill village Homo sapiens and has brought us this far. Somewhere, I once heard that there were only two kinds of people in the world: the givers and the takers. The takers always eat better, but the givers sleep better. I don't believe Papa and Mama ever had a sleepless night.

13

Joseph Louis Barrow

Once I read a profound and timely statement somewhere that "the wonderful aroma of a dream can completely overpower the bad odor of failure." Through history there have been many stories that encourage and provide hope for the desolate, disadvantaged, and those looking for a better tomorrow. When I think of this, I always remember one of my local heroes, who grew up not too far from our little town. If anyone had reason to feel life was going against him, it was Joseph. I cannot recall a single person that was admired and discussed more in the mill villages than he was. He became a product of his time and place, but he never gave up on himself.

Why couldn't Southern Reality allow him to arrange his life in such a way that systematically, by rote or chance, the hurtful and undesirable aspects would have passed him by? Unfortunately, life isn't fair and it doesn't work that way. We must face it as it happens. The everyday has come dangerously close to our wheelhouse, a captive of the white-hot maw of society's imagination.

In 1914, about fifteen miles as the crow flies from where I grew up, a young boy was born. It was out in the derelict countryside of Chambers County—near where my sawmill, farming progenitors came from—close to Lafayette, Alabama. His name was Joseph Louis Barrow. He was one of eight children. His father was a poor hard-luck sharecropper and was in bad health most of his life. Sharecropping would always leave you poor, no matter how hard you sweat. Only the good Lord knows how much cotton Joe must have picked.

Sadly, his grandparents were former slaves. The old clapboard house he lived in swayed rather precariously to one side and his mother had two

121

jobs just trying to keep the family fed and clothed with a roof over their heads. Materially, he had nothing to call his own and was rarely in school, having to help out at home and in the fields. It was a desperate, problematic, uncompromising, and discouraging life. In addition, he had a very bad speech impediment, which compounded his hardships, contributing to his frequently missing school. He was always picked on by other kids. It must have been like living on a hot stove. We all want to know more, but in darkness, even the light is a stranger. He had little to look forward to, yet he trudged on in perseverance. You would think he had been listening to Winston Churchill when he said that we should "never, never, never give up!" Maybe he had.

Joe Louis, as he was later professionally known, became Heavyweight Boxing Champion of the World in 1937. I remember the date because it was the eventful year I was born and that Point University was founded. He successfully defended his crown against the best boxers in the universe an incredible twenty-six times. He also interrupted his successful career to spend two years in the army during the critical years of World War II to help defend his country. Many years after he retired from fisticuffs, a journalist was interviewing him one day in Las Vegas. He asked, "Joe, when you were a kid, and everything that possibly could was going against you, exactly what was the specific circumstance in your life that made you successful?" Joe Louis, who was always quiet and somewhat introverted, said what became very famous words: "I just did the best I could with what I had."

That was his challenge, and it's still our charge today: to just do the best you can with what you have. You see, Joe knew that he had nobody else that could do it for him, and he couldn't leave anything on the table. As he entered the realm of adulthood, he knew he had to decide which parts of his life and his discontents were no longer actually necessary and that he could do without. Of course, that's true for all of us unless you are in the fortunate one percent or live near that neighborhood. In the real world, the return on personal investment that we bring to the marketplace will determine our success or failure. Joe Louis clearly understood that. That's why his exploits were a constant point of conversation in the mills, and he has been one of my long-time heroes. Anyone like him that could produce a great success out of the unbelievable impediments in his life makes our minuscule problems look like a Sunday walk in the park. Today a tall bronze statue stands on the Chambers County Courthouse lawn. This statue honors the county's most famous son, one that came a long, long way against unthinkable odds. He is an example for everyone, living the American dream and telling us that we should never give up.

Many years ago, after his exploits, I drove by the house where Joe was born in Chambers County. It was in a dilapidated condition back then. It's amazing to contrast that house to the man himself, perhaps the greatest boxer the world has ever seen. When you think about it, you begin to realize that success is not about where you begin, but where you end, what you are able to do with what you have been given to work with.

Growing up, I was a lot like Joe Louis, but I lived in a more easily defined sententious landscape of dreams and quelled hope, one of practicality and rationality much better than he faced. For me, it was a most enjoyable task to engage the radiance of others that are also out there, trying to survive each day just like me. Because the real bottom line is to love people as kindred spirits, kith and kin, each on their own quest. I often think, perhaps like Joe, that life itself is only an exemplary piece of our bent and contrived speculative fiction. I aged into my own blessed career of expansiveness, until it was finally over and I hung up my proverbial boxing gloves for good. The Brown Bomber would have been proud—as was my wife and family.

Now, after extensive experience, I eventually opened my mind and came to a definitive conclusion that Mother Nature knew exactly what she was doing in the beginning of time. To help us maximize our potential, she gave each of us an antagonist to help hone our skills and keep everything about life in balance—Joe Louis had Max Schmeling; the good has the bad; Jesus had the Devil; Democrats the Republicans; Hillary had her Trump; and Auburn has Alabama. Yet there is one bit of wisdom I have yet to figure out: the imbalance between husband and wife. Why does Mother Nature always make the wife superior? Oh heck, I keep forgetting. She was the one that established the rules of the game, not Father Nature. Joe was just lucky she was on his side.

There was one thing for sure that I think Joe learned along the way: that the crazier the world gets, the more abstract fairness and truth becomes. Yet, I think he knew that miracles—like him—that we see here on Earth on rare occasions are not really so unusual; they are just common everyday occurrences in Heaven. If the opportunity had been available for him to work in the mill and to be a weaver, machine fixer, or shift supervisor in the late 1930s, he would never have become the greatest boxer in the world.

Joe grew up in a harsh, market-driven jungle culture that identified and stratified him through society's grounding forum. He, in turn, tried to take his physical and mental attributes and tailor his future to the demands of those market forces. Like us all, he wanted to improve his life—as well as that of his family—and his prospects in the grim world he faced. One never can be ambivalent and must always stay focused on the objective. Joseph Louis Barrow did. He was a fighter, one of the best in the history of ever. In the same context, I'll bet if you had asked Joe, he would have said, "I've seen very few people changed by my opinion, but hundreds changed by my example." Just like so many little kids growing up in a mill village, Joe knew he didn't have to prostrate himself before reality; he could change it with forethought and effort, and he did.

I think Joe Louis, in contemplation of his life in the whole, would agree that Southern Reality has a peculiar way of attempting to compensate for some of the tragedies it inflicts on individuals. Perhaps it has a benevolent mode we never see, trying to placate us for its own downside. Sadly, it doesn't do that for everyone. Now I don't want you to get me wrong. I have great confidence in the future, because the moral universe is far-reaching and always bends toward justice, regardless of its path. If you don't believe me, just ask Joe.

14

High School

We woke up early one fall morning in the mill village, utterly unprepared as teenagers, and had no clue how hard the new experience of *adulting* was going to be. We had never been there before, so it was a new world. It was easy to plummet into life's taunting trap as we moved right ahead from the baby crib—through youth, pubescence, juvenile adolescence, and past the dazzle of early teenage years—without a clue. Our parents never did any genetic testing to see if we were actually qualified to be grown-ups; they just opened the front door and pushed us out into a scary, dog-eat-dog jungle called high school. We were innocent, premature young adults in learning, with all kinds of crazy thoughts going on, completely lost inside our slowly developing teen bodies and fragile minds. No one even thought to inoculate us against hormones, weak tendencies, and scores of the worst temptations and allurements in immaturity. We didn't understand all that we knew and didn't know all we should have understood. Growing up soon became a series of open awkwardness separated by lost periods of self and *me-ness*. So we had to learn all that hard human nature stuff on our own. It was called a high school education.

Life, from its incarnation, and in all its many wonderful attributes and manifestations, is still a perishable commodity. It must be consumed before its "use before date." We don't always understand that when in high school, because most of us have yet to find ourselves and we are too naïve by half. A teenager's thoughts are more in the hormonal curve and less on adulthood, which, in a public realm of anarchy, is over the next hill waiting in ambush. As teenagers rarely do, we pursued life with anthropological rigor, because one has to be wide awake to do so and teenagers rarely are. We spent a major

Valley High School, 2018.

part of each day just trying to avoid reality. However, if I could have just gotten rid of eight or ten vices, I would have been near perfect.

If you run into an old classmate with a wrist tattoo saying "Reality Sucks," an ear stud, or a nose ring, they are trying to tell you something about themselves. Or maybe they are still trying to find out who they really are. Every journey has a beginning and end, but I don't think a person can ever know where they are going unless you first know where you came from. It takes a while before we do and that obscure, almost indecipherable period of discovery is called "high school." It's a place where friends are very special, because they become the family we choose for ourselves. Of course, at this age we all prefer a photoshopped image, but there was no hoity-toity, because underneath the mind's trap door is a bottomless pit of uneasy self. In contrast, today we need a revolution in manners, instilling better common sense, tolerance, acceptance, and respect for our human nature.

Ever since I was a kid growing up in a mill environment, fall has always given me a thrill of anticipation. But it also gives me a little shiver of delight, bringing shorter days and cooler nights as summer comes off the grid and school starts, with Halloween, Thanksgiving, and Christmas on the docket to inspire the imagination and engage the heart. Then one day I discovered that football was just part of the season and went wild. I have been lost in the throes of fall ever since. In man-speak, football helps gravitate toward the common threads of humanity left over from the primal call of male history, advancing toward the pain and suffering we think is necessary in life. Although disappointments are hard to swallow, I think the bottom line is that football is just a "guy-tude" thing. It certainly has a way of turning up the dial and infecting our thinking, especially as teens.

Teens at the high school stage are rarely straight arrows, thanks to a lack of a clear fixed identity. We were more an accumulation of contradictions, paradoxes, and reaching inconsistencies waiting to be formed. We were hoping to someday be fully accepted by family, worthy in the eyes of our peers, and respected and loved by all. In our high school years, the opaqueness of memory brings interesting and fuzzy tidings, along with an element of humor and superficiality. We walked arm-in-arm in the new cliques we formed, in the shadows of some beautiful days, trying to catch a smoother ride on the comfort of one another's elusive slipstreams. And we enjoyed many nights watching a big moon cut a hole in the darkness to show off its beautiful stars. Imagination becomes our primary defense against the ordinary. I faintly remember those special times in junior high and high school when we played football, baseball, and basketball—especially the many bruises and breaks. There were times I danced with a bad limp, tried to breathe through a broken nose, and wore a cast on my hand for a dislocated finger. Not everything we did ended in success. Although, if we are lucky, even failure can become notable when we learn and move ahead. So it was with me. I was a hardheaded kid and never settled for anything just because it was easy. I had my full share of harsh Southern Reality and too many times I thought I also had a big share of someone else's. We quickly discover that we cannot erase the past just because it doesn't fit the present as we want it to. In spite of my shortcomings, I well remember our celebrity Valley High School graduation speaker for the class of 1954. I don't recall his name, but he was very generous with his words and didn't charge anything for speaking that day. He was worth every penny we paid him.

High school is all about entering the privileged world of teenaged make believe as a hormonally bumbling misfit. We were worried about passing, and anxious about experiencing first love, the gossiping cliques, and trying to figure out who we really were—underneath our many facades—all at the same time. One tries hard to shed the immature vestiges of junior high school while being certain that everyone else is smarter, clearly more popular, better looking, and destined for greater things than you. Sound familiar? And some things just don't get forgotten. As a student, I was a long way from perfect. That's probably because my perspective was uneven and even slightly indulgent, but nevertheless it charmed me with a trademark of warm-hearted humor and a satirical acceptance of reality.

You think as an awkward freshman that high school will last forever, but it's here today and gone before you know it. I especially liked it because I no longer had to order from the kid's menu. The first two weeks of school we sat in class as optimists, carefully evaluating and eyeballing one another before making a move. Back then, I wanted to be brief and tight when I was writing and loose and uninhibited when dancing. I couldn't wait to apply the Pythagorean Theorem and calculus to real-world problems—how disappointing that was. There were so many times we thought we were safe from harm, when we were just in the eye of the storm. As mid-teens, we were greatly concerned about living an unlived life and not being accepted by our peers, which we feared more than death itself.

There were several guys in my group that never learned where the library was or what it was for. If they are not dead by now or did not drop out of school, I'll bet they are still there, wandering around. There were also two or three football players that were always late for class, which I guess for them was right on time—and they liked to make an entrance. It was also interesting how early on, while on a learning curve with some of the people you started dating, you quickly began to feel like you had mistakenly wandered into the wrong party with a group of strangers.

Of course, we were all a litle flighty at that stage. When a senior, I remember two different girls telling me that someday I was going to regret never asking them for a date, but for the life of me, I cannot remember their names. Looking ahead, on the week of graduation, several girls had already picked out the dresses they were going to wear to our 10th class reunion. For some reason, my senior picture in the class of '54 yearbook made me look like a wet behind the ears freshman; boy, how I wish I looked like that now. Back then, from time to time, I needed two #8 or #14 screws to repair my bruised ego, the size depending on how bad the damage was. Sadly, I guess, in reflection, most high school seniors hadn't quite figured out whether the party was over or just beginning. Of course, none of us knew back then that we would spend most of our lives chasing bright shiny things around in circles and overlook what was by far the most important thing of all: each other.

I worked hard at giving myself admirable constructive advice, but I was incapable of accepting it. Teenaged wisdom seems to come from drawing strong, definitive conclusions from insufficient evidence. Yet I was usually afraid I would head off in the wrong direction and learn to master everything that was not worth knowing. I never minded not being movie star handsome, because high school romance is not complete delirium like losing your mind, but there are many common symptoms. All girls eventually develop strong boyological urges, and boys are clueless. I dated this beautiful blonde once that finally discovered the center of the universe and was terribly disappointed when she found out she wasn't it. The cold winds of self can be as drafty as a chamber-pot in winter when it causes us to ignore others. Every person has a sane spot somewhere, but there were many of us that never could find it. The only constancy I ever discovered about high school was its inconstancy. Of course, we all have a need for a little "me" time; we just shouldn't overindulge.

First love usually involves a little naïveté, along with a bit of foolishness and a whole lot of curiosity. As a middle-teen, I remember kissing a pretty girl for the first time and playing my initial tennis match on the same day. I haven't set foot on a tennis court since. I tried hard and learned to avoid every single vice except temptation. Papa told me once that there would be times in life when you would even have to vote for your opponent instead of yourself; it's called sportsmanship. I found that he was right, and I did it several times. At the moment, that thought was rarely on my agenda. My primary concern was, with all the critical problems in the world (mine included), where was Superman going to find a phone booth?

Back in the '50s, we went to Callaway Gardens in Pine Mountain

(Chipley then), Georgia, and to the beach and backwater on weekends. But girls never got sunburned in the delicate places they do today. Romance was in full bloom, and the primary joy of reading those old high school love letters today is in knowing that you don't have to answer them. I had one girlfriend that was absolutely and completely intolerable, but that was her only fault. We all loved dancing and rock and roll music; in fact, it was a lot better than it sounded and our dancing was a lot better than it looked. To our class, most things were stranger than fiction, and you learn one should not be afraid to tell a pretty girl how you feel. It's much less embarrassing than changing your underwear in public—but not by much. But we never let school interfere with our goal of getting a good education. When we were young, we thought money was the most important thing in life. Then as we got older and wiser, we knew it was, by a vote of our 60th Class Reunion of ninety-six percent to four percent. When we finally graduated from 12th grade, we made a pact that we would all live within our means—even if we had to borrow money to do it.

All the girls in my class were older than me, and it was puzzling how in the past fifty years they had all gotten several years younger, especially the widows and divorcées. The lines in our faces came from the paths of least resistance. Age doesn't matter. Actually, most wrinkles aren't dangerous unless you remind women that they have them. They come mostly from where smiles existed at one time or another. Regardless of how much a person's maturity may affect their appearance, one can reduce it by at least ten years through just smiling—if you still have all your teeth, or good facsimiles. Looking back, we have great compassion when a friend suffers for some reason, but it's hard to find peace and comfort with someone's great success: a poor self characteristic. Each age has its own playthings, but playthings of the older generations are the memories of youth. As teenagers, we always had a rationale for drinking water. It seemed more egalitarian than drinking Budweiser or Schlitz, was considerably cheaper, and much less likely to cause a hangover or death, because our dads would have killed us.

My good friend Terry Bishop, now vice president of a large bank, tells me that he and I had comparable athletic talent back then. (We were an

VHS Class of '54, 45th reunion in 1999—Terry Bishop, Jackie Wilks, and Gerald Andrews.

unmatched pair on opposite ends of the line in high school days.) Of course, that's Terry's opinion, he is getting old, and it was almost sixty-five years ago. The way I recall it, I was much better than he was, and for the past twenty years or so, each year, I keep getting better and better. Claire says I've become a legend in my own mind. I'm not sure if she meant that to be a compliment, but I'm sure it was a small decision. I'm not really sure how good I was, but someday I'll ask Dr. Gwen Gibson. She lived three houses up the street when we were growing up. She taught all the boys in our class to dance, and with two left feet, I needed help. No need to ask Terry. Poor fellow, his memory is really beginning to slip. It has actually become a little disconcerting because all my schoolmates are getting so old and their eyesight so bad that they don't even recognize me when I see them. I seem to be the only one still holding together. It's kind of sad, because they look a little bedraggled and have a lot of wrinkles in their faces, which are very similar to my character lines.

By serendipity, luck, or providence, I recall that I was fortunate enough to play football in high school. Unfortunately, it was against Jimmy "Red" Phillips from Alexander City, Alabama, and "Big Ben" Preston of Eufaula, Alabama—two of the best that ever played the game. If I live to be a hundred, I'll never forget it. I'm almost there, so maybe my memory is improving. When it comes to football, the state of Alabama takes a backseat to no one, and Jimmy and Ben were good examples. They were selected High School All-State, made first team at Auburn as freshmen, became All-SEC, All-Americans, and All-Pro. They played on the 1957 Auburn National Championship team. Southern football is very simple: you can either play it or you can watch it. Most boys and young men transition through both universes and never depart from the latter, unless it's feet first.

I will never forget the fateful night we played Eufaula for the state championship, in the mud after a full week of torrential rain, when we helped inaugurate their brand new stadium. They kicked off to us. We took it and marched straight down the field, and I caught a beautiful seven-yard pass for a touchdown. I remember coming back to the huddle and loudly saying, "We've got 'em on the run, boys." How stupid can a sixteen-year-old be? That was the last time we saw the ball. They beat us 36–7. I remember

1953 Valley High School football team.

thinking that we should have given Ben Preston one of our high school jerseys because he played in our backfield all night. Then, on second thought, I decided to keep my mouth shut, because it was my job to block him and keep him out—or not. As an energetic and fast but not too bright kid from a mill village, I thought I was a pretty good athlete, and I foolishly considered making a long-term career out of the game. But after encounters with Ben and Jimmy, slippery serendipity changed my cryptic mind and career. It was kind of peculiar how that change in my mindset happened.

After the big Eufaula game, I was sitting there in the visiting team's dressing room in quiet repose and great pain. I had a trophy display of deep scrapes, dried blood, and dark bruises. I was half undressed and thinking, with my nose in a splint. (We didn't have face guards in the early 1950s, and I had broken my nose three times over the years). I could hardly move and looked like an emergency in dire need of ambulance service. I was black and blue and bleeding from several improbable and embarrassing places on my torso. Now, I was a good Christian boy before that game and was a much better one afterwards because I prayed every time Ben Preston crossed the line of scrimmage toward me, which was every play.

Then, while sitting there hurting, out of the blue, I had a glorious epiphany that I should go to Auburn and study engineering. It's absolutely amazing what a miraculous effect God—and a ferocious All-American lineman—can have on a sixteen-year-old churchgoing Southern boy's perspective about life. The greatest blessing I recall that year is that when we played Alexander City, Jimmy "Red" Phillips played on the opposite end of the line from me. That was Terry's end; maybe that's why he went into banking.

For those less-informed regions of the United States, the South has three religions: church, high school football, and college football. Not necessarily in that order. Now which Protestant service, Catholic church, or Jewish synagogue you attend doesn't really matter, as long as you show up on Saturday or Sunday. They don't call it the Bible Belt for nothing. In our Greater Valley community of 25,000 people, we are a bubbling cauldron of churches. If you read the last page in the *Valley Times-News* on Friday, there are 136 churches listed by identifying names. Of course, that doesn't count the twenty to twenty-five "small" churches that aren't noted. Yet, there will probably be as many people in the stands to see Friday night high school football in our three public and one private high schools as there are in the pews on Sunday morning.

Now, in my wildest dreams I could never be a butterfly, because I wouldn't know how to start a hurricane a thousand miles away by just flapping my wings from my present perch on the Alabama and Georgia border. However, the University of Alabama and Auburn University flapped their football wings many times over the years and caused hurricanes on football fields all across America. One of the lessons I learned along the way was that successful people don't have dreams. Instead, they establish and meet goals. So it has been at Auburn and Alabama on the football field for decades. Authenticity—and a winning record—always spirits you to the head of the line in style. Yet no one should ever believe that this transcending "moment" is here to stay.

Of course, which college team you pull for on Saturday is not a life-or death-decision; it's much more important than that. It's a career survival issue, and a biography changing experience. The team you call your own causes more marriages, families, and churches to split up than the Devil. In my weaker moments, I have sometimes wondered if football wasn't just the Devil working incognito. Now, in Alabama, where I grew up, the best church attendance is not on Christmas or Easter, nor high holidays. The best attendance is the Sundays when the Auburn and Alabama football coaches came to speak. I have heard it's part of their recruiting technique. The coaches say it's not true, but for some peculiar reason they only show up each year in the towns where the best football players are located and at the churches they attend. This is quite a coincidence to occur year after year after year. I always thought the license for deception had a steep price, but maybe not where football is concerned.

The present coaches—Gus Malzhan and Nick Saban—have always been good public speakers. They have preached many more sermons to their players and university boards of trustees than most congregations have ever heard, and they were just about as effective with one as the other. They are still the highest-paid coaches in America. Yet, today they have very low annual salaries of only $7,000,000 each, on seven-year contracts, so you shouldn't really unreasonably expect the world in their win/loss performance year after year—so they say.

The first thing a new preacher in town is asked is, "Are you for Auburn or Alabama?" His response will determine how long he stays. Some newly called preachers have been asked to leave after two weeks. I heard one was even asked to depart before his first sermon, when on the fourth day he was there, he foolishly changed allegiances. When you have 150 churches for only 25,000 people, it results in a lot of transition and moving around. I understand college football and church are the historic basis for coining the phrase "fruit basket turnover." Don't get me wrong, I love college football and Auburn, but sometimes the season can get very long. Why, once I spent a whole year with my family and team on just one fall Saturday afternoon in Tuscaloosa. However, over the years, many a time I have seen an elephant in the room, and it wasn't always from Alabama.

One of the greatest lessons I learned in high school was eye-opening. I discovered that fame alone will not fulfill you, or make you whole. It perhaps warms you up a little bit, but it is warmth without substance and will leave you in a lurch when you need it the most. We all have a fear of being ordinary, when it should probably be our objective. It has absolutely nothing to do with the fact that a cat has thirty-two muscles in each ear. Middle age is the point we begin to exchange our strong opinions and bent emotions for more definable medical conditions. But I had much rather be sixty-five years young than fifty years old. As we gravitate from high school toward tomorrow, we openly renounce the errors of youth, so we can engage the mistakes of advanced age. Starting out, our objective is to get wise before we get old. Few ever make it. The more my age elevated, the harder it became for me to believe that added years always brings wisdom.

Then, as we bend toward greater longevity, we realize how wrong we were in middle age, thinking that in the future we would feel much better.

After high school, it was interesting to find that all the things we had planned to do were illegal, immoral, fattening, or too expensive. Of course, at a high school reunion you should never talk about yourself in front of others; it will be done behind your back as soon as you leave. A good listener is not only welcome, but they will learn more than anyone else and won't have to lie about themselves. From observations, sometimes I think that high heels came in vogue when women got tired of being kissed on the forehead. Maybe that explains why all females at reunions wear elevated shoes, as well as two or three of the guys. As the class of '54, we became dedicated to giving good advice, because we were too old to provide bad examples. At eighty-plus, we were all trying to figure out exactly when the "old enough to know better" would actually kick in.

Realistically, the first one hundred years are always the longest and hardest. Before and after I retired at seventy, I was asked to do a lot of public speaking at different venues. I got so good at it that I could get the preparation time for a thirty-minute speech down to just four weeks—if I worked on it full time. At our 60th reunion, about the only thing I noticed about baldness and the commonality of its presence was its cleanliness and neatness. Somewhere between the ages of forty and forty-five, men begin to have thoughts about women, but before that, they simply have feelings. However, by the time we are old enough to know better, we have forgotten everything we once knew. There were several girls at the last reunion I used to date that didn't even recognize me because they had changed so much. There was one class mate I hadn't seen in many years that really surprised me. When her fourth husband died, overnight her hair turned from white to strawberry-blonde, she said from grief. I think fourth and fifth marriages always provide the promise of hope over experience, but I didn't tell her that.

One should be careful about trying to warm your hands on the success and accomplishments of others. As the election day of 2016 for president of the United States rolled around, I was still trying to figure out which of the two most undesirable candidates to choose between—the one that gives me constant migraines or the other that gives me dysentery. However, I have come to expect weirder things in recent years, and to tell you the truth, it doesn't greatly bother me which one, Republican or Democrat, is elected to the office. I figure that under the best circumstances about the only thing either winner could do productively is to give us a brief respite from the Kardashians. However, I was paralyzed with fear the other night, and woke up in a cold shaking sweat. I had dreamed that my Valley High School graduating class of 1954 had won the national election and would

VHS Class of '54, 20th Reunion at Riverside Country Club, Lanett, Alabama.

be running the country. It was my worst dream in years in a twisted nocturnal world of nightmares. However, I haven't fully adjusted to President Trump, but it looks like he will take the cake. It seems we each have to run the final obstacle course of our own biases. So when no one is looking and someone does the right thing, it shows you who they really are—and what they learned in high school.

We have tried to have a class of '54 reunion every five years through our 60th affair. Being far away at times, I didn't make it back for them all. But it's funny how, when I saw my classmates again for our last gathering, I discovered that I had become somebody else.

15

Night Watchman

Opportunity doesn't always arrive in our presence unheeded. More often than not we must knock on its door and ask to be let in. If it doesn't answer the call, then we keep knocking until it does, because nobody knows what might happen until we take the initiative. At sixteen, the future is typically formidable and maybe a bit overwhelming—for me it was. No one pays you any heed at that age, and life has yet to develop a plot line. Everyone has to make their own space.

My first job in the huge local manufacturing plant, which used two million pounds of cotton each week, began when I was a senior in high school in the oppressively steamy Yarn Dye Plant. I worked every day from 6 a.m. to 8 a.m. before school, from 3 p.m. 'til 7 p.m. after school, and eight to ten hours on Saturday. This amounted to about thirty-five to forty hours each week at the fantastic rate of sixty-one cents an hour. I must have done a good job because before long I was given a two cent raise. When I started college, I was able to switch to cleaning employee restrooms for three months. Then I got a job as a night watchman to better accommodate my daily class schedule. I commuted eighty miles round-trip Monday through Friday to Auburn University while working as a night watchman eight hours Friday night, sixteen hours Saturday, and sixteen hours Sunday. Each watchman's hourly round was walking one and a half miles and turning thirty-one clock keys, which took forty-five minutes. That meant walking twelve miles on Friday night, twenty-four miles Saturday, and twenty-four miles Sunday. On holidays, and when school was out, I worked sixty to eighty hours per week, walking 90–120 miles.

After three or four weeks, with my heavy school demands, I found I needed more time on weekends to study textile, engineering, math, and science courses, an exceedingly tough curriculum for a full-time working boy. So I analyzed the watchman's job while working out a new algorithmic way to perform the function. The approach I came up with would give me over fifteen hours of study time, in one-hour increments, in the guard station each weekend and still meet all written requirements of the national insurance company that covered the Corporation. I went back to my supervisor—Mr. Partridge—and reviewed the one-page written rules from the industrial insurance company to be sure that was all that was necessary to meet my job duties and responsibilities. Three weeks later, when I came to work on Friday evening, I had a note to go see my supervisor.

Mr. Partridge, to put it mildly, was quite upset. The insurance company had read clock-tapes of the past few weeks and said I wasn't following the rules. I explained that I had followed the one-page written instructions to a "T," and had even reviewed them with him a few weeks earlier to make sure exactly what was required. He remembered. I went on to explain that I had met every single written ordinance but had revised the method used to create more time to study. The rules said to "make one, one-and-a-half-mile round each hour, turn thirty-one keys on the watchman's clock in sequence, and carefully observe for fire, water damage, and plant security, as well as any other significant situations requiring special management or Police/Fire Department attention. Don't ride the elevator and always use the stairs in the multiple four-story buildings." I did exactly that but I did it differently—to my personal advantage.

Instead of walking the one-and-a-half-mile round in forty-five minutes, I could run it in thirty minutes. If I did back-to-back rounds at the end of an hour and beginning of the next hour, it would provide several back-to-back one-hour rest periods in an eight-hour shift. That would mean four hours of total study time, and three were in one-hour increments. This new approach gave me at least fifteen one-hour increments every weekend, a major study addition. It still met 100 percent of all written insurance requirements. Mr. Partridge finally understood and told me to go back to the walking regimen of the old original practice—and no running. He'd talk to the insurance company and get back with me in a few days.

Two weeks later, he left word for me to come by the office. He had reviewed with the insurance company and they understood what had actually been done. Now they had written new instructions that were expanded from 1 to 2½ pages in length. This established new detailed requirements for night watchmen. He said this was being discussed with all other industrial insurance companies in the United States and, in the future, would be required as standard practice by everyone in the U.S. The rules had clearly and explicitly eliminated the innovative, more convenient practice I had implemented and were now much longer, more stringent, and rather laborious in spelling out what to do and what not to do. It was now crystal clear, and no longer ambiguous. In retrospect, I can't help but grade my idea "out of the box" on a curve because it didn't break any rules and its intentions were good. Even though it failed, it was still out of positive ambition to accomplish a specific purpose—which it did. Of course, I could have lost my job, but I didn't.

I continued to wonder what went wrong in management. How could all industrial insurance companies in America, covering trillions of dollars in corporate assets, not have done a better job explaining what was required? This was not only important for fire protection but also a critical economic and security responsibility. It reinforced my perception that even the largest national companies didn't have all the answers. How short-sighted and ineffective they were if an imaginative sixteen-year-old could get them to change, or at least bring better transparency to their requirements. It became clear to me that almost everything could be improved for the better, and it was simply up to me to find the best way to do it.

16

The Plant Janitor

In their day, almost every small mill village looked like the finery in a bride's trousseau—something old, something new, something borrowed, and something blue. Each had its own enchanting blend of birth, personal history, success, failure, proud tradition, conservative culture, and warm hearts. It's that unique yet differing balance that made every little hamlet one of a kind. By inherent nature, they were confining by their infiniteness, each measured by neighbors living in goodwill and harmony so close together. The narrative of anxiety was usually in distant future tense, because everyone felt that their little towns and their jobs would last forever. As time passed, I came to believe that we were not the creators of our own special civilization, just the final product of that evolution—and the end of the road wasn't very clear. There was one thing for certain: not one village ever wanted to be notable because of their lack of notability. Looking back, it seems life was much more serious and sharp-edged than we liked to pretend, perhaps to keep it from scaring us.

For more than one hundred years, people lived in their own unguarded, mostly unincorporated little towns, each in its own unique world that was more fragile than we ever imagined. A mill village had a calm collage of thousands of human voices, all saying the same thing as each presented a monologue about itself, but not selfishly. One's interior lives and better nature were shaped by the same entity: a benevolent Company. I could say that as a child I never felt adversity. In fact, we had as much materially as almost anyone else that I knew, and more than some. I could have had, all things considered, a little more materially, but no more fun. Yet, in so many ways, I was the rich little poor kid in a fading depression and dragging

141

recovery era for everyone. I quickly learned that one should be determined to leave as little up to chance as possible. I was just a kid when common and ordinary things burst into bright primary colors, awakening the mind. As a little boy, I rarely saw a wide American landscape without hearing the soft strains of "God Bless America!"

No one completely owns their personal story, because others are always involved. Along the way I found an aesthetic that had somehow prefigured my own. I discovered an important truth (since confirmed) that it only takes two people to make you, but a family and whole village to raise you. You should never outsource the upbringing of your child to someone else, but the mill village helped. Give me one man or woman from a mill village with a good mind and honest convictions and I wouldn't trade them for ten strangers with strong opinions. I especially came to favor plant janitors. We can also take lessons from older successful individuals, who have a tendency to adrenalize their ambitions and alchemize change; I did.

As I grew tall in stature, things began to transition as a creative transformation started to gorge on the world around us. Creativity, by its nature, may have a singular anatomy, but it usually has multiple possibilities. Seeing the many problems waiting to be resolved, I took a deep breath and dug in. I wanted to help expedite the needle of progress, so I learned how to chase problems around in some pretty tight concentric circles until I discovered the true value of algorithms and squares. It was a comfortable, nonconfining cage of childhood, nurturing and protective but sparsely decorated. Like a June-Bug on a string, you could fly just far enough away to stretch your wings and exercise, but no further. Gradually the answers were becoming easier and better defined. I found that few things are as interesting and energizing as an uninterrupted conversation with oneself. If we could have just gotten far enough away from the real world to triangulate reality, maybe we could have produced better answers. At the same time, each day there are mid-sentence fast forwards to cope with, which try to head us off down rabbit holes.

In a small town where everyone knows you, you shouldn't let your human nature get lost in your psyche's junk folder. Self-effacement is not for the faint-hearted, as it brings a lot of dark light to the horizon. Trust and every other aspect of life is marked and in turn must be supported by truth, as everyone tried to toe the mill village line. It's always tempting but not much fun to see what one looks like from the inside of their head. Because, in our mind, we anxiously tend to observe ourselves and our lives at a distant remove. By our human nature, as we age, we become more experienced and flexible and inhabit a handful of different characters trying to find oneself. Similar to reality, life is structured by its own artful pauses, and as we begin to reach into insight and sentiment, it becomes more recognizable.

There is also an otherworldly undertow of empty actuality we need to pay more attention to, because so much of life takes place outside the lines and is not always observed. We are never sure how unfiltered our thoughts are. In little mill towns we prayerfully thought our life could be turned around and better balanced, even the plant janitors at the bottom of the ladder. For a lucky few, they did, but for many more of us it rarely did. It was just more of the same each day. Not bad, even mentally comforting in so many ways, but less economic progress than we would have preferred. We became hemmed in by the everyday making it hard to escape. Without microscopic observation, which we are not very good at, some significant things are turned down to a whisper, easy to miss. Few days are frictionless and can be like a curtain drawn across a mystery, because truth has a peculiar way of performing alchemy on our thoughts. Now when we look back, the past can seem like a foreign country, but it's a distant dream of yesterday and we are fortunately ahead of the curve and in little danger of getting hurt today because yesterday has already happened. So it was, growing up with the mindset of a mill villager.

The new language of change that I discovered was full of money. If you could learn the business vocabulary from the letters produced by the alphabet trees, the reaching dialect of education and transformation were full of value. Yet in those days our time vacancies became crowded to running over. Life, in its many manifestations and demands, can also be partial in the positive support of a person. Maybe it was for me; it's hard to say. You learn that as opportunity comes bouncing down the street, you have to run at full speed to catch it. You must engage it straight away and not miss a trick or challenge. Of course, a truly creative eye can consistently see more than a disengaged mind or lazy gaze can ever hope to view. Too many people see each day through ambition's narrowest prism, but I carried some weighty baggage as a young man. By fate and providence, some of us were able to avoid that disadvantage. I also discovered that living is never frictionless, not even to the fortunate 1 percent residing at the pinnacle of the economic pyramid—although that wasn't the street I lived on. Neither did I live on the street with the new moneyed elite: the 9.9 percent.

There were so many wonderful people in a mill village, in all sizes, shapes, ages, and colors, particularly the plant janitors. They were individuals that had an extraordinary empathy for others, especially those down on their luck and needing a pick-me-up. I never once remember hearing a single person say, "That's not my child," or "This is not my village," or "It's not my responsibility—let someone else do it." When I was a little boy, my heroes wore costumes and capes, flew through the air, were strong and powerful, and fought against injustice. They were fantastic and very popular; they were the "good guys." As I got older, and grew taller, my heroes were the same but changed their look. They lost their costumes and capes, but still did the same thing. The funny transition was that my heroes began to take on the names and faces of people I knew, that lived on my block, down the street and across town. I surprisingly discovered that mill villages were filled with people like that. I began to understand that compassion is always guided by an inner light and no one is any older than the age of their heart.

One learns that leverage can often be the secret to success, but how do you obtain it when located on the bottom rung of the ladder? I wondered exactly what reality was, because sometimes it seemed to come completely out of left field when you are unprepared. Then one day it became clear that it was stuff that couldn't be concealed or papered over, so I gradually learned to see the everyday through more generous, forgiving, and invested eyes. I decided I needed to pool and dump my solitudes, bad attitudes, and worries and just get on with life. That's where I found myself at sixteen, starting out, as a college student, in the most mentally degrading job in the mill: as a plant janitor cleaning employee restrooms. If there is a worse place to start, I don't know where it is. After analysis and considerable thought,

I came up with a plan to try to create opportunity, but I was going to need a little help.

I knew that women were more conscientious than men about cleanliness, so that would be my secret strategy. I cleaned and left the men's restrooms in a first-class condition, probably as good as or even better than anyone had ever done before. But I decided the women's restrooms would be perfect, spotless, nonpareil, the best they had ever been or could be. They also must have a special distinctive cachet, an added touch—and so they did. After the first week, women began thanking me for how clean, neat, and well stocked their restrooms were. After a couple of weeks, when someone made that comment, I said, "Thank you, but would you please do something for me?" Almost everyone said, "Of course, if I can. What's that?" I responded, "Would you also tell the overseers, Mr. Whitten and Mr. Bramlett, what a good job I do? I have to be able to work somewhere next quarter, and if I can't find a job that fits my course schedule, I won't be able to go to college." True to their word, they responded in kind.

Several times both overseers told me how complimentary the employees had been of my work, both women and men. I thanked them and said, "Would you please do me a favor?" Fortunately, both of them said yes. "Then would you tell Mr. Addison in the personnel department what a good job I'm doing for you? I need a job somewhere next quarter to meet the difficult schedule of engineering classes or I can't go to Auburn."

They said they would, and they did. Each also said that if Bill couldn't find anything to come see them, they would work something out. I firmly believe they would have, but Mr. Addison came through for me, quarter after quarter, job after job, for five years, even after I received a Co-Op Scholarship. There is great power in the spoken word, especially when it's sincere and a legitimate request for help. But when you combine that with an honest, warm smile, you have a direct connection to a pure heart. It's something that will melt one's defenses faster than a Hershey's bar on a hot Georgia sidewalk in mid-summer.

The big things are important and affect our every day, but it often ends up being the little things that make the difference. There is always one irresistible quality in a person that's impossible to ignore: kindness. It's a trait hard to define in a college or job résumé. Many years later, the personnel director told me a story. I remember it well.

He said, "I looked up late one afternoon and the lady janitor that cleaned the front management offices was quietly standing at my office door. She said, 'Sir, I'm sorry to bother you, I've never done this before, but I want to recommend someone to you. He works with me as a restroom janitor—'cept he works out in the mill. I've never worked with anyone like him. He knows the name of everyone that cleans restrooms and sweeps the floors in the mill; there must be two dozen of us that do that. He always smiles and calls us by our name. He has respect for everyone, colored or white, even those that do the lowest jobs in the mill. That has never happened to me before. He's always willing to help us when he catches up. Women specially are always forgettin' and leaving purses or somethin' else behind, and he sees they get them back. He's one of the most honest, thoughtful, hardworking people I ever worked with, and I've been here fer over twenty-six years. I like to be around him; he makes me smile and feel good. He's trying to work full time, drive back and forth to Auburn every day, and has to pay his own way. If he doesn't have a job, he can't go. I want to recommend him and ask that you help him. Don't you think you could find somethin' for him to do in this big ol' mill? I've never done this before, and I hop' I'm doing it right. I have nothing else to give, but I recommend him as many times as I can.' I told Maudie that day that she had done it just right, and I thanked her."

Well, when he told me, even this many years later, it was hard not to puddle up a little bit, because I knew exactly who it was—and now she was gone. She was an extremely quiet person who kept to herself. I doubt that she ever finished the sixth grade in school, and I know how difficult it must have been for her to come forward to reach out and do that for me. I never forgot it.

The personnel director said, "You know, thoughtfulness is a very unusual trait in a person. The mind holds on tight and remembers, long after the experience is gone. People overlook plant janitors, but they will always pay attention to the supervisors, overseers, and managers. It was also the only time I can ever remember having a janitor come to me and recommend someone for a job that wasn't a family member. It's hard for anyone to overlook such a generous spirit that respects everyone. It's also interesting that one day your wife Claire ended up working for us in the personnel department as a secretary-receptionist while you were in school. She was smart, pretty, thoughtful, an exceptional person and super employee. I wasn't at all surprised."

He continued, "You know, it's not easy to explain kindness, thoughtfulness, and common courtesy on a résumé. It's clearly a learned talent. So I did everything I could to help find you a job somewhere every quarter for five years so you could work and go to school full time. I remember those days well, when you were working nights, long weekends, holidays, vacations, sixteen-hour shifts on weekends. I don't believe there were too many job patches in the plant you missed, if any. Why, you must have run twenty-five to thirty different jobs during those years, maybe more.

"At the time, it never crossed my mind that someday we would all end up working for you, but I'm not greatly surprised. Wherever you went, you were probably the youngest supervisor, overseer, staff manager, plant manager, general manager, vice president, and president in the Company. I recall that, as you moved around in the organization, everyone reporting to you was usually much older. I liked the way you compensated by completely breaking traditional Company protocol in numerous ways. I well remember that to make people feel more comfortable, you always insisted that everyone call you by your first name, even the plant janitors. I thought that was neat. We should always love and respect people and use things, not the other way around; you did that."

That was the greatest compliment I ever received.

Papa always said I would meet many people in life, and everyone would deserve some degree of importance and respect, regardless of what they do. All people need attention and recognition, even if it's a simple smile and hello even janitors. But to each of us, nothing is more important or sounds as sweet as hearing someone call you by your name. That means you are somebody.

As a kid, you don't have to go far to see a long way in your mind. In a problem-infested world, there were many times when I believed that a fair, equitable world just didn't exist. For a person living in a country hamlet, even in its ordinariness, almost every moment was a compact drama of identity, riveting in its being, composed mostly of results—or not. It wasn't an original plot, but one played out on stage by humans for thousands of years. Now it was my play, and I was the actor in the proscenium, trying to make a favorable impression. However, when reality is turned into an un-bridled, competitive three-ring circus, there is always the possibility that the lion will win. So always be prepared, and have your whip and chair handy.

When it's all you know, there is a certain order and prettification in the continuous rows of neat little white mill houses, with black asphalt roofs and manicured yards, all lined up in a row on long continuous oak-lined streets. Everything had its place. There were hundreds of precisely designed and planned Company-owned homes that were well-maintained and mani-cured throughout the village. The rent at one time was one dollar per week per room, gradually increasing over the years as rent was subsidized by the Company to obtain the best employees. In 1961, the Company decided the homes had served their purpose and were offered to those that lived there at exceptionally low prices and good terms. Almost everyone had pride in their pretty little habitats, flower and vegetable gardens, and sculpted shrubbery. Yet, other than the plant managers and some of the overseers' houses, few landscapes were fully color coordinated like the nicer homes in West Point, where the corporate executives and merchants lived. We heard that in West Point a few even had personal landscape gardeners, whatever that was.

When the homes were sold to employees, the Corporation still insisted that the plant managers and assistant managers live in the nice Company-owned homes adjacent to the mills—as they had done for one-hundred years. The managers came to me in 1974–1975 requesting that we discontinue this practice because of real estate inflation, tax, and other good economic reasons that over the years had become detrimental. I agreed and convinced corporate management (Grady Webb Jr., Dewitt Duskin, and CEO Joe Lanier Jr.) to remove this requirement. After several meetings, the practice was finally discontinued.

Every person was attempting to climb their own mountain, to have more and do better than the day before. We were trying to move another rung up the economic steps of income and prestige. Some made it and some didn't, for various reasons. The mill village was actually a simplified tale of historic America in miniature. For a newcomer, it was a small town quickly becoming a coarse weave of strangers, welcoming and curious, who became friends and neighbors. Everyone was supportive, each important in the whole, with no one considered marginal. They seemed to always be there for one another, and harmony was obvious to those that had eyes to see. There was gratitude on the part of the recipient and magnanimity on the part of the giver. Many were members of second, third, and even fourth family generations in the same village.

There were always the realistic touches that weighed heavily on the sense of wellbeing, on both the inner and outer selves. In a small town, everyone attempts to camouflage their own frailties from others, but you can never hide them from yourself. People lived so close together that your personal life was familiar to everyone else. You witnessed your neighbor's basic strategic plan, which encompassed the common realities of all families: that of sickness, success and failure, living and dying. Divorce was a rarity in those days, almost never heard of—the family came first. A mother and dad seemed to always be there. I never recall a child born out of wedlock. Now, everyone was not a saint, nor semi-perfect, but it didn't come close to today's more challenging and semi-bonded familial environment. All the while, the human condition was waiting in ambush, around the corner and behind every tree.

In our town, we were slightly south of simple. I found that churches were always a good place to pray, but so was home, at meals, in school, at ball games, indoors, outdoors, at meetings, every morning, and each night before I went to sleep. As I got older, I found the same was true in big cities. You just have to let life unfold and learn to lean into it with love and trust. Perhaps we should just love others and outsource all the rest?

Life is not accidental. Actuality has a blunt way of bullying, arriving to take your milkshake right out of your hand and drinking it while you're watching. It's the Homo sapiens' nature to be given to reflection, and we have a collective longing for the simplicity and comfort of the past. Yet, yesteryear is long gone and never to return. We have perhaps heard the old joke, "How many Southerners does it take to change a light bulb?" It takes twelve: one person to change the bulb, and eleven to stand around talking about how bright the light used to be before it went out. We all become rueful about the withering legacy of our past as we permit life to happen more by accident than design. Everyone has a normal tendency to take tantalizing glimpses over our back shoulder at how things once were and we would have liked for them to remain. The art of losing is one of the easiest tacks to master, because it takes no thought and little effort.

We are part of every created thing whether we accept it or not, as wisdom patiently waits for us to catch on to "who" and "what" we are. The unexplainable process is called faith. Some have it, some don't, but we all need it to survive in today's world. Those that have it are blessed, and those that don't should never stop searching. It's there waiting for you. For me, I found it long ago, when I was twelve years old, in a tiny mill town in Alabama. Yours can be found where you least expect it.

We humans oscillate between fact and fiction, and for some reason, history always needs a kick in the behind to wake us up and get us going. As we grow older, wisdom and insightfulness has a way of grasping our thoughts and shaking us awake, ready or not. I discovered that whether I have a $25 or a $1,600 watch, they both tell the correct time and neither can change reality. You can also get drunk as quickly on a $6 bottle of wine as one that costs $250, and after a few glasses they both taste about the same. The funny thing is that a drunk man's words are usually what a sober man is actually thinking. The surprising bottom line is you can also be just as happy in a one thousand square foot home as one that's ten times larger, frequently even happier. I had flown almost 3,000,000 miles before it dawned on me that the economy class seats arrived at the same time as the business and first-class seats and were a lot cheaper.

When I was young, I wanted to be rich, but as I got older and wiser, I discovered that I had much rather be happy. But when growing up, rarely does one's talent match our ambition. I also found that the people who really love and care about you will never leave. They will always find a reason to be there for you, even if it's undeserved. And it doesn't really matter whether you reside in a mansion, a penthouse, or a mill house. One must learn to live his or her fullest the first time around, because we are only passing through. At the end of the game, win or lose, like Monopoly, it all goes back in an empty box. Life is all about balance, enjoying the little treats that come along, usually bringing their own indulgence. With exhilarating innocence and the unguarded mortality of youth, I realized that someday I may become smarter but never any younger.

Mill villagers didn't weigh in on any particular subject—even plant janitors. They usually just minded their own business and got on with daily living, without fear of inner life and what was to come. They trusted the ordinary flavorful taste of the everyday. Simple living was about their only luxury extravagance. I think they depended upon truth giving their thinking confidence and the strength of its staying power. Honesty of the people who lived there had a special satisfying sensation that was completely trustworthy, and nothing could easily modify it. We all liked to experiment with our various cloaks of identity, in pastel dreams, trying to figure out who we really were. Yet, without thinking, too often we tumbled down into deep rabbit holes, a crazy land where honesty and facts don't matter. They are meaningless concepts in the political circus, signifying much but meaning little. Truth always seemed to be compounded and enhanced by our own improvisation.

As we get older it becomes more difficult to keep a careful genealogical listing of all the people we once were because there were so many. Truthfully, we rarely showed our real self to anyone. It's hard to see straight through the many masks we wear, especially when the meditative self is in control. Stagecraft has a way of ending up an important part of life's equation. Sometimes we even become unrecognizable. I tried to stay on nodding terms with who I used to be, even though there were times I didn't always like myself back then. Yet, I discovered early on that one of the greatest satisfactions and enjoyments you can ever have is to help lift up others when they can't lift themselves.

It was always interesting to me that we end up spending most of our lives looking for integrity and our natural authority. Then we are surprised when we find that wisdom had actually been looking for us and had been waiting all this time with the plant janitors in the mill village.

17

152

My Town

As we mature and age, we begin to realize that everything is relative except right and wrong, as we have come to live in a world characterized by its unordinariness. Yet for some peculiar human reason, we all still learn to wear our alter egos with the ease and comfort of an old flannel shirt. Few things are better than straightforward discretion. Everyone wants to grow up to be a legend in their own time zone, but few ever make it. I have never seen a good manager, wise leader, or productive politician of any kind that was also full of his own ego. It certainly didn't work in a mill village, even for a good plant manager who was also king, mayor, sheriff, judge, and jury in his unincorporated village kingdom. With all of his reaching authority, he was fully responsible for the economic performance, company property, employee good will, physical mill village, and continuing health of the plant and manufacturing operation. But, like the military, he had to pay great attention to fairness and the wellbeing of all the people under his command in the greater unincorporated community.

In fact, a plant manager, or even a vice president with many plants under his dominion, does a lot for his town(s). The time I spent in jail as a manager, general manager, vice president, president, and CEO should have been embarrassing, but it wasn't. In fact, it wasn't even the first stretch. I had been locked up before, but the various times were for a good cause: to raise money for charity—to be bought out of incarceration. However, these occasions were better than when I was dunked in a water barrel or the moment I had to kiss a pig for a good cause. That was the wettest snout I had ever seen. It was actually worse than the two nights I stood in the street, in a freezing rain, with a plastic bucket in hand collecting money for a hospital fund drive. Even harder than the many occasions, from 6:30 a.m. 'til 7:30 a.m., standing in the rain and cold with my two sons at mill gates passing out political cards for people we supported during voting season. Perhaps the most dangerous was when umpiring softball games between bitterly opposing teams. It was impossible to win, because regardless of the outcome, one team or the other would be mad. If I had a choice, I think I prefer being in the king's and queen's court at a powder puff football game. But it's all in fun and for a good cause: growing up in small towns, building camaraderie.

Every little village, for decades, had its own movie theater. It cost a total of twenty-five cents to go to an all-day "picture-show" and buy a bag of popcorn and a Coke. Today, if you were to attend a movie at the multiplex, you would have to take out a loan at the local bank, especially if you took your girlfriend. The small town theaters are all gone. Every community had a recreation department for most Company-employee activities, along with youth and sports teams from five years old up to seventy and even older. There were always lists of scheduled functions every week: special events, along with numerous recreational activities—dominoes, cards, bingo, civic clubs, church get-togethers, school functions, library visits, sporting contests, and community presentations. Everyone enjoyed participating in something. The Company maintained all the homes, corporate property, provided a free Kindergarten, paid your health insurance, and helped financially support hospitals, plant/community nurses, public education, churches, and sports programs through elementary, junior, and high school.

In our particular situation, the seven little towns—West Point, Lanett, Shawmut, Langdale, Fairfax, Riverview and Huguley, each with their own elementary and middle school systems—eventually divided into four high schools, three public and one private. These were West Point, Lanett, Valley, and Springwood. In 1968, Springwood, a college preparatory private school founded on Christian principles, was established in Lanett and opened in 1970. I was one of the original founders. It is still doing an exceptional educational job today, some forty-six years later, with 100 percent college acceptance. It has also had foreign students attend from sixteen different countries. The Company and executives were very generous in supporting all the educational programs, as well as the hospital and healthcare in the greater area. This scenario played out all across the South and in most small manufacturing communities around the country. You scratch my back, and I'll scratch yours—loyalty is always a two-way street.

We all have to give back for progress to be made. For several years, like many fathers, when my boys were growing up, I coached Little League Baseball. In teaching the game I always tried to keep a balance between instruction, discipline, and love—a three-legged stool. That may sound like a weird combination, but it works. I discovered that truth many times when I took my players home at night around 8 to 9 p.m. after a game or practice. I saw so many homes dark when I dropped them off, no one there, frequently without a father present. As parents we burden too many of our kids with our own personal baggage, which they can't unpack by themselves. There were many times when those boys would come to practice early in the afternoon because they had nowhere else to go.

It dawned on me one evening that some of those kids—especially in the summer—had little attention, affection, or sustenance all day and now were hungry and had to try to scrounge up something to eat at night. Yet in their need, they never once complained or asked for a single thing. So I told them that every time we won a game or had an exceptionally good practice, I would take them by McDonald's, Burger King, or Dairy Queen and buy them a hamburger and Coke or a vanilla milkshake, which I wanted. Of course, during the season it could become a little expensive. Usually I would have to take the same four or five boys home, so it wasn't so bad. About that time, the games and practices became much more energized and fun as we grew closer as a team.

Kids, deep down, really need attention and discipline; in fact, they crave it. They want their parents to be parents: always present, involved, and in charge with rules. Those were the signals I always got and felt. If you want to keep them out of trouble, give them direction, love and stable, secure, happier childhoods. It enables them to realize that if they are doing some-thing they shouldn't, especially in excess or if it's wrong, that you will remove them from its harm. It's a chance to let them learn about a more benevolent world of affection, care, thinking, and understanding. Every child is simply

Opelika Little League All-Stars, Alabama State Champions 1968.

trying to locate their place in the world. If they can't find themselves, just pray they find someone better to guide them.

So many times I felt that there, but for the grace of God, go I if I had not had such a wonderful family and hadn't been so busy trying to survive. It hurt me wondering what those boys' futures were going to look like under their circumstances, and it would have been satisfying and fun to help give them a better life. One year there were two in particular. They were handsome eleven- to twelve-year-olds, grinning young fellows with wavy black hair and dark eyes full of light and life; they reminded me a lot of Junior. I would have liked to have taken them home with me every day. We moved the next year. I have always wondered what happened to them. Life never comes with "no strings attached;" there is always a Catch-22. We keep too many of our thoughts at an intellective remove, usually over our heads but still reaching for our hearts. Part of life's fun is following our scattered breadcrumbs to see where they will eventually lead—or don't.

The funny thing is that during the five years that I coached, in three different towns, we won four league championships, two regional titles, and one state championship. I came to the conclusion that, in the three-legged stool of coaching, love is by far the strongest and most important leg of all for kids.

It would be fair to say that our little Fairfax mill town, built from 1915–1916, was not one of the more sophisticated enclaves in America, but it did rank pretty high on the Alabama scale. George Washington never slept there, but many wonderful people did. We were threadbare strivers looking for an ascendancy of abstraction, bidding to reshape life's playing field—and many of us did. The peculiar thing about introspection, and the decisions we make, is that it has a way of causing us to think about ourselves, when we already do too much of that. We then end up becoming too uncomfortable in our mental state of perpetual self-examination. Yet, it was free-trade reality and technology that eventually ate and devoured mill villages, small towns, and big cities all across America.

In our little town, we had our own water filtration plant, and all water came out of a tap. If anyone had said that one day it would be dressed up in fancy plastic bottles and cost more than gasoline, they would have been laughed out of town. Even that which is prettified with fancy labels usually comes out of someone else's city pipes, and we dense folks pay big time for the marketing of plain tap water. Most of those naive individuals with thick wallets don't come from the mill village. Back then, health food was anything that was considered edible and prunes were for medicinal purposes only. We saw oranges, walnuts, and bananas only at Christmas time, when all school kids received a small bag of fruit and a toy from the Company Santa Claus. He visited every school and community. The plant manager wanted no child to be overlooked or left behind for any reason, whether their parents worked for the Company or not. For some, it was about all they got at Christmas.

I don't know why it is but we never seem to fully appreciate something of true value until after it's gone. Maybe it's just part of our human disposition. At Christmas in the mid-1950s, Fairfax Mill brought to the greater community a beautiful merry-go-round, with free unlimited rides for the children (and all adults so inclined) in the mill villages. It was placed across from the mill in the center of the softball field behind the recreation center. It arrived in early December every year and remained through the holidays.

Christmas 1968—Fairfax Merry-Go-Round.

The multiple attendants for children's safety were Fairfax Mill employees that worked in the machine shop. This included me and my dad the first year and each year I was a student at Auburn. Over many decades we took our children, grandchildren, and great-grandchildren for rides at Christmas. We enjoyed those excursions with a child's glee, a hoarder's zeal, and a postman's passion. The benevolence of the mill to the Greater Valley continued for over fifty years until the plants closed. A few years after that sad event, the city of Valley opened it back up and has continued the merry-go-round practice in the Langdale community. By now, multiple millions of free rides have been given to kids, adults, and visitors from surrounding towns. For large numbers of families from miles away, it has become a family Christmas tradition. And like us, although the mills are gone, they are there every year, with a new generation of "mill villagers."

When I was a kid, we thought that oil was for use only in automobiles and combustion engines, with lard and animal fat earmarked for healthy cooking. Curry wasn't a spice we had ever heard of; it was the surname of the family living in the third house on the right on Maple Street. Never once did I see anyone place their elbows on the table without getting a knot on their head, as manners were taught at home and in school. Today it seems to be voided by both. Only twice did I ever talk back to my Dad, and the ensuing experience was so painful that I didn't believe it was worth ever doing again. I didn't.

Although we had nothing materially, every kid had as much as they ever needed to play with, which was called "outside." Iced tea had its own standard Southern recipe: the one-to-one ratio. One tablespoon of tea to one cup of sugar, unless you liked it real sweet. Now, granulated sugar got good press in those days, and doctors didn't get involved with medicinal guidelines. It was in abundance in every dining room, but cubed sugar could only be found in fancy uptown restaurants. Uptown was West Point and was a completely different world to an eight-year-old living on Cusseta Road and points south. We were weighed too much by a city's profound sense of mystification, coupled with an overpowering awe of the many downtown retail stores. Never did I realize back then that someday I would be in the retail business, big time.

Back then we were only at the start of our learning and remembering but already deep into our questioning. I always got clothes for Christmas and birthdays instead of the stuff I really wanted. You were better off if there was only one child in the family rather than four, where the presents were divided four ways. Practicality always presided over toys. In those days, we were all just hoping, searching, like everyone does, for our own slice of earthly actuality. It was pretty clear early on that in the broader world, for the disadvantaged and poor, hardship and trouble always knew your name and where you lived. Yet, in America back then, it was not where you were "from" that mattered the most but where you were "going," and everyone seemed to be intent on "going" where there was better opportunity. Some of those opportunities occurred at home where you grew up. Success was dependent upon about 15 percent of what happened to you and 85 percent of what you did about it.

Life is clearly about fuzzy black and white issues that arrive at your front door in several undefined layers. The real world exists in one hundred shades of gray, and you have to pick the right one or you lose. I learned rather expeditiously that whatever we decide to do, we usually have a choice, so learn how to make the right one. Fantasy may be fun, but eventually we discover that reality is the name of the street where all the action takes place. A smart child swiftly discovers that a good teacher can open the door of knowledge and a bright future, but you still have to walk through it yourself. I had my own smiling, folksy style, but I think in addition it was sincere and friendly. I guess I also had a sentimental heart, reaching out to others because I always had empathy and liked people.

We had no GPS in those days, so our direction was usually hit or miss. Rearview mirrors were very popular. Headaches and ambushes were constantly waiting around the corner or over the next hill. My wise grandfather called that "the learning curve of life." It was a head exercise of the most ambitious order, as we each looked around for our own beanstalk to climb. There were still some around. If you're lucky, you learn early on that life is really all about sweat equity.

I probably beat up on politicians more than they deserve, but I doubt it. Most, when running for office, want you to think they are a tasty box of Kellogg's Frosted Flakes. But they don't want you to read the label on the side of the box to see there is little of nutritional value inside. However, mill folks were not easily fooled. We especially tried to avoid people who were like the rooster and thought the sun rises just to hear him crow and those that couldn't think clearly because it takes their mind off themselves.

We knew that Winston S. Churchill and Vladimir Ilyich Lenin didn't play on the same football team and that Al Gore spent his entire life in D.C. inventing the Internet and expediting global warming. In recent years, it has been transparent to everyone that Donald Trump wore a toupee, Hillary Clinton made her own pantsuits, and Lady Gaga was just a typo. It is ironic to me that, in their hallowed and privileged perches, Hillary was once a Republican and Trump was a Democrat. Just goes to show how swiftly the weather and political winds can change when you are high up in the clouds. We knew what was going on and were anxious to take part. We understood there was a perpetual battle between rules and principles. Of course, one must understand that rules don't always work because they are subjective to man's whims. At the same time, principles are more important, foundational issues and can change lives. The wise man in the mill village always knows the difference.

Of course, in earlier days, wisdom embraced almost everyone in our neck of the woods, except the boys who foolishly kept swimming in Moccasin Creek. If our parents had known that, they would have killed us, assuming we had survived the snakes. Even so, I didn't mature enough to start keeping company with city girls until I was a middle-teenager. When I say city, I mean West Point, Georgia. It was the big retail town in the Chattahoochee Valley, the shopping metropolis and where most of the big executives lived. It also had close to 3,600 people and two synchronized stop lights; we didn't have any in Fairfax or the rest of the towns in the Valley. It was amazing to just stand there in downtown West Point, as a little boy, on the corner of Highway 29 and 3rd Avenue. You could watch those pretty coordinated red, yellow, and green lights blink on and off, on and off, all day. Amazing! Just like a colorful Christmas tree, year round. I used to wonder how they did that. We couldn't wait to get us one in the mill village.

They didn't have to burn down the school house to get me out of the third grade, because I skipped it. A lighted torch would have helped accelerate the education of a couple guys, though. I remember one fellow in particular at Fairfax in the eighth grade. He had played football, baseball, and basketball for several years longer than the rest of us. He was also pretty good. The teachers had to excuse him from class twice or more every year to go vote. Boy, we all envied him, but not when he went to the Red Cross to donate blood or had to be considered for jury duty. Of course, I don't ever remember him being chosen for a jury; it took too much thought.

The greasy pole climb at the recreation department on the Fourth of July for prizes was more challenging than trying to hem up the greasy pig they let loose, but the lawn mower races and three-legged sack contests were hard to beat. And few things were up to the level of bobbing for apples with pretty girls. That was almost as enjoyable as walking them home from the movies for a goodnight kiss, but less exciting. It's amazing how that activity got more interesting as I got older. Wait a minute, now that I think about it, I recall our Fairfax Junior High motto: "Study hard—you are only young once, but you can be stupid forever."

One of the more exciting events in the fall was midget football for pre-junior high school boys, sponsored by the Company recreation departments in each of our mill villages. There was also the cheerleading participation for girls. There were perhaps 500–600 total boys in the Greater Valley that took part in midget football alone. The mystery event at the end of the season was the huge banquet put on by the Company for all players and coaches, usually in Lanett. At that event, twenty-two participants from the total were selected by the coaches as Valley All-Stars. The fun part, beyond the special recognition, was the beautiful miniature gold-plated footballs given to the winners at the banquet each year. I was fortunate and received three but now only have two. I let my girlfriend at the time wear one on a chain around her neck. When we broke up, she refused to give it back. She said I gave it to her but I didn't; I only let her wear it. That was another rude lesson I learned the hard way: Never fumble away your football regardless of the game you are playing.

There was no room for middle ground during Iron Bowl week. This was the most divisive college football competition in America: Auburn versus Alabama. It usually took place the last game of the regular season. Students

My 1982 football ticket stub of first Auburn vs. Alabama game played at home at Jordan-Hare Stadium in Auburn.

were friends year long and played on the same sports teams, but then it came time to choose sides and school colors. Growing up a football fan in the state of Alabama, the Auburn versus Alabama game was and still is the biggest deal of the year—almost any year, any sport. One grows up immersed in the hard rivalry, and bragging rights go to the winner the full 365 days that follow the monumental event. The week of the game, you hang out with fans for your team, whether or not you liked them otherwise. If your team draws the short straw, you'll hear about it for the next 365 days, every day, until the next time. Now, don't get me wrong, I adore the University of Alabama members of my extended clan. They are my kith and kin. But they are not included in my will.

Each year I looked forward to the old-time family reunions, and I found out there is always at least one more idiot there than you expect. My dad would have killed me if it had ever been me. I once asked my mother why there were so many fat and skinny women at our extended reunions. She said, "Son, you have to understand. For a woman, life in a mill village is not really fair, in a number of ways. That's why Southern women come in so many different sizes and shapes—so it's to each her own." I'm not sure that was an answer, and I didn't understand it, but over the years it never changed. I have been afraid to ask Claire what she meant, because I probably don't really want to know.

Growing up as a near-destitute teen in a small backwater, surrounded by a lot of interesting people, tightened everyone's belt up a notch or two. At times it was similar to a one-ring circus and my grandmother was the ringmaster. When you don't know that there is anything better, you reconcile and enjoy what little you have, regardless of how limited it may be. Under the circumstances, it matters not whether it's a communal bed in a boarding house, one room in the local Fairfax Hotel, a small two-room house in a miniature village, or a four-room rental. It could even be a grand thirteen-room colonial home on a hill in Alabama, a beautiful 1720s farmhouse on the ocean in Kennebunkport, Maine, or a sumptuous penthouse in uptown New York City—even a home high up in the mountains of North Carolina. I was blessed and lived in all of these, plus several more. We discover that life is lived as much in the mind and spirit as in the body, heart, and soul.

In the real world, we are just ordinary human beings that are ongoing works of art still on the easel. Too often we mistakenly think we are a finished product, but not so. Nostalgia's always there undercover, fueling our resentment toward transformation, longing to return to yesterday, but we can't go back. We are stuck with who we are, so be sure it's someone you like—or change.

Someone told me once, long ago, that America is like a unique box of crayons. Some are pretty and some are not, some sharp and others dull; many are almost used up and others have never been out of the box; some have peculiar sizes and names and others are just ordinary. We are all different colors but still we snuggly reside in the same box.

To a child or an adult, everything is relative to what you have and know. One's experiences are not just examples but are made within themselves. Of course, every mistake in life counts, if for nothing else, toward experience. That's been proven time and again as our sense of self is always internalized. However, I discovered early on to always be careful in the problem solutions you devise, because you never want to "Peter Principle" yourself out of the picture. Neither do you want to become your only best friend. Sometimes I think we just prefer less truth than life provides.

18

English Class

The vast majority of teenagers in the Greater Valley that were able to go to college never picked cotton, but instead became pragmatists, adept at navigating the many curves in the road and the mounting hum of economic anxieties; also, they attended Auburn. Their parents, who hadn't been able to go, taught them the importance of education. Carpooling for the daily seventy-four mile (round-trip) commute was one of our most popular activities. Many outstanding mill village kids in the 1950s took a long shot from center court and made the basket. There were many times I wondered if I was trying to cross a bridge too far. So each day I just came in costume as myself. Now, I wouldn't say that I was behind the curve, but in my first English class I discovered that for sixteen years I had been speaking prose and didn't even know it. English class, with all its manifest themes and variations, was entertaining, informative, and intimidating. Being an "Auburn Man," I had learned up to this point that every hand was worth shaking, every neck worth hugging, and every check worth kissing—that is, until I met my first English professor.

Life, in its own rhythm, is always an origin story—not fully predictable but exciting just the same. It usually depends upon the writer, and how he/she learns to color within or outside the lines, leavened by their thoughts and delicate touches. It also depends upon the hues and shades he uses to brighten or dull the pictures. In our little town, English was the *lingua franca*, backed up by our Southernese and redneck otherness. But wait, I'm getting ahead of my story. I would not consider myself a historical novelist or creative writer, either of fact or fiction. I was much better at doctoring problems in the corporate and community environs as a change alchemist while producing innovative ideas. Initiating creative language was just not my thing. I never recall a day when I thought myself proficient at finding the proper words or sentences waiting for me underneath the alphabet trees.

Even with that handicap, I taught creative analysis in my October years as the executive-in-residence and visiting professor at a leading university. Along the way, a very interesting thing occurred. To scratch a longtime itch, I came to teach others and was instead taught. I wanted to explain and influence, but came to better understand. I always had a rather creative and structured management predisposition, good people skills, and an engineering mentality. It involved a mindset that focused on working with people to improve tangible and fungible things.

I like universities because of all the profound, accumulating knowledge living there. The freshmen continue to bring a little in and the seniors rarely take any out, so knowledge just sits there and accumulates, year after year, in a big pile that's free for the taking. Confidence is the valuable property of youth that thrives in inverse proportion to one's experience and wisdom. Auburn, with its wide-ranging academic opportunities, was an eye-opening reprieve for a mill village kid, but there was also much to be abstracted from a warm encompassing past nestled in my comfort zone. At the same time, you eventually learn that life doesn't always indemnify you for stupid mistakes.

I would never enter a claim of participation in the upper echelon of English students when I was in college. In the true sense of the word, I was quite far removed from a docent of the first order. I can assure you that we didn't have an expansive bookcase of hardbound first editions at home; to tell the truth, we didn't even have a bookcase. In fact, I was instrumental in helping hold down the average class grade—all the students loved me. I found that, for an inexperienced individual, I was more used to massaging facts, evaluating, and applying logic while using rationality and science. Creative writing for me was like trying to climb a greased pole and hem up slippery words at the top with a simple mind. A creative bent made it most enjoyable and to my liking.

I am a little embarrassed to tell this story but it is painfully true. At the time I was a sixteen-year-old first-quarter freshman in the College of

Engineering at Auburn University. When the quarter began, we were asked by our English professor to write a theme paper reflecting one's perspective on politics. I was slightly nervous in class because I was a little short on reading the classics; they were the books everybody needs to read, but no one does—especially in a mill town. Now, my professor could harangue with the best of them, but he never inspired me enough to want to jump up and jog around the block. That first day I had a choice of being assigned to Shakespeare's favorite seat: 2-B or not 2-B. Naturally, as a freshman, I made the wrong decision.

That same quarter I was taking an elective course in Greek literature and philosophy (which I liked) and was studying Plato's *Republic*, including his various concepts of government. So I prepared a nine-page handwritten paper on the positive aspects of Plato's Benevolent Dictator. I thought it would be interesting and make a big impression on my professor, and it did. I think he liked his literature straight, clear, cold, prejudiced, and dead. Now if I could only learn to open and shut my eyes as easily as he did his mind. Being 1954, the hostility and tension between capitalist and communist ideologies were rapidly heading toward an apogee, but growing militaries, economic competition, and philosophical conflict were the farthest things from my freshman mind; I was just trying to survive in the real world in which I found myself.

In a few days, when my paper was returned, up in the right-hand corner of the front page was an 'F-minus' in large, bold red letters. Yet on the nine pages there were only three simple comma corrections. The narrative logic was traditional rhetoric, while the handwriting and presentation were clear and legible. I thought it merited at least an A-minus. I sat through the class session, internally fuming, and went up to my professor immediately after class. I handed him my paper and tactfully said, "I would like to discuss my grade, and under the circumstances, I don't think I deserve an 'F-minus.'" He looked at me over his glasses and sarcastically responded, "I agree. You don't deserve an 'F-minus,' but it is the lowest possible grade I could give."

My mouth fell open. Gathering my composure, I calmly asked him to please explain why. I had always been a good student, and up until that point, in my exposure to academia, I thought an 'F' was the lowest grade you could receive for any reason. He frowned, squinted his eyes, and rather loudly said, "Are you a communist?"

"No, sir, I'm a capitalist just like you," I explained.

"Then why did you write a paper glorifying communism, praising a Benevolent Dictator?" he sternly asked.

"Well, I was studying Plato this quarter. It was on my mind and I thought it would be a different twist on politics, and that it might get your attention. I thought you might think it creative. I understood this was an English class involving grammar, presentation, writing, sentence structure, and the ability to clearly express one's self. I didn't know we would be graded on our personal political philosophy," I responded.

"Now. . . you. . . know," he intoned, looking over his glasses and slowly repeating each word.

It was a lesson rudely learned, and one I never forgot. Fortunately, by the end of the quarter, my initial grade punishment had been positively resolved and we were on mildly improved personal terms—not great, just better. Of course, from that low point at the deep end of the pool, there was only one way for me to go and that was up. During the quarter I discovered he could compress more words into the smallest ideas than any other teacher I ever had. It seemed he liked plain simple students, because he went to great lengths to make us all ordinary. I think he didn't believe he was profound until he couldn't understand his own words. Fortunately, I discovered he was an atypical college professor.

From this experience, I learned that the single most essential ingredient in the recipe for becoming a writer, speaker, or leader—on any topic, for any purpose—is the reader or listener; not the conceiver or presenter of the inspiration, but the recipient, the interpreter of the iteration. If the reader or listener misses the point of the thought (or, even worse, misinterprets the idea), then all the effort is for naught. It is also much better to keep it simple and over-communicate rather than under-communicate. That is true in public speaking as well, but that's another subject for another day.

The communication process permits us to express the intuitive wisdom that comes from within our tiny grey cells. It matters not whether those thoughts are spoken, written, or shouted, because they must navigate through crowded mental space that is charged with the echoes of all the other voices that have paved the way. It is like competing radio signals trying to come through on the same mental frequency, or multiple thoughts at war with one another. The convergence of life and reality peels back some of our challenges, helping us to better articulate our thoughts and emotions as we place them into the more correct and understandable words. So it was in English class, and in other opportunities for communication as well. We are weighed by our abundance and emptiness, oscillating dualities vying for our attention, and fortunately they seem to stay in balance to make life worthwhile.

Now, where higher education is concerned, there were many academic honors for exceptional students. Some graduated cum laude, a few less graduated magna cum laude, and fewer still (the highly intelligent) graduated summa cum laude. For me, I did even better. I graduated, miraculously, and my parents were more pleased than all the rest.

Reality is not a state of mind; it's a fact. My dad always told me that being unique and standing out in a large group was a personal compliment, and at the same time that "special" acclaim should strongly support one's potential promotion opportunities. I'm not sure the 'F-minus' exception in English is what he meant. Neither did I realize at the time that I was going to college while working forty-plus hours a week, with many sleepless nights, so I could graduate in five years, go into management, and have the "privilege" of working sixty-plus hours a week with even more sleepless nights.

19

Creative Change

I learned early on that every upside or improvement in the status quo usually has some kind of negative consequence for someone or something, somewhere. Sometimes it's anticipated. Other times, not so much. That's when it jumps up and bites you. It's the destructive other side of the coin of creativity. When you live in the microcosm of a small town, where everyone works for the same company and you know one another, there is usually some unexpected aftermath to one's actions, especially where change is involved—even if the net effect is positive. Regardless of our age, we have to push ourselves to think better or the lazy genes will take over. I was still early in the process of finding myself, although it seemed to be picking up speed and moving at a faster pace.

When I was eighteen years old and a junior in college, I received a three-year co-op scholarship (including two years of paid college) to work a quarter in various departments in the mill as an intern and then go to college for a quarter. To this day, it was one of the best things that ever happened in my career. I also had to continue working full time when I was in school to pay my living expenses. Before the summer work quarter in my junior year had started, the plant manager, Mr. George Harris, called me to his office to discuss something that I hadn't expected to be on my plate that day. Something in the conversation sharply piqued my curiosity. He said, "The overseer of the Inspection Department will be having gallbladder surgery and will be out of work for seven or eight weeks. Would you like to act as interim overseer while he is on medical leave?" I was very surprised and flattered because in that era, no one ever became an overseer until they were forty to forty-five years old with twenty-five years experience, even if

Weave room at Fairfax Mill in 1960s.

an interim. Age, experience, and tradition ruled the day, and I was just a teenager.

This department was responsible for the plant's primary weaving quality control function, a critical cost control area of accountability. I had previously worked in that department for two weeks and had expressed my concern about inefficiency and high cost, which I thought could be substantially reduced with study. Perhaps that was the reason I was offered the management opportunity: just to see if I was right and had initiative, or was only a young kid blowing smoke.

Mr. Harris never said, and I never asked. I would also be the youngest person working in the department by several years and would be in charge—interesting potential dynamics. I had always wanted to be a creative sommelier and improve things, and here was my first big break. I also knew that whatever I did, whether it be good or bad, would have a huge impact on my future in the rapidly growing company. In the understated if not contradictory message in capitalist meritocracy, a successful leader will have a statue dedicated to him or her in the town square, while an unsuccessful one, regardless of the effort, will be lined up and shot at dawn by a firing squad of board members, civilians, and politicians. I seriously thought about that possibility. Yet, whatever I did, I wanted to be sure to avoid the ordinary boilerplate expectations. At the same time, in every problem or opportunity we tackle, we should always try to offer up a little decision based in normalcy that would make sense.

During the next several weeks in the temporary management slot—in my spare time and in the evenings—I couldn't shut down my creative instincts, even when I was off the clock. So I carefully and quietly measured all the functional jobs on three shifts step by step, including employee efficiency, machines used, equipment design, practices, schedules, task frequencies, and operating procedures. I laid out a detailed plan while carefully evaluating data. Then I re-engineered on paper all the jobs by changing duties and frequencies, which greatly increased our extraordinarily low employee efficiency. An effort had evidently never been made to improve economics in the department. Status quo ruled the day. New management measurement and cost controls were developed to ensure high performance. There were a couple of key bottleneck areas that needed to be eliminated. I then completely redesigned the inspection tables, cloth trucks, and other equipment for increased speed and efficiency and came up with a major department reorganization and a surprising recommendation.

For the first time in Company history, I boldly proposed that we install expected production standards on quality control inspectors. It had never been done before anywhere in the Corporation to this degree. The resulting economic potential surprised even me. I calculated that from ninety-six employees, we could eliminate thirty-seven jobs and reduce total employees to fifty-nine, a 38 percent reduction in direct cost that freed up approximately 25 percent of the total floor space being utilized by the department. This was badly needed for warp storage in the adjacent slashing department. There would also be huge quality feedback savings by reducing inspection response time to the weaving operation.

This transition would require a capital investment for newly designed, modified machinery. Cost estimates were prepared from my drawings by Mr. Reeves, the overseer of the plant machine shop. I designed a complete new department layout and retraining procedures for all the remaining employees. There was an economic payback in less than four months, which was totally unheard of for such a major functional revision. It usually took several years for a payback, even in a highly labor-intensive industry. It would also improve product quality control by reducing defects through initiating more expedient (by about three hours) feedback to the weaving operation. I didn't know how much that was worth, but I knew it was very big—on an annual basis, perhaps almost as great as the labor savings. The Company was in a growth mode, and I figured that in the large diversified plant, we could retrain and place in other departments thirty-four of the thirty-seven employees being eliminated. The Company could retire an additional two individuals, and normal attrition over several months would take care of the last one.

The twenty-six page proposal I had prepared, with narrative and machinery design drawings and detailed cost and savings, was typed in confidence by a secretary in the production office, where I had worked the prior quarter. When the department overseer returned in seven weeks, I reviewed the concept with him in private. I thought he would be elated (which was naïve—inexperience on my part). Instead he was extraordinarily hostile towards me, feeling the proposal was a negative reflection of his past management—which in reality, it was. Relationships can take on a sharp edge, with no visible saturation point, when emotions get involved. Fiction and fantasy had been milking Southern Reality for years, but it was time to cease. Two weeks later, in my summer work exit interview, I presented the proposal to Mr. Harris and the assistant plant manager, Mr. Pease. They were quite surprised but extremely pleased at the potential.

As recommended, test machines were made in our first-class machine shop. The proposed changes were reviewed, jobs were evaluated by the industrial engineering department, and within about six months the entire proposal was implemented. Of the proposed thirty-seven jobs, thirty-six were actually eliminated and floor space was freed up as projected. I did not know it at the time but that summer was the beginning of my transition to becoming a young corporate Problem Doctor. Management was elated, because it solved two problem areas—quality control cost and the slashing department's desperate need for space.

I was just a junior in college and only eighteen when I achieved the sort of celebrity and attention that strivers my age, and much older, only dream about. Yet, it wasn't easy, nor was it simple. I spent many a hard day's night invested in that opportunity. I was unknowingly, at that very moment, using the focused algorithmic concept I later developed and called the 10-Step Creative Analysis Process. Yet, there was also a downside—the "creative destruction" aspect—of a positive event. The inspection department overseer, a former friend, never spoke to me again. The operation was highly successful, but the relationship died.

However, I learned that one should never be afraid of the apparent, because it's there for everyone to see. The problem was a full disclosure of economic opportunity. It had been waiting for years for someone to come along and set it free. Yet, if you impinge in any way on your next door neighbor, be prepared for the fallout. One should always be concerned about the duality of truth and consequences. Over the ensuing years, I wondered more than once if I had passed my "use before date" as an ingénue Problem Doctor. However, fate was always kind and came to my rescue time after time. That unusual project celebrated its sixty-second birthday this year. I would never have believed back then that reality was benevolent enough to present a gift with my name on it. That one unique incident launched a lifetime career as a Problem Doctor that I could not have imagined. I quickly learned that a Problem Doctor's job is to change things—which most people don't like—and you rarely receive a kind word without a serrated edge.

When one grows up in a harshly competitive world, one can't help but feel the pressure. You assume you don't have all the time you need when you start the race at the back of the pack. You know you have to make up for lost time, because there are a lot of people ahead of you in the management queue. So, as a poor kid, I had to become a master of self-creation. I searched in many mirrors for the meaning of my own reflection as I moved up the ladder from one job challenge to another. I didn't always like what I saw, but I had to admit that it was a truthful image at the time. I clearly remember the tangible sense of who was actually looking back at me from my mirror every morning, and the one who should be there never left my mind. This was a heady, dizzying experience, but a fully illuminating one.

Sometimes you even get to stretch muscles in the mind you didn't know you had. Whether you like it or not, in a truly contested career, you eventually reflect four things: the narrative of self, the results, one's résumé, and the marketing of your skill set.

At that particular time, creativity finally gave me a unique voice. I had not yet become a full self-described extrovert or an innovator, but finally—with that success—I no longer had to speak loudly for people to listen. That had never happened before. I discovered that little miracles happen every day; it's just the big ones that attract our attention. Now management was all ears to my thoughts, and at eighteen, I liked it. I decided creativity would become the touchstone throughout my career. From that point forward, I don't remember any future recommendations being trivialized. At the same time, I learned that having to make hard decisions—for various reasons—is always a Problem Doctor's paradox. From the beginning to this very day, one of my favorite things to do has been tweaking the status quo. One should never forget that life is always about self-actualization.

In those younger days of fight and challenge, I was highly active in business and sports and was energized. Now in my December years as I have gotten older, become more conservative, and finally retired for the fourth time, things have changed. I think that early tomorrow morning I might wake up and go on a six-mile run. Or I could also be lucky and win the mega-millions lottery. Either way, the odds are about the same.

20

A Cool Girl

Ah, the preternatural analytic of life that's hard to self-invent is romantic attraction. Nothing ever tastes as good as love feels. You either relax and accept your fate or become asphyxiated from the tight grip of the afterglow. Pouring gasoline on a fire will never reduce the flame. Life is finite but hope is infinite. In its own special way, mutual affection is a form of open and closed reciprocity, and can even be found in a bargain economy and a mill village. It is no small burden to possess something as valuable as someone else's trust. Sometimes I think attraction is simply poetry of the imagination, music in search of the words. Once the love bug bites, there is only one antidote to cure the disease: marriage. I have discovered that the happiest couples are those who both think they have married way over their head. Regardless of how intensely one looks, it's difficult to find the extraordinary in the ordinary.

Adoration at first sight is also a great time- and labor-saving device. At the same juncture, romantic relationships are always an existential crisis in process. When one is smitten, romance is the finite within the infinite. It's like a complicated virus that only affects one or two people at a time; but if not given attention, it can be damaging—even devastating—to the normal performance of the heart. That's why "I love you" is an ordinary remark that has extraordinary power, but it always involves risk. I have never seen a statistical or theoretical analysis that can measure the evocative strength of secret thoughts and emotions. Life in its generosity tries to give us what we want but not always in the way we expect it. It offers something beyond the tunnel focus that can entrap the mind, because reality has a perverse way of trying to trick us. The heart is fragile, breakable crystal, so be careful

175

Claire Smith Andrews — A Cool Girl in 1980.

how you use it; there are just some yearnings that are not easily expressible through language.

In deep cognitive thought, some memories last forever in our neck of the woods. Perhaps the greatest claim to fame in my life was the day the coolest girl in school, Claire, reciprocated my feelings. She had long-term possibilities and was worthy of not only attention but admiration—if I could ever get on her agenda. She had me at hello, with her bright twinkling eyes and a smile full of mischief, fun, and compassion! It was an uneasy feeling, like when you first had a crush on someone but knew they were out of reach. I liked everything about her, including her faults. In this case, Cinderella had a lot more going than just glass slippers and a pumpkin. From across the room, through smoldering glances, I was immediately attracted by her *je ne sais quoi*—that special something hard to define. I was gobsmacked from the first moment I met her. Of course, no one is perfect until you fall for them, and after that it's too late to recognize their faults. Like me, she wasn't wealthy (her mother was the postmaster in Riverview and her father had a small business), but money can't buy class, character, or authenticity. Of course, it can purchase beauty to a limited degree—but she didn't need it. She was an anthology of delights.

Women don't get to make fools of men, because most of us beat them to it. I wouldn't want a female to know this, but all males are essentially the same; we just have different faces so you can tell us apart. The sad thing for women, which they don't realize, is that all men are created equal and below average. Men should be on guard and remember that women are smart and should never be underestimated. After all, they invented windshield wipers, fire escapes, laser printers, and most important of all, bulletproof vests. For me, I never argue with Claire. It's like reading the tiny print on a lengthy computer software licensing agreement. I usually give up, ignore what's said, and just click "I agree." Love is never a given; it's always an aspiration.

For years I was footloose and fancy free and had been able to avoid the opportunity of making some unfortunate young lady miserable. I was the fellow that never made the same mistake once and had never told my wife a lie—because I didn't have one. I'm not sure I was a good catch, but if so, it was doubtful I was a keeper. Then I met Claire. When I first saw her, I got a little tingly feeling up my spine to my brain. I later discovered it was common sense departing the premises. It was the shank end of a spring that I will long remember. When I first saw her that day with her best friend, who I knew, I started looking for a new way to metabolize heart palpitations. In high school, she was two years behind me but good looking, smarter, and more talented, kindhearted, friendly, and popular than me. She was selected "Most Likely to Succeed." She had bushels of friends and admirers, but I had her. It was a win-win situation for the home team. In a dating mode, most of our thoughts are for private consumption. I knew I had to jump high to clear the acceptance hurdle in her case. When I was around her, I stood as close as intimate decorum would allow. When I spoke, I had a hard time finishing a sentence; my words wandered all over the place.

God recognized early on that men like two things: danger and play. So he invented women, who became dangerous playthings.

Claire is a resplendent name, and she was the first "Claire" I had ever heard of. It is supposedly English, inherited from her aunt. Today, every third baby girl born in America is named Claire. I tell her, "It's because of the great example you set in your earlier years, in your many accomplishments. It had nothing to do with the renown you gained in marrying me." For some reason, I didn't make any points with that last remark from the smart, pretty girl from Riverview. Now note, I didn't say "pretty smart" girl; I said "smart, pretty" girl—a big difference in the Southern vernacular. She said, "Must I remind you that you only had one nickel to rub together when we were married?" I responded, "Yes, I well remember. But now I have two, and that's a 100 percent improvement." On the day of our joined boy-girl partnership, I found out that I had agreed to give up privileges that I didn't even know I had.

There were no dollops of pretension; what you saw was what you got. I took a shot and invited her to Easter Sunrise Service at Callaway Gardens in Pine Mountain on a first date in 1956. How could a girl from First Christian Church in Riverview turn down such an offer? To go in a non-hooded 1940 Ford Coupe, with a loud modified muffler, was an added plus—or so I thought. She said yes. Now I just hoped my car would get us over there and back, or it would have probably been our last date. It did. It wasn't. I was ineluctably hooked. I was never a perfectionist and was very practicable. Our druthers usually become character studies of people and things that don't exist, but she was different. To be honest, she was so pretty, smart, and talented that I didn't also expect her to be able to cook. Wow! What a pleasant surprise.

Claire used words like breviloquent, which had never before been mentioned in a conversation in a mill village—certainly not at the boarding house where I lived. I didn't know if you lived it, wanted it, ate it, or if it was dangerous. However, breviloquent was not a lightly chosen word, because she never did anything in a casual or unthoughtful manner. Not wanting to appear stupid or at loose ends, I didn't ask her what it meant, and I still don't know for sure. But I think it means brilliant, eloquent, and focused, which fit her to a "T." She always made me think of all the wonders of the library, which was one of my favorite places—and still is. So many interesting things to explore.

I was never bashful, but I spent nearly all of my time in high school trying to learn how to ask girls out because they were all at least one or two years older than I was. For a high school boy, being turned down on a date features all the enjoyable spontaneity of a visit to a dentist for a root canal. I knew that if Claire said no, it would leave me with only two options: to leave town forever or commit suicide. Neither choice was very appealing. I discovered that the heart has a thick accent when it hurts. Personally, I have always been a little afraid of clearly communicating with her, because then I risk figuring out what she is actually thinking. I'm not sure I want to go there—yet. I was blown away when she started talking about a meaningful pH balanced diet with granola and wheat germ. We didn't have either of those in our mill village, whatever they were. Yet I knew I was missing something in life that couldn't be filled by a Cocker Spaniel or German Shepherd. Everyone wants to be connected to a whole person, especially a pretty one. With her there was always plenty of quiet presence.

When romance is involved, it's hard to say the words without hearing the music, because it always alters the mindset for the better. I have discovered that most Southern men (maybe the entire male species) are easy to figure out. Every man I have ever known falls deeply in love with any woman that will listen to him talk. Perhaps just paying attention is the greatest act of love, because it takes at least two people to balance the romantic equation. Yet, modern coupledom is not easy. But don't get me wrong—men are not all anti-domestic. There are probably upwards of 3 percent, from time to time, that don't mind doing a little cooking, house cleaning, and yard work to please their spouse, although I've never met one. One's actions are the best way to interpret a person's character and values. However, love is a lot like politics: the more you know, the less you understand.

To develop a strong relationship, time is needed. Brevity may be exciting and even elegant, but ultimately it's usually empty. I will never forget the first time Claire came to dinner to meet my people, as is Southern tradition. We were sitting around my grandmother's big dining room table in the boarding house in loud talk and laughter. The table was heavy laden with fried chicken, pork chops, meat loaf, a dozen vegetables, garlic creamed potatoes, cornbread, hot buttered biscuits, and banana pudding—high Southern cuisine. I was a little anxious, to say the least, not knowing how it would go. I knew I was in way over my head and grossly overmatched. It was a very unusual courtship risk (and truthfully, probably unfair) to initiate someone as delicate as she was into that environment for the first time. It was such a large unruly crowd. Of course, temptation is like an envoy from a palliative dream inviting us to join in. We all long for romance because it's deeply imbedded in our DNA. In fact, that's how we got here in the first place.

As usual, Claire was absolutely captivating, charming, and quietly holding everyone's attention. She was all of 5'2" tall and weighed a whopping 98 pounds soaking wet. She was selected Class Favorite, Class Beauty, voted Most Likely to Succeed (that didn't mean succeed with me), was class vice president, an Honors student, and had won the Miss Chattahoochee Valley Follies Beauty Pageant a couple of years earlier. There is absolutely nothing wrong with intellectual arm candy. I hope you are starting to get the picture. She was an accomplished musician, playing a clarinet in the high school marching band, although in her modesty and humility she said she was more of a "toter" than a "tooter." She had scruples and was always a lot more demure than me. She was an expert in decorum in all matters of taste, great and small. She was all one ever needed.

Now being both wise and health conscious, she believed in a balanced diet of vegetables, fruit, grains, nuts, and fun. I have finally come to believe that fun and nuts was the reason she liked me; she never said and I was afraid to ask. For years, I was misguided and thought it was my fervent romantic passion and great muscular physique that attracted her. Now I don't think so.

Underneath our febrile façade, Southern men are really quite vulnerable—some are even mildly human. Most of us are just an "alternative male" anyway: ordinary, middle class, heterosexual, football loving, honest, employed, and with our own failure built right in to who we pretend to be. Usually we are too busy trying to make a living to have enough time to work on our intuition and relationships and to upgrade our Southern Reality.

Togetherness in an affiliation is important, because you have to choose each other, every single day, over and over, or it doesn't work. Successfully married people already know this.

What you are probably thinking by now is correct, because I was clearly not in her ball park. In fact, even in my halcyon days, I wasn't in the same league. Intellectually speaking, she was ready-witted, leaving me in the shade, and she was uber-wise in an all-knowing Southern female perspective. Not only that, she was a portmanteau, always brief but eloquent and to the point. She never would let anyone know how smart she really was. Love is actually an ancient recipe anyway, made over and over with the same artisanal ingredients. Even so, today, I still get in the last word. It's usually, "Yes, ma'am!" Years later, when we lived in New York City, the only thing of value that I ever remember doing where she was concerned was to tactfully convince her that a new mink coat would make her look fat. Boy, I was nervous that afternoon, because I got a lot of eye-rolls.

Claire had been surprisingly nosed out, in a large graduating class, as valedictorian by Gilmore Meadows—the football team waterboy and manager. Gilmore went on to Auburn and Ohio State University to get his Ph.D in nuclear physics. I always admired him for being so smart. He

A Cool Girl in New York City, Central Park in 1998.

is the only person I ever knew that made a living working with something that no one else had ever seen: atoms. I'm still not sure they are not a scam, and nuclear fusion isn't just a figment of perverse scientific imagination. Perhaps the important lesson here for football players is that you should be kind to your waterboy, because someday you may end up working for him.

She was controlled, fastidious, and meticulous to a detailed fault. Claire balanced well with my ordinary, casual, extroverted scruffiness—which I guess is the way the good Lord intended the conjoined Southern marital equation to work. But I'm not about to raise my hand and ask 'Him'—or 'Her,' as Claire says. Yet, with all of those unbelievable attributes, something seemed to be missing that particular first evening at the boarding house. Then, in her warm, soft voice, she said, "I am an Auburn girl and that's where I'm going to school." Everyone around the big dining room table smiled and nodded approvingly through the long, loud, standing applause. It was love at second sight; I was hooked, and that was over 60 years ago. We were bookended with one another. None of her wonderful qualities have faded since that eventful day. She's very dear to me and we still try to go to every Auburn football game. About twenty years ago, I began to trust her completely and now let her carry the cooler with the beer.

Men, by their weak nature, are very simple and easy to figure out. All females need to know about them is that you don't have to tell him jokes to make a good impression—you just have to laugh at his. Women will eventually discover that love is blind, and marriage becomes the real eye-opener. Females have a tendency to fall in love with broad shoulders and a big smile and then make the mistake of marrying the whole person. Romance has a way of filling up the heart as the brain empties; that is, if one can think at all. It's also the most painful emotion, except for all the others. The only way a woman will ever change a man is if he is less than one year old and still wearing diapers, which most are. So when you are selecting a mate from the crowd, looking for the pick of the litter, be sure and get one that's already housebroken.

We eventually learn that affection is not something you see with your eyes but with your mind, as thoughts travel on the way to your heart. And yes, opposites do have a peculiar way of attracting one another. Yet they don't always keep that magnetic pull. Much of the effort is still left up to you. It's a lot like a Rube Goldberg contraption: a machine with a lot of intricately moving parts. One finds that attraction is not an easily definable condition. It doesn't really involve words, but more unexplainable emotions coupled with the unfathomable mind and a warm disposition. But in its own way, affection is both complicated and easy to understand. It's when someone else's happiness is more important than your own. It's the tie that binds; it's the bee that makes the honey. The endgame is that we each have an innate way of accepting the love we think we deserve. Attraction isn't something you go searching for and find; instead, it usually finds you when you least expect it. So it is with the complicated lives of the Homo sapiens. However, it doesn't matter what challenges or objectives you encounter in life; everyone still needs someone to respect, laugh, cry, and act crazy with. A good marriage is where the meal is better than the dessert, and a wife is only as old as her husband makes her feel.

Claire also saved me from many embarrassments and potential disasters, teaching me things I didn't learn on Combs Street, in school, at the Fairfax Hotel, or at the boarding house. Thanks to her, I learned which fork to use, the right wine to order, which suit and tie to wear, never to forget my Auburn lapel pin, how to be a good host, which hand to shake, and what to do at a black-tie affair. She taught me to never drink from the finger bowl, because it contained only water. She even taught me how to be an effective conversationalist, when to talk and when to listen. She was all that and a trophy wife to boot, immaculate in any setting. Of course, she was an Auburn graduate, always comfortable at a cocktail party or the finest restaurant in New York City; curious on a trip to Paris, London, or Cairo; knowledgeable at the United Nations; astute at the Museum of Modern Art or a Broadway theater; organizing a children's birthday party or a formal dinner; or attending the Metropolitan Opera. And perhaps most important of all, she reminded me to never forget to pick up my paycheck each month. And to think I had to go three whole miles, all the way to Riverview, to find her.

In summary, Claire was always extraordinarily pretty, intellectual, personable, talented, prim, and proper. She easily cemented her position in the cool-girl pantheon long before she met me, and it hasn't diminished.

Where she was concerned, I always had admiring overtures. The sun has a special way of lining a dark cloud's edge in silver, just as she does mine. I guess, in retrospect, her only downside was me. However, I won't tell her if you won't. I guess, like Jonah, she didn't change directions and take the boat to Tarsus; she just followed her heart. I never did understand what she saw in me and I have always been afraid to ask. I learned long ago that the enigmatic mind of an ordinary Southern woman is absolutely unfathomable—so don't go there. Their minds and hearts always seems to vibrate at a completely different frequency than men.

Also, women are much smarter than men. Males become entangled more in their own deceptions, while females frequently cause more trouble than they are able to cure. But they look cuter while doing it. One day Claire said, "I think I've put on some weight. Am I starting to look a little fat?" I said, "You ask me that and want an answer; do you think I'm stupid?" She just smiled and two days later went on a diet; she only weighed 106 pounds then. I came to the conclusion that we need an old school conscience-raising session periodically, if for no other reason than to reckon with the problematic state of reality. But we don't like it too much, because it's like looking in the mirror and seeing the real world that we try to avoid. Now, I don't want to give anyone the impression that I favor girls over boys in any way, because I don't. I have seven grandchildren, two of which are boys, and I love them equally.

After all these years, Claire still prefers to drive when we go on a trip because she says that, statistically speaking, she is less likely to have an accident than I am. She reminds me that she is right because I had an accident—once, fifty-six years ago—when my tire blew out. You will always see me in the passenger's seat. I'll be the one wearing the safety helmet. I could tell you with a clear conscience that we lived happily ever after. However, that was only six decades ago, and 'ever after' isn't over. Besides, she, in her effervescent Southern female mode, says I am still on probation and she may return me for an improved replacement. Even as an elderly Southern male bell-bull, I have never fully understood the constant and universal validity of love. Now, for all you gentlemen readers, I have a word of advice. You never want a girlfriend (or even worse, a wife) that believes

*Celebrating
25th wedding
anniversary
in 1981.*

diamonds are a girl's best friend. That means she has never had a dog and is probably a cat lady.

Claire once told me, "Married women speak an average of 21,000 words a day, and married men only speak 7,000. After their husbands die, widows speak only 10,000 words a day, because they don't have to repeat everything to their husbands at least twice." I said, "What?" She said, "You probably have the distinction of being one of the better husbands in the mill village, which is absolutely nothing to brag about."

Of course, I think life is meant to be not only experiential but also a verbal timepiece from the beginning to the end. After sixty-two years of marriage, I have discovered there is nothing left for me to learn the hard way. I think I have already experienced it all; I can't believe there could possibly be anything remaining on the agenda for me to screw up. The good Lord wouldn't be so cruel. In my case, the greatest wisdom I have gained over the years is in knowing when to keep my mouth shut. Now men, I want to offer you a word of caution. Always be flexible where your sacred cows are concerned, because when you get married, every one of them will sooner or later run into a butcher.

I think some of the happiest people I have known are those that made life like a sheaf of delicate notes and loose details kept in a notebook of ideas and adventures, rather than a rigidly-prepared formulated future. Human nature is surprising. I have frequently found that a perfect couple becomes so because they are so imperfectly matched and simply complete one another. When the kids and grandchildren started to think about getting married, I told them they should ask me for advice instead of their (grand)mother, because I made a much better choice than she did.

Being strongly and emotionally attracted to someone is not just a fulfilling and transcendent experience, but also has a tendency to gridlock the mind. Chemistry is an important and critical part of a relationship. If the equation doesn't balance, the formula won't work. One must also look for the center of gravity, temperament, and balancing point. When you find it, you eventually discover that love and affection give you an extraordinarily sharp pain in the solar plexus, just from the ordinary anxiety of each day. I have never understood the logic of overweight men—they would be much wiser to burn up calories by just reaching for their mate instead of their plate. To be perfectly honest, true love is not unique; it's simply the joint process of consuming someone while being consumed.

Yet regardless of the downside, love is without a doubt still the best thing God created in the history of ever. I'm still trying to figure out if that's from God's promise or Adam's plea. What I know is that the real world always finds time to lob in a few stress grenades into every relationship—even in a little mill village. Now, in my old age, I am not at all egotistical. Yet sometimes I look at my wife admiringly and say in my humility, "Wow, she is one lucky girl to have married me!"

21

A Boy and A Bike

Truth and compassion always tug at the heartstrings. Juxtapositions emerge in great contrast to what we might expect, while the importance of intelligence, education, creativity, hard work, affluence, and opportunity moves to the fore. We learn that people can be vastly dissimilar in many ways, and for different reasons. Most of these variances become painfully obvious. They also reflect the cause and effect of disparaging reality and the bell curve of intelligence. We each see and hear the world in our own way, and we don't all pass the standard litmus test for authenticity. We become so tightly coiled up in our personal thoughts that we sometimes lack the courage or will to tackle our own afflictions.

Most of the adults I knew who lived in a mill village had become a little cynical of the changing political winds. They believed that if voting was really important, and if it made a difference in running the country, then the politicians wouldn't let us do it. Each mill village, out of dozens I have visited, had its own unique personality and political outlook. It simply reflected the management and the people that lived there. In my earlier Problem Doctor days, when on a new assignment around the country, I wanted to get a feel for the town and the community, as well as the people's perspective on the plant management. So on the first few days of a new job, I would take a little time in the afternoon and go to the stores and restaurants, introduce myself, and talk to the proprietors and customers about the community, Company, and mill management. Talking with people, off the record, was the best way to feel the pulse of public sentiment. My objective was to be the least interesting person in the room, which wasn't a great stretch for me. It was also good public relations time and an opportunity to show interest in the community while adding some positive comments about the Company.

One hot summer afternoon, on a new assignment, I had stopped at a small café to get a "vanilla shake of milk" (my weakness). It had six or seven booths, three or four tables, a jukebox, and maybe ten barstools at the counter. There were only three or four other customers present. This place was similar to one my mother once owned and ran when I was about four years old. I was talking with the waitress and saw, out of the corner of my eye, a little boy ride up on his bicycle. He was perhaps ten or eleven years old, needed a haircut, was barefoot with worn blue jeans, and had on what I think had once been a white t-shirt. It looked as though he hadn't had a bath in two or three days, which was not unusual for the summer when kids were out of school. He reminded me of my own summer days.

He came in—confident, head held high—and sat down at the counter two stools down from me. He looked over my way and nodded his head hello. He asked the waitress, "How much does a hamburger with all the trimmings, fries, and a Dr. Pepper cost?" She said, "Fifty-five cents." He took

The one and only William the yard man.

the change out of his pocket, placed it on the counter, and carefully counted it. He paused for a few seconds and wrinkled his brow, calculating in his mind. He said, "Well, how much does a hamburger with all the trimmings, fries, and a glass of ice water cost?" She said, "Forty cents." He thought for a second and said, "Then that's what I will have." While the cook was preparing it, I smiled, introduced myself, and told him I was new in town.

His first name was William, but everyone called him Will, and he said his father and mother had moved here about three years ago from La-Grange—another mill village. His dad had gotten a better job. His parents were working on the second shift at the mill and would be home at 11 p.m. He was an only child, and during the summer, he did yard work. When the waitress delivered his hamburger and ice water, I said, "Will, I enjoyed talking to you. I hope you have a good summer and find plenty of yard work." He smiled and said, "Yes, sir. Me too. Hope you enjoy working here; we like it." Two minutes and perhaps four gulps later, the hamburger, fries, and water were gone. He got up and smiled and said, "Goodbye!"

The waitress came over to clear his plate and said, "Lordy be! He left me a sixteen cent tip. He passed up a Dr. Pepper and drank water so he could leave me a tip. What a thoughtful kid. But, you know, I've seen something like that happen many times since I have been working here."

Like William, we all reflect our parents, family, how we are raised, and what we are taught—positive, negative, or indifference. I have always found there is far more good exhibited in small towns than otherwise and it didn't really matter where you were from: north, south, east, or west. Somehow I believe it has become part of our American DNA over time. I pray we never lose it. I have thought about William several times since that day, many years ago. I expect he later became very successful in life, and may one day have ended up running that mill where his parents worked, if it hadn't closed.

I vividly remember the perspective of one of my favorite heroes: the great baseball pitcher Satchel Paige. He is best known for throwing more strikes than any player in the history of the game. He was almost as well known for his reaching wit and wisdom. Someone asked him one day, "How in the world can you throw so many strikes over the middle of that tiny home plate?" To paraphrase, he said, "Well, there is really nothing to it. It's the easiest thing in the world to do, because home plate stays in the same place; it never moves."

It's hard to hit the target when the rules, values, and principles keep changing. Today they seem to be shifting every inning, making reality more problematic. It has become much tougher to look to the horizon and see tomorrow, but maybe we would be wise to listen more closely to the wisdom of yesterday. We clearly need to focus more on Jesus Christ. His target is clear; it never varies, never changes, never shifts, never moves. It's the same today as 2,000 years ago—consistent, immovable. I learned the hard way that a truly happy life primarily depends upon your objective and where you are placing your full attention and trust.

Attitude doesn't just pop up out of the grass by chance, like mushrooms on a hot, wet, humid day. It is usually the natural response of the heart to audience demand. We want to fully understand the words but also see the performance. What's truly sad is when continuity of trust is on its last legs, that which holds us together. It now avoids truth and tries to rob us of our raison d'etre—our reason for being. When that occurs, we have come to make a choice of diagnosis over prescription, retrospection over solutions, and a preference for minutia over the whole.

The wise man knows that you should be friendly and learn from others, because everyone you meet knows something you don't. Life in the whole is important, but what we do each day matters the most. We do not want to be like the housekeeper who leaves dust in the corners and under the bed. In the real world, you do not become what actually happens to you, only what you accept and choose to be. I think William had already absorbed that lesson at an early age, having learned that thinking gives the imagination something to do while the tongue rests. Satchel Paige would have been proud.

22

Sarah Jim

I have been blessed to travel the world and visit many prestigious museums: the Louvre and Musee d'Orsay in Paris, Metropolitan Museum in New York, Vatican Museum in Rome, Hermitage in St. Petersburg, British Museum in London, Rijksmuseum in Amsterdam, Uffizi in Florence, Tokyo National Museum, National Museum in Beijing, and the Egyptian Museum in Cairo, among others. I enjoy art of all genres and would have loved to have been an artist, but I came up short in something called talent. One day soon, I'm going to take another stab at the canvas and brushes. But the greatest artistic creation I have ever seen was not a picture you hang on the wall of a museum or a cold dead sculpture, but a dynamic, living and breathing hominid artifice by the name of Sarah Jim McGraw—my mother. She was the uncredited star of the family. If I were an artist, I would never paint her in anything other than bright living colors, which would compliment her beautiful red hair.

People come in many flavors, colors, sizes, shapes, and textures. Others are spicy, occasionally a little bitter, a few sweet, and some even savory. Sarah Jim had all those flavors, but you just never knew which one you would get. Her life was filled with interesting, delightful, and unexpected anecdotes, and every event was delicious in its own special way. It's hard to live vicariously in one's thoughts alone, or reside long in the house of oneself—and she never did. Truth is a promissory note, a formal I.O.U., from one person to another with guaranteed dependability. It's an unwritten agreement that both parties will continue to believe in its worth and value. Truth was just another word to her, like so many others—love, family, friends, trust, integrity, character, and faith—that she would hold dear all her life. Courage is many things; it's necessary to stand up and speak, but sometimes it's even more important to sit down and listen. She could do both.

She was an incomparable work of artistry because of her big heart, toughness, ranging personality, and many creative distinctions. Jim is a rather unusual name for a female, but it fit her perfectly. Mother's four sisters and her brother were named after people in the Bible, as was Sarah. When she was born, someone said, "Oh, she has beautiful red hair and looks just like her Uncle Jim Chase." So it became Sarah Jim.

I have been told by many people that I am more like her than anyone else

*Sarah Jim
— 1935
All-Star
Basketball
Player,
Fairfax High
School.*

in my clan, and I consider that the highest compliment I could ever receive. She was red-headed, Scotch-Irish, smart, talented, loving, compassionate, quick tempered, funny, big hearted, caring, and scared of no one. Sarah Jim was forever young, with a lot of extra juice—even into her eighties. She firmly believed that everyone she ever met had the right to be greeted with a smile and I learned that from her, reinforced by my grandfather.

Mother grew up in a family of eight with six brothers and sisters, a place where breakfast, lunch, and dinner included sizzling offerings of conversation and strong opinions—no one was bashful. She once became an underage bodyguard when kids, in fun, bullied her older sister Naomi in elementary school. She got into numerous confrontations for that very reason with older students. I am told she didn't always win, but she never once backed down. Sarah Jim understood early on that problems and bullies rarely give up without a fight, so one must always be prepared; she was. She struck a good balance between delicate and tough, but was always faithful to her identity and big heart. There is nothing I have enjoyed more than when she would release her genial features into a big smile. It would light up the whole room—even in the dark.

Mother and Dad were married for sixty-eight years and were exact opposites in temperament and personality. He was extraordinarily smart, mechanically talented, strongly focused, an outdoorsman, serious, hardworking, and a good leader. She was funny, loved life, had great conversational and people skills, was a good athlete, was musically inclined, and was multi-talented. Sometimes I think that she might have been a character actor trapped in a normal person's body, but never in a conservative person's mind. In real life she had a great curiosity—more of a dreamer—and dreamers in history somehow usually end up being heroes; she was certainly a hero to me. I think Mother and Dad were both very mature at a young age and understood that reality is where all the action in life takes place, while probability and the hypothetical are where the imagination resides. They never got the two mixed up.

She seemed to know that the heart was declarative and not just a decorative organ designed to try to influence others—and she didn't. What you saw was what you got, sometimes to her detriment. She was always ready for anything new. One day, when I was about nine, I said, "I think I'm going to become a creative person; is that okay?" She said, "Sure, go right ahead, go for it!" The best classroom I ever attended was sitting at her feet. Whenever she told me that I had made her day, it made my day. No matter how serious my problems or burdens were as a kid or teenager, I still needed someone to make me chuckle and go crazy with. She was always there and ready. She made me laugh a little louder, smile a little brighter, and made my life a little fuller. If I had a rose for each time she made me smile, I would have a full rose garden to walk in every day for the rest of my life.

Mother had the most beautifully harmonizing alto voice I have ever heard. Like an angel, even if discounted heavily by my prejudices. As a mid-teenager, she was in a girls quartet that traveled around Alabama and Georgia, performing at churches, schools, theaters, and community groups. Later, she sang in a church choir and at family gatherings for as long as I can remember. She was a smiling, unshrinking performer and a truly free spirit. I was told by two ladies that played basketball with her in high school (one of those being Ruth Yarbrough) that she was the best defensive player in the league. Ruth said, "The coach always gave her the other team's top scorer to guard, and she would shut them down to just a few points a game, time and again."

Sarah Jim McGraw was a fantastic dancer and an indefatigable jitterbugger. She was a great cook, taught primarily by my grandmother. When I was a little boy, she opened a café and ran it for several years. It was constantly packed with customers and friends, the big band swing music always going. She also loved to discuss politics with people and was strongly opinionated. But to her, patriotism itself was never a divisive political issue; she was All-American, through and through. Over time, the long hours of standing on her feet all day and running a business became tiring and stressful. So she went to work in the local Fairfax finishing plant cloth room as a machine operator, where almost one thousand women were eventually employed producing Martex towels.

She enjoyed the outdoors—especially hunting and fishing with Dad—at our cabin on the backwater and was a very good shot. She loved to fish with treble hooks and caught two fingers one day. As she removed the painful hooks, some of the grace she was known for was left out of her comments, and she told me not to listen. When I was about eight years old, they taught me a brand new sport: frog-gigging. It was mother's favorite activity and was done at night, on the backwater, in a boat with a sealed-beam automobile headlight and a car battery for power. I liked it probably for the reason mother did—because it was downright dangerous. We would get in the boat and Dad would operate the small trolling motor. Mother and I would sit in the bow of the boat. I would handle the light, and she would handle the ten-foot long frog gig. We would troll about forty to fifty feet from the bank, shining the bright light along the water line. When a frog on the shore saw it, they were blinded by the intensity of the light and were afraid to jump. We would direct the boat toward the bank and gig him. Typically, we would get twenty or thirty frogs a night. Fried frog legs tasted great, like chicken, and Mother knew just how to prepare them.

I thought I was grown up when I graduated to doing the gigging and she handled the light. The dangerous part of the nighttime excursion was the presence of water moccasins in the water's edge and on the overhanging tree limbs. They were poisonous and aggressive. We always carried a .22 rifle or .410 shotgun for that purpose. Rarely would a night go by that a snake or two didn't get into the boat, but no one was ever bitten. Normally we would take the paddle and toss them back into the water. However, I do remember three distinct times we shot out the bottom of the boat with the shotgun trying to kill one—mother twice and me once—and we killed all three. In the pitch dark night, we were lucky it wasn't one of us. Fortunately, we were near the bank each time it happened and were able to wade ashore, but it ruined the boat every time. Later we laughed about it, but not at the particular moment.

One day, when I was about thirteen years old, she asked me to help her do something. I said, "OK, be glad to; what?" She said, "Teenagers don't have enough wholesome things to do during the week, and I would like to start a chess club at church on Thursday nights for teenage girls and boys." I remember the conversation well. I said, "Mother, you don't know anything about chess. Have you ever seen a chess set before? You don't know how to play and I don't either. I'll bet there's not a single set in town. Probably not in the Greater Valley."

How did she respond? We went to Columbus and bought what we needed and a book on how to play the game. We practiced in the evenings and in about four weeks started the first chess club for young students the Greater Valley had ever seen. The church purchased the other chess sets and boards for the club. More than thirty teenagers showed up the first Thursday night, and she maintained around that number—twenty-five to thirty-two—for three years. They loved it; so did I. Sarah Jim was the best player in the group. It was always those unusual, unexpected everyday fun things with her that made life important, memorable, and meaningful to me.

I was the only grandchild in the local Andrews/McGraw clan until I was in high school, when my brother Larry was born. I had started attending college at sixteen, before he was ready for Kindergarten. He became a very talented self-taught musician (with Dad and my grandmother's help), learned to play the rhythm guitar, bass guitar, keyboard, wrote numerous songs, and had a good voice. Somehow I missed out on all those musical genes, although I sang in the high school glee club and in the church choir. He grew his hair long, down on his shoulders as teenagers did back in the Beatles era, to the consternation and dislike of most of the older, traditionally-oriented generation.

One summer afternoon I came by Mother's home. Her car was in the shop for maintenance, and she asked if I would take her to West Point to get Larry a pair of shoes. I said, "Of course." We pulled up in front of Quality Shoe Store, which was next door to a hardware store. The store's owner and another man were standing on the sidewalk in front of me, talking and smoking cigarettes, when Sarah Jim and Larry got out of the car. She smiled and nodded hello as they walked past the two men. The big burly owner of the hardware store said, sarcastically and loud enough in a bullying voice for mother and Larry to hear, "That long hair's disgusting. If that was my skinny kid and I had a pair of scissors, I would cut it so short that he wouldn't look so much like an ugly girl."

That was a very bad mistake. He said the wrong thing, about the wrong person, at the wrong time, in the wrong way, and I knew it as soon as the words left his mouth. In spite of his lack of civility and common sense, he should have known never to anger a redhead. Even I knew that. That's important when she's mildly upset because you infringed on a loved one, especially when she has a pair of sharp scissors in the proximity of your head. On this particular day, he had thrown caution to the wind, and her sunny side wasn't up. He had made a prejudiced, bullying mistake and converted a casual summer moment into a substantial event. Bad judgment can travel halfway around the world before an idiot knows it has left his mouth or has to face the potential downside of his egregious comments. Mother didn't say a word. She just put her hand on Larry's shoulder and said, "Wait here."

She turned around and calmly walked up to the man, stood a foot from his face, opened her purse, and pulled out a large pair of very sharp scissors—the kind that every woman working in the cloth room had. She offered them to him and calmly said, "Here's a pair. You go right ahead and cut his hair if you would like, as short as you want. And when you get through, then I'm going to take these same scissors and skin your ugly head and probably cut off the tops of those two scroungey-looking ears of yours."

It was so brash and unexpected that the man didn't say a word. He just turned red and went back into his store. She calmly put the scissors back in her purse, never changed her expression, and she and Larry went into the shoe store. I heard it all clearly, but she never mentioned it until I asked about the incident on the way home. The message was loud and clear: never mess with Sarah Jim, and I didn't.

Over the years, Larry's band, the Stolen Children, played at universities and other public venues all over the Southeast. The Stolen Children were booked by Grant Sullivan, his cousin and a student at Auburn. They were very good and cut several records, a number of the songs written and performed by Larry himself. Many years later, they changed the band's name to Silver. Claire and I heard them many times, and Mother and Dad traveled to see them perform whenever they could. They were even invited to play as a "precautionary stand-in" (at the end of the show) on the famous weekly

Ed Sullivan television show on CBS at New York Studios off Times Square. My dad made the arrangements to New York City and chaperoned them during rehearsals all that week, including every night in the city, which I imagine was quite a challenge. The only question that I ever had was who chaperoned my dad? That night they were ready in the wings on stage, but there was no time, so they didn't perform.

Mother had a subtle sense of humor, often with a "gotcha" moment. I guess I inherited mine honestly. I had never flown before and now, as the new twenty-two-year-old financial controller for the nonwoven fabrics operation, I was headed to New York City for the first time to make a financial presentation to the marketing/sales force. I had prepared comments on product costs, financial reports, and P&L analyses of operations. I was looking forward to the trip, but was a little nervous anticipating my first flight at 35,000 feet. I told Sarah Jim of the concern, and bless her heart, she tried everything she could to calm my nerves and anxiety. She said, "You know you are much safer in a plane than on the ground in a car, bus, or train. In fact, flying is even safer than doing work around the house." After talking with her for a while, I was feeling much better and I relaxed. Then, with a sly grin, she said, "Oh, by the way, be sure and take out plenty of flight insurance. You never know when you might need it. Just make me the beneficiary."

During a period when I was vice president of manufacturing for the consumer products division, Walter Chapman was director of human resources and very good at his job. Sara Jim worked in the cloth room of the Fairfax Finishing Plant and had an exemplary record, once having worked a fourteen-year stretch without ever missing a day for any reason. She was so personable and thoughtful the employees and supervisors gave her an A+ rating. Several told me so.

One afternoon Walter called me on the phone. "Are you sitting down?" he asked.

"No, I'm standing up at my desk talking to you," I replied.

"Then sit down."

I said, "Walter, what's the problem?"

He said, "Alvin just fired your mother. It had nothing to do with what

Fairfax Mill, Cloth Room, towel hemmers in 1974.

she did. It was not about her or her job, but she is no longer employed with the Company."

It turned out that one of the over edgers was called into the office by the supervisor and overseer and told if she didn't improve her productivity they would have to terminate her. This was her third and final warning. So she went back to her station and started crying. Mother saw her and went over to see what was wrong. She said she was raising two children by herself, had no help, no family, nowhere to go, and had to work. If she lost her job, she didn't know what she was going to do.

Mother got upset, went to the supervisor, grabbed him by the hand, and took him in to see the overseer. She read the Riot Act to both of them, and they fired her. The interesting thing was the overseer was one of her best friends. They were in high school together, and Mother and Dad had been out to dinner with him and his wife the prior weekend. I have always wondered what she must have said, but I don't really want to know.

She was such a good employee that, after the standard two-week termination period, they hired her back on the same job. Everything was fine and she was again an exemplary employee. About two years later, I was working in Maine when the phone rang. It was Walter. He said, "Are you sitting down?"

"Walter, don't tell me. . ." I said.

"Yep, she was fired about thirty minutes ago. Similar situation; it was just a different person involved," he explained.

If we had been unionized, which we weren't, Mother would have made a great union steward—maybe even president of the union. In two weeks, they hired her back. She just had a big heart and didn't want to see anyone mistreated. She always told me that the best way to improve my appearance was with a smile, but she also knew how to frown and wasn't afraid to do so.

About a year after the last firing incident, I was living in New York. Mother called one Friday and said the Company had just offered her a job as a supervisor in charge of 106 employees, and she was thinking about taking it. The pay was good, but she wasn't certain because of the extra time and responsibility required. What did I think? We discussed it, pros and cons, and she said she would let me know what she decided.

The following week Walter called, and the first thing he said was, "Are you sitting down?"

I said, "Walter, don't you dare tell me she has been fired again."

He laughed and said, "No, she just accepted the job as supervisor about fifteen minutes ago and I think everyone in plant management and all 2,400 employees were delighted. She is one of the first female supervisors in the Company."

I said, "Walter, if you start calling and giving me more good news instead of bad, I might even give you a raise some day—maybe in three or four years."

He said, "You know, I haven't told you lately, but I really do like you. In fact, I've got a crush on you, and I think I'll give you a big hug next time I see you."

I said, "Walter, that's not good news. That's bad news and it scares me, and it won't get you any extra points."

That night, Mother called to tell me about her promotion. She served in supervision for about ten years until she retired. She thrived on it, never met a stranger, and loved working with people.

After Mother and Dad retired, she had to stay busy and use up an unusual amount of excess energy for her age, so she went to see friends. She and her older sister Ruth traveled around the country—and a few times outside of the U.S.—with different travel groups and volunteered for just about everything that came down the pike. She was always talking about Ireland, and I told her I would take them there. But she didn't like to fly. She said she would be ready as soon as they finished constructing a bridge between Boston and Dublin. Sadly, she never made it. She enjoyably babysat her grandchildren (and later her great-grandchildren), loved to teach them new games, and taught them all how to cook.

She sang in the church choir, helped Dad with his carpentry and construction projects, and assisted him in building rooms and garages on houses after he retired. She became a deaconess in her church and had a big vegetable and flower garden. One day, I went by a project Dad had started: adding a rather large family room onto someone's house. He was on a ladder, carrying a load of shingles up to the roof. It was very noisy from the hammering, so I yelled at him and said, "Where is Mother?" He just pointed up to the roof, where I heard the noise coming down but couldn't see. It was Sarah Jim nailing shingles on the roof—and doing a good job. She had just spent most of the prior week helping him put up 2x4 studs and framing for the walls.

That wasn't enough activity for her, and since she was a fabulous cook, she started baking cakes, muffins, and cookies for friends, neighbors, and several restaurants within a thirty-mile radius of Fairfax. I stopped by to see her when I was passing through town once and we got to talking about her baking. She specialized in delicious and thin eight- and ten-layer French torte-type cakes. Chocolate, caramel, red velvet, fresh coconut, banana, Lane, and Italian cream were her most popular—and of course, her famous sour cream pound cake (which she taught me to bake). She didn't know how many she cooked every year but told me to take her ledger and add them up. I only reviewed two years out of the dozen or so in her ledger, and she had baked 786 cakes one year and 812 the next. She had also baked over 12,000 cookies each year, and I didn't have the patience to check the number of cupcakes. I do know that over ten years she burned up three electric stoves and I don't know how many mixers.

She loved baking, but never charged enough compared to her cost and the going market. I had done an economic cost-benefit analysis for her about four years earlier and suggested she increase her prices by about 30 percent. She said, "I know I need to, but if I did people might not buy as much—and some couldn't afford it, or might not stay as long to visit and talk when they come by to pick up what they had ordered." I think one of her greatest pleasures back then were those thirty minute visits every day with people she knew.

When we lived in New York City; Kennebunkport, Maine; New Jersey; North Carolina; and other places, Mother, Dad, and my Aunt Ruth loved to come for visits. Ruth was the oldest of Mother's sisters and my favorite of an expansive family. She never had any children and always said she didn't need any because she had me. I was a handful, and all she ever wanted anyway. I went everywhere with Ruth and my Uncle Jesse. Having buried two wonderful husbands, Ruth died two weeks after her one-hundredth birthday.

For a country boy, the rhythms of city life in high relief were hard to dispel, and I loved it. It had a similar attraction for country girls. One summer, when I was working in New York City, I invited Sarah Jim, Ruth, and their sister Naomi to spend some time with us. I told them I would take off work all week and we would explore New York together for their first extended visit. Mother loved the Big Apple and was always ready for another bite. I had also scheduled trips for us to take them to the Pennsylvania Amish country and down to Princeton University, about ten minutes from where we lived in New Jersey at the time. They flew in to Newark Airport, where I picked them up.

For the first full day after they arrived, I had arranged for a night in New York City that they would never forget. I told them to be ready by 5 p.m. and dressed to the "nines"—sharp, long dresses; high heels; coiffured hair; and New York attire—and they were. I looked out the window at about five o'clock and said, "OK, girls. Excuse me! I should have said Cinderellas, not girls. Our carriage awaits." I opened the front door and there at the curb was a big black limousine two blocks long—or at least it looked like that to them. Claire was the only one that had ever ridden in a limo before, which I knew. For some reason they just didn't have many of those in the mill village. The chauffer was standing there in his crisp, black, double-breasted uniform and cap with the door open. It was spacious and comfortable, equipped with fresh flowers, champagne, light hors d'oeuvres, candy, and soft music for the one-and-a-half hour ride into the city, just as we'd ordered. Four ladies from a small hamlet in Alabama were utterly flabbergasted, a dream from which they didn't want to wake up and a memory to top all memories. It certainly beat taking the long uncomfortable trainride into the city, which I did most mornings.

We arrived in Central Park on time at the famous Tavern on the Green restaurant, where I had booked reservations in the Crystal Room. It was filled with numerous beautiful chandeliers (and was to me one of the most striking dining rooms in the city). They were blown away, because they didn't have anything like that where they grew up. Not even a stop light. To three elderly ladies from Alabama and Georgia, New York City was electric and delicious, like seeing life in vivid color through a looking glass. We enjoyed a wonderful dinner with wine, fascinating fun conversation, and watching the "beautiful people." When we left the restaurant, the limo was waiting for us. On a glamorous starry night, we drove through Central Park, down 7th Avenue, and onto Broadway. We were headed toward the theater district for an energizing musical, with great center-orchestra seats. We left the theater at about 11:00 p.m. and the limo took us to one of the city's bustling bars for after-dinner drinks, soft piano music, and two smooth vocalists. It was a typical exciting New York night on the town. The chauffer then took us home and we arrived around 1:30 a.m. We were out for the evening for eight hours or so, an excursion those three ladies would never forget. If I had arranged the same entertainment every night for the rest of their lives, it would still fall short of all they had done for me. I won't mention the cost of the evening, or the week of limo rides, airline tickets, sumptuous dinners, and evenings at the theaters, for it was completely meaningless under those special circumstances.

Another time I was traveling from the West Point office to New York

City on business. I was up there every two or three weeks, but Claire had a conflict and couldn't accompany me, so I invited Mother and Ruth to go. The Company had three nice apartments in the city and I was using the largest one—the penthouse at the Dorset—and it was right in the middle of town on 54th Street, only a few blocks from Radio City Music Hall and our office in the McGraw-Hill Building on 6th Avenue. I had product design meetings and marketing conferences scheduled in and out of the office on Monday, Tuesday, and Wednesday (including Ralph Lauren) and would be taking the evenings and rest of the week off to show them around. So during the early part of the week they would be turned loose in the city by themselves for the first time.

New York City is quite dynamic, very dissimilar, and a little dangerous compared to the small towns they were from, where you rarely had to look both ways while crossing the street. The city was so different in that aspect— you had to watch the traffic both ways, even when you were standing on the sidewalk. Mother was always smiling and full of fun and foolishness, coupled with seemingly unlimited energy. I asked her about that one day. She said, "A person that doesn't know how to have fun is probably no good at working either." I haven't forgotten.

They were pretty sharp and had traveled quite a bit, and I really wasn't worried about them or their safety. I was, however, a little curious about how they would react when alone in the city. New Yorkers are mostly courteous and don't mind giving you street or landmark directions. In fact, most take great pride in knowing where they are themselves. I arranged their daily schedules, with written instructions and trips lined up using taxis. They would have lunch at different sidewalk cafes with tables on the street. It was a completely new experience, because they didn't have those in the Valley. They were a little nervous starting out that first morning, but after that they were home free. Every evening they would tell me where they had been, what exciting things they had done, and how nice and friendly the taxi drivers were. I can still visualize two soft-spoken elderly Southern ladies extrovertly conversing with their drivers, who were not used to such friendliness, courtesy, and a "thank you" from passengers.

That week we went to three Broadway plays, to Radio City Music Hall to see the Rockettes, and to Carnegie Hall for a concert. I took them by our corporate offices, the beautiful show rooms, the design studio, and to meet some of our management/employees that worked in and out of the city—approximately two hundred people. We toured the Empire State Building, FAO Schwartz, Macy's, Saks 5th Avenue, Tiffany's, and Cartier's. We went to Rockefeller Center to see ice skating, on a tour of the United Nations, to the Metropolitan Museum of Art, on a carriage ride through Central Park, to Harlem, Greenwich Village, and many other typical sitesee-ing locations. I had been a member of the Harvard Club of New York City for many years, and we ate there three times that week while enjoying the ambiance of the beautiful mahogany paneled walls—lined with historic oil portraits of famous Harvard Alumni—and great food, which they loved. We went to the elegant 21 Club for dinner one evening, where I told them they could have anything they wanted. After careful thought, they ordered wine and the 21 Special—the gourmet hamburgers, if you can believe it. Of course, they were much better than Burger King. We also went to the famous Carnegie Deli for their famed mile-high pastrami sandwiches.

One day we had expensive $1.00 street vendor hotdogs in Times Square for lunch and topped it off with Lindy's celebrated New York cheesecake, which Mother learned to bake. I took them by The Engineer's Club, where I often stayed, across the street from Bryant Park and behind the famous 42nd Street Public Library. (I believe the largest in America, if not the world.) I showed them where I found the deceased victim of a stabbing in beautiful Bryant Park early one morning at around 6 a.m., when I was walking to work. The body was sprawled on a park bench, and I called the police. I wanted them to understand that the city could be fun, but was also dangerous. Over the years they made various comments about that trip—especially that notorious park bench.

The most memorable thing involving that particular visit was none of the above, but something the Company President Kjor Kjorlein (my boss) arranged for Monday, our first evening there. He had met Sarah Jim many times before and thought she was super special. He was intrigued by my position in the Company and my mother getting fired twice. Almost every time he was in the area and visited the manufacturing plants, he would ask me to take him by to talk to my mother at work or at our home in the evening. She was witty and continually made him laugh and feel good. He was always asking her to come to New York. He had met Ruth once, maybe twice before when I introduced them on plant tours over the years. When I told him I would be bringing them to New York City with me, he insisted that I bring them by his beautiful apartment on Park Avenue for a cocktail party Monday evening. Kjor had invited me there many times over the years, and he and Ginny were always gracious hosts, whether it was just me or an apartment filled with people.

Park Avenue is a pleasant yet unique street for a satisfied mind. It's a place where you have no place else to go if you live there, because you have already arrived. It's not a street for walking or hurrying, but an avenue for strutting, dawdling down to loud applause. It was then and now a full-blown international address, where everyone is hastening to their own destiny. Always a pleasant place for contented minds while subject to a retail clientele who needs little, desires nothing, and wants everything. It's way uptown, closely paralleling Madison Avenue, and a place in which it's difficult not to be distracted by one's own creative and active curiosity. Life itself is always a huge gamble built on not much more than hopes and dreams. That's the best way I know of describing Park Avenue. If you live there, your dreams have probably already come true. Conceivably that's why Monopoly added it to their fantasy game board—because for most people it's not real. It was a little hard for Mother and Ruth to fathom it at first glance. Surprisingly—well maybe not, knowing them—they quickly adapted to a radically new environment.

Now the girls had a chance to see it firsthand. The president of Spiegel's (a good customer) and four of his lieutenants from the Chicago office—two ladies and two gentlemen—would be there at the Kjorlein's that evening. Mother and Ruth had never seen an upscale Park Avenue apartment before, nor how the "other half" lived. Nor had they been to a real New York cocktail party. So this would be a celebrated new experience for them. Also, 5:30 p.m. was perfect timing because we had to leave by 6:45 for dinner reservations I had made at Patsy's: the famous Italian restaurant near Carnegie Hall, which we were going to that evening. We entertained customers and business executives quite frequently at the Kjorleins' apartment—a perfect venue, with thirteen-foot ceilings, fabulously wide moldings, tasteful New York décor, and beautiful art on the walls. But more importantly, they were wonderful people and gracious hosts.

Claire and I learned much from Kjor and Ginny—not only because they were special mentors, but also because he had become one of my best friends. That was very important for a young mill village boy and his beautiful and charming wife, both eager to learn the corporate ways of New York City. In a few short years, I had become an exceedingly young executive. I had also become what I term a corporate Problem Doctor, and I needed all the help I could get in a highly competitive and magically morphing business world.

Sarah Jim and Ruth were a little nervous when we arrived at the Kjorleins' on Park Avenue that evening, though not as much from the pending cocktail party as from the five visitors from Chicago they had never met. In addition, they didn't like the taste of mixed alcoholic drinks, but enjoyed champagne and wine. They were perfectly dressed for a New York night out in their long, tasteful attire; beautiful hair; and makeup—polished and refined, just like the New York "in" crowd. The Kjorleins and Spiegel contingent could not have been more congenial. Kjor suggested that mother and Ruth sit on the sofa and everyone else pulled up close to them in chairs while they became the center of attention as we talked. The cocktails, wine, and champagne flowed freely, passed around time and again. You didn't run into this type of environment in any mill village they had ever seen.

They must have been asked a hundred questions about growing up in small towns in the South, working in and supervising a large manufacturing plant. Sarah Jim and Ruth responded in fun with the most humorous comments. They seemed as comfortable as if they had been in their own homes. It was probably like what they had been doing for years in the three local elementary schools: telling little kids at show and tell what it was like growing up in difficult times as little girls in a mill village before, during, and after the Great Depression. Kjor continued to fill their glasses with champagne and wine while they both reached for the hors d'oeuvres every time they were passed around. We all had a wonderful time. We stayed at the apartment until after 6:30 p.m. when we left for dinner and the theater.

Kjor was taking the Spiegel's group to dinner at 7:30.

When we got in the taxi and headed toward Patsy's, I said, "Well? Give me a report; how did you like your first New York City cocktail party?" Ruth smiled and said, "Their home was knock-dead gorgeous. Not many like that in a mill village—or at least I have never seen one."

"Well, I was a little nervous at first, not knowing what to expect," Sarah Jim said. "But everyone was so nice and friendly that I began to relax after that third glass of champagne."

"Yeah, I noticed that when you fell off the sofa and Mr. Kjorlein had to help pick you up off the floor," I said laughing.

She just grinned. Ruth said, "The only thing I couldn't understand were the hors d'oeuvres. They were good, but not nearly as sweet or chocolatey as the candy we make at home; not at all what I expected."

"Ruth, Mother, those hors d'oeuvres were not supposed to be sweet. It was not candy but pâté—goose livers. I assumed you knew that, as many as you were eating," I replied. I thought they were going to throw up, but then Mother started laughing. Ruth and I joined in on the joke and it set the trend for the evening. They laughed all the way to the restaurant and would start snickering and chuckling throughout the concert. There was never a dull moment around those two girls. In their easygoing nature, they had no trouble at all smiling and laughing at themselves and the foolish things they did, didn't do, and should have done.

I guess I inherited those McGraw genes, because I like to make people laugh as well. The Andrews were more serious, focused, and contextual, but the McGraws were always full of fun—a great combination. For the rest of the week and long after, when having a glass of wine or champagne at dinner and special festive occasions, they would smile and say to one another, "Would you like some hors d'oeuvres with that?"

There are a million stories about Sarah Jim and so many more I haven't said. There was one tale she never got to hear—or participate in. One day, many years later, after I had retired for the fourth time, I was in Capital City Bank in West Point. As I started to leave, the vice president of the bank, who was a very attractive lady, stopped me. She said, "I've been meaning to tell you something for a long time and always forget it until after you are gone. Many years ago, when I was just starting out in life as a young single girl, I was a machine operator in the Fairfax finishing plant and your mother was my supervisor. She was the best manager that I ever worked for and everyone loved her to death. We would do anything she asked. She was calm, smooth, smart, and had a big heart. She knew her job well and was one of the best supervisors in the mill.

"She truly cared about the people that worked for her. Good managers understand that supervisory relationships come to radiate a characteristic closeness, as well as a soft ambiguity—close enough to connect, but not far enough away for discomfort. You could discuss any problems you had with her, in complete confidence, because she knew that everyone had problems. One day I remembered her and knew you were her son, so I kept telling myself to stop you and tell you what a wonderful lady she was."

I thanked her and we chatted for a couple of minutes; then I left. It was not the first time I had received such remarks over the years. I guess they hadn't heard about her temper, and twice getting fired in her younger days, but perhaps in the bigger picture it didn't really matter to them. I got to thinking about that scenario one day, and I would bet she was the only supervisor in the 140-year history of the Company that had been fired twice for insubordination. The most serious conviction Mother ever had was that life should not be taken too seriously. She had a happy heart, always bigger on the inside than the outside, and her love for others was so simple that it was almost incomprehensible.

Sadly Sarah Jim didn't get to hear that particular story firsthand, because she had died three years earlier at age eighty-eight from Alzheimer's. That evening, in my prayers, I told her what had been said. I am certain she heard me and smiled, because she always did when I talked with her. I have wished on many, many occasions over the years that I had told her one more time how much I loved her before she was gone. When the merry-go-round makes its last circuit, it's all about love—nothing else. Yet I have learned that for all people of faith, life doesn't end with a period; it ends with a semicolon, and so it was with mother.

Some days drain us, and other times we drain the days. Which one of those it will be for you, only you can decide. Don't ever let someone else determine that for you. We owe nothing to improbabilities, because life is all about the reality that takes place around us. Sarah Jim always lived in the present and was a mirror reflecting light on the world. Reality may sometimes appear to be just an illusion, but it has a lot more staying power than fantasy, especially if you grew up in a small mill village. From the time I was a little boy, she was always there to make me smile, but then one day she was not. Even so, she taught me that the heart is always concerned with what the mind is telling us to do.

I don't believe that love can be graphed, weighed, or even measured—love just is. So never wait until someone is gone to tell them that you love them, or how important they are to you. Tell them now, while they can still hear you and enjoy it.

23

Boy Scouts

During a highly animated youth, and for many years after, the Boy and Girl Scouts were my favorite of the ranging community activities for young boys and girls in our village. They are both pretty much volunteer organizations. They were also, along with the church, a very important part of character building everywhere I have lived. And so it was in every mill town. I was an active member in my early years, and one of my greatest disappointments in life is that I never made Eagle Scout. Other things came along and I let them get in the way. But as an adult, I served for a long time on the boards of both Boy and Girl Scout councils wherever I was living. I also participated for a number of seasons in various capacities at the George H. Lanier Council of the Boy Scouts of America, located on the border of Alabama and Georgia. This included serving for an extended period as vice president of finance and raising money to support council activities and programs.

Male behavior is strongly flavored by the backdrop of a quintessential youth laboratory: the Boy Scouts, which was made especially for shaping boys into men. There is a distinct and enduring benefit to all males in its ethos, and society is the beneficiary. To our detriment, there are a diminishing number of young men exposed to this unique educational experience and character-building adventure today. This is despite the reality that they will be sorely tested in many ways in their futures—through morals, ethics, and values—by the growing complexities of life, which reveal one's integrity and character.

In 1977, I was asked to serve as president of the George H. Lanier Council for a two-year period (1978–1979). I accepted and decided we should make plans and establish goals to reach our full potential—whatever that was. At the time, we were ranked about 200–210 out of 334 councils in America and the territories. For decades, we always seemed to be in the third quartile of the pack, falling near the middle (160–200). The measurement of council performance by the national office was based on a list of quantitative and qualitative criteria. It included number of boys served, council growth, advancement in rank, new troops established, camping activities, merit badges, volunteer leadership, community service, and other areas of meaningful evaluation determined by the National Boy Scout Office.

You can't get far with just a generalized preamble to thought, so I performed a creative analysis to see where we were, how high we could possibly rise in the national hierarchy of councils in America, and what it would take to reach our goals. From there we initiated a full-court press, with a major concerted effort of leadership training and goal orientation initiated throughout the towns and cities in the council. We implemented several new programs and objectives. By the end of the first year, we had climbed up to around sixtieth in the nation—the highest we had ever been. At the end of the second year, we were ranked the number one Boy Scout Council in America. In 1979, just four of the many recognitions our council received included:

- Boy Scout Council of the Year in Georgia.
- Boy Scout Council of the Year in the Southeast.
- Boy Scout Council of the Year in America.
- Boy Scout Council President of the Year in America, in addition to Georgia and the Southeastern United States.

We were told by the national office that—with the large number of ribbons, trophies, badges, plaques, and flags we had earned from many competitions during the year—our council had probably received more awards and special recognitions than any council in the history of scouting. Yet perhaps the greatest personal satisfaction for me was the new troops we established for boys with mental and physical disabilities (youth and older adults). Because of the physical and mental requirements, they had previously been unable to participate in scouting. Their amazing success and enjoyment was the main highlight of my many ventures in Scouting.

We learn in working with others that life, like Scouting, is always a team sport and truth is a biological necessity of humanity.

There was one particular night that I vividly remember. Our corporate business wasn't going very well, and I had to leave Atlanta the next morning on an 8:05 a.m. Delta flight for New York. That meant I had to get up around five. I also dreaded the trip because of the problems waiting for me in New York City that had to be resolved. It wouldn't be painless. I was in one of our far-away Scout districts the evening before the trip for a Court of Honor, making awards, giving merit badges, and recognizing the advancements of the scouts and volunteer leaders in the district. Being council president, I needed to be there to participate and speak to the gathering that night. There were perhaps six hundred people in the audience,

George H. Lanier Council, Boy Scouts of America, the Number 1—Boy Scout Council of the Year in America in 1989 out of 334 councils: from left, Gerald Andrews, Council President; U.S. Boy Scouts Chief Executive presenting awards; Ed Babb, Scout Executive of George H. Lanier Council.

mostly parents, relatives, and numerous volunteers. There were many, many Scout troops we had to work through, slowly—one at a time, boy by boy. I was tired, had a headache, and was concerned about the late night and my early flight the next morning. Perhaps I was feeling a little sorry for myself. The troops were entering through the back of the auditorium, hundreds of Scouts marching up one at a time to be recognized as names and awards were called out. It was a long but very important evening.

As I sat there in my sympathetic stupor, the umpteenth troop emerged way in the back of the room and started marching toward the podium. At a distance, this was the most disorganized group I had seen all evening. There were tall and short Scouts; not all had on complete uniforms; and they were not in step. I had never seen anything like it. As they came closer, I noticed that some had grey hair and others beards. I thought, "What in the world?" The closer they came toward us, the louder the applause from the audience grew, until it became a standing ovation. I had never in all my years seen so many smiling faces on Scouts. They were each so very proud of themselves, because rarely in their entire lives had they ever received such applause and recognition for anything. It was one of the troops we had started for men/boys with mental or physical disabilities in the hopes that they could grow in Scouting regardless of their age or ability.

Some wonderful volunteers led these groups in our council. When it dawned on me which troop this was, I stood with everyone else and applauded. As each person's name was called out to thunderous acclamation, they stepped forward, grinning from ear to ear. I watched in amazement, thankful that I had played a small part in this effort. Each was recognized, and it was one of the greatest pleasures I have experienced anywhere, anytime, and for any reason! I'm certain their families felt even more so.

I arrived back home after one in the morning and was in bed for a short nap before getting back up. I realized as I drove back home that I'd forgotten about the business problems facing me, and my headache was miraculously gone.

At the end of the year, we were selected the Council of the Year in America, and I was selected Council President of the Year. I also received the Silver Beaver award, one of the highest recognitions for volunteer leadership in

Scouting. The recognitions were graciously accepted, but what had been the most meaningful for everyone involved was that we had introduced more boys to the world of Scouting than at any time in our Council's history and because it included those "boys" that had never before had a chance to be recognized in a positive way for their personal accomplishments.

Hard work, and reaching out to others, left a high watermark on Southern Reality once again. When we do something for someone, there is a continuously occurring aftertaste of the pleasures and successes of one's hard-earned achievements. It's something difficult to replicate. Over the years, when employing someone, I have always given special consideration to anyone who had earned Eagle Scout, and there was no loose afterthought. Looking back, perhaps the saddest part of life is not what we become but what we could have been. The Boy Scouts always encourages the better angels of our nature.

24

Healthcare

Ishouldn't be—but have always been—amazed at what towns and cities can accomplish when they work together for a common cause. Richmond Terry was a good and dear friend. We literally grew up together. He and I attended the same high school and college, played sports for the same teams, and worked for the same corporation. One day he called me about joining the board of trustees at our local hospital and nursing home. Little did I know where my decision would eventually lead. I had been asked once before but turned them down. Yet, for some curious reason, this time I accepted.

I enjoyed working with doctors, nurses, patients, hospitals, nursing homes, and healthcare organizations because medicine is the only profession I have ever found that continuously works to put itself out of business. The healthcare industry doesn't make any money if everybody is healthy.

In 1989, during the hostile takeover at West Point (Pepperell) Stevens, I joined—at Richie's urging—the board of the George H. Lanier Memorial Hospital and Nursing Home. It was a mid-sized hospital and the first one founded under the Congressional Hill-Burton Act of 1950. It served fifty thousand people on the Alabama-Georgia border and was bounded by the Greater Valley in Alabama and West Point, Georgia; therefore, most of its patients came from mill towns. My corporate plate was running over, but I was always interested in learning something new and strongly believed in giving back to the community that had nurtured me. I accepted the invitation to become a member of the board. I had been vice president of the County Mental Health Association, worked with the Red Cross, and was even a member of the Five Gallon Club for donating blood, but this was a whole new medical ballgame.

After becoming a member of the organization, I must have initiated too many questions, made too many recommendations, and solved too many problems because in six months I was asked to become president of the Chattahoochee Valley Hospital Society and Chairman of the Board of Trustees. This group ran the hospital, nursing home, and medical park and served as liaison between physicians and all related healthcare activities in the broader geographical area. By this time, I knew the crisis nature and magnitude of the situation. With great foreboding on my part, I accepted because of the critical need of the community. Perhaps I wasn't as wise then as I am now.

The needs were almost overwhelming, which placed the hospital in a questionable position of viability. There were serious problems between the CEO, administrative staff, physicians, nurses, hospital employees, and the board of trustees. There was a huge void in operating leadership, while finances were in crisis mode. Dissention was prevalent among the doctors; there were difficulties with quality and quantity of nurses; operations were in dire need of management attention; new and upgraded facilities were required; and there were pressing legal proceedings to contend with. In addition, there was a desperate need for millions of dollars in capital funds

EAMC-Lanier Hospital and Nursing Home in Valley, Alabama, in 1980.

for updating and renovating the hospital, along with the acute demand for restructuring the total long-term debt.

There was a sharp decline in West Point (Pepperell) Stevens management and employment in the area. We also experienced double the percentage of nonpaying and indigent care customers, compared to the two larger competing regional hospitals. This alone had cost several million dollars in P&L operating performance over the prior two or three years.

The federal government had substantially reduced Medicare and Medicaid reimbursements to small- and middle-sized community hospitals. Hospitals serving rural communities were receiving less in funding than larger facilities for the same procedures, in effect forcing small hospitals out of business and funneling medical services into larger facilities across the nation. Evidently part of the strategy worked because, in a two year period, over 1,200 small hospitals across the U.S. closed, with hundreds more to follow. We were teetering on the abyss and didn't want to join the parade to oblivion. Fortunately for both myself and the hospital, I had been President of the Retail Stores Division for WPP. We had built a good management team and were on target for our objectives, so I had enough personal time to apply to the healthcare issue. (I did stretch my work days, evenings, and weekends by many hours to help support the hospital.)

I could write an entire book about this experience and what a great job the trustees, hospital staff, physicians, volunteers, and community did in coming together to address the crisis. We prepared a Creative Analysis identifying the most pressing problems. The CEO and some of the staff were terminated, replaced, or reassigned, which improved communication and morale. We worked to restructure hospital debt and obtain additional funds for renovating facilities through our mortgage holder, Alabama FHA. This governmental organization, which had obstinately held the purse strings and a reasonably small amount of debt, wasn't responding to our needs.

We recruited new physicians and nurses. A scholarship program was later initiated with a local college that had a nursing curriculum. (I had been on the college president's advisory board and knew the people involved in the nursing program.) Hospital employee and community morale was of serious concern, so special attention was given to each area of healthcare, including physicians and the public.

There was serious disengagement between approximately three dozen physicians on staff—family physicians versus medical specialists. They weren't working together in the hospital's best interest. I personally spent uncounted hours (mostly in the evenings and on weekends) one-on-one with each physician soliciting their support. I was doing more listening than talking because everyone had their own ideas about the problems. After individual meetings, we brought all physicians and board members together in a Saturday session in a neutral location: my corporate office conference room. We discussed the precarious viability of the hospital and what we had to do to preserve healthcare as we knew it in our area, including working together for a common cause. It began to get better—slowly.

The FHA continued dragging its feet. They refused to visit our hospital to review facilities or discuss the situation. In such an untenable financial dilemma, we initiated a major public relations and fundraising effort called Project Help. We engaged all the communities serviced by the hospital in the Chattahoochee River Valley. I also served as chairman of the initiative and spokesperson for the effort. Because of the desperate plight of small hospitals across America, we drew the attention of a national TV station in Chicago. They sent down their mascot to help, and they also gave us national news coverage. We quickly raised approximately $1.25 million from the community and local corporations, a short term Band-Aid that gave us a little breathing room.

To deal with the FHA, we arranged a meeting with U.S. Senators Howell Heflin and Richard Shelby of Alabama in Washington, D.C. We explained that the FHA evidently didn't want to assist us, even though they held the existing hospital debt. We were not behind in payments of any kind or with any of our economic covenants of responsibility. There were approximately fifty thousand people in our health care market that depended on our hospital, nursing home, and related physicians. Fortunately, FHA was under Senator Heflin's area of Congressional oversight and both Senators Heflin and Shelby seemed surprised at their procrastination. They agreed to un-jam the roadblock.

The following Monday morning, Alabama's FHA executive called saying that we had gone over his head to Washington for help. Evidently he was upset because it had come back to "bite" him. He was a bureaucrat of the first order, and after ranting and raving finally invited us to his office in Montgomery to discuss resolutions. Under the frustrating circumstances we had experienced to date, I guess I was a little vindictive, so I said, "I'm sorry but we can't come to your office. We are very proud of our facilities and, after talking for months, you have yet to see our campus. You should, so you come up here." After another explosion and many excuses, he reluctantly agreed. We met in two days at the hospital to initiate restructuring the debt to our satisfaction, and we began to right the listing ship.

After almost two years of active engagement, all the major initiatives on the Creative Analysis docket were fully enjoined in battle or had been completed. We established a new hospital foundation for fundraising and related needs, and I served as founding Chairman. A new outstanding interim CEO was brought in before Bob Humphrey, a very capable young man, assumed the position permanently. Douglas Dewberry was eventually made Chief Financial Officer. He did a superb job and followed Bob as CEO. The physicians slowly began to work together as the nursing squeeze improved. We also introduced new awards and recognition programs for healthcare leadership. Additional funds were borrowed for capital improvements, the overriding debt was restructured, and more physicians and nurses were recruited.

The hospital began major renovations and new equipment was purchased. Over the next few years, a new assisted living center was added, new physician's offices were built, and a new outpatient center was constructed onto the hospital along with a brand new surgical wing and a major upgrade of the emergency room. There were also significant improvements in patient rooms and public areas. In essence, there emerged a new first-class hospital, prepared for the foreseeable future.

This was an exercise in dedication and a lot of hard work. Inspired hospital and community leaders from the mill villages placed the healthcare of the metropolitan area above their personal interests. This transcendent process continued long after I left in 1992 for New York City. The hospital has since

The George H. Lanier Hospital and Nursing Home, Operating Board and Physicians in 1989.

been under outstanding leadership, and it continues to move ahead. The lesson for all of us is that it happened while several thousand small hospitals across the hinterlands faltered and closed under similar economic burdens of pervasive and forced governmental pressure.

Although there were many, many deserving people responsible for this almost miraculous resurrection and transcendence, they haven't received the credit they should have. Since I was the one carrying the flag, I received more recognition than was justified. I guess that's the ultimate compensation. If you are carrying the colors, you either get undeserved credit or you get shot. In its benevolence, the Greater Chattahoochee Valley Chamber of Commerce selected me as "Citizen of the Year" for this leadership effort. There were numerous recognitions to follow.

I would have preferred to remain in that capacity for another year or two to assist in the continuing effort and stabilize the changes taking place. However, West Point Stevens decided it needed me in New York City to help invigorate the company's merchandising. Hospital board member Bill Scott became chairman. He had been instrumental in the turnaround and was one of the most capable community leaders and critical thinkers I have ever worked with. I did remain on the foundation's board.

When I made periodic rounds at the nursing home and hospital, it concerned me that so many people were lonely. Many patients had few visitors or family attention. I would pick out four or five of these neglected patients, and then every two or three weeks send them an anonymous fun card. I would sign it from "Someone who loves you and believes you are very special" or "X-X-X—a Secret Admirer." It gave them a warm feeling and made their day to guess who it might be from. I never told them who had sent it. Compassion is simple. It means mind and heart need to blend together into one whole. I have come to the studied conclusion that there is no melancholy static holding up the universe; it's all left up to you and me.

Approximately four years after I left, the George H. Lanier Memorial Hospital—under CEO Bob Humphrey—was evaluated in a special study conducted by HCIA, a national healthcare information company and an HR management consulting firm. It was selected as one of the Top 100 Hospitals in America based on nine measures of clinical, operational, and financial performance. The little mill villages that could? They did!

25

Three Dr. Peppers

We rarely forget those things we discover when we are young. The best lessons of all are those that we personally experience. One should constantly try to set a positive example for others. There is always someone watching not only what you say but, more importantly, what you do. My grandmother's boarding house was an unusual place where you could copyright your life, and many adventurous people tried and did so. She had six young, male boarders who worked in the local textile mill. She also prepared close to 125 meals each day, five to six days a week, depending upon how the mill was running. Mostly they were for people who worked in the mill, the plant offices, and for students at nearby Valley High School.

Today we wake up each morning to a murky duke's mixture of change, with a lot more abstract, fuzzy lines and plot points to uncover. Thinking back in advocacy, tracing the contours of elusive times, I can still conjure up the richness of those earlier mill village days. Some might even call it subsistence living, although everyone had their own touch of cleverness and little patch of blue sky. Yet life is always relative, because what you know and remember rescues valuable experiences from certain death. Back then, trust was so rooted in strong relationships that it didn't need promises for support.

My grandfather John Brown Andrews, whom we called Papa, never owned or drove an automobile. In an unincorporated town of 3,500 people, he walked almost everywhere he went: work, church, fishing holes, to visit friends, and the grocery store. In the afternoon he would go to the homes of many elderly shut-in friends (male and female) to visit and cut their hair, gratis. I have wondered many times if perhaps, in the confusion of surviving, he missed his calling to be a school teacher or perhaps a barber. He knew from dealing with people that there is rarely a misleading impression about niceness and honesty.

One Saturday afternoon circa 1945, he walked over to Combs Grocery Store (about three miles round trip) to get me, my grandmother, and himself a Dr. Pepper. My grandmother drank only Dr. Peppers in the Kingdom of Coca-Cola and subsequently got everyone in our family addicted. God bless Texas! When Papa returned, he placed a brown paper bag on the dining room table with the sodas, pulled three nickels out of his pocket, and placed them on the table. "Oh my goodness, I gave Mr. Combs a quarter and he only charged me ten cents for those three drinks. It should have been fifteen cents. I don't want him to think I tried to cheat him out of a nickel, so I've got to go back and give it to him," he said. He left immediately to walk back to the grocery store before it closed. I remember it well because he asked me to walk the three miles with him, and I did.

Now fast forward with me fifty-plus years to 2001. I had some time on my hands after my third retirement, so I purchased a beautiful 1930s-era brick apartment building in West Point, Georgia. The building, located directly across the street from Point University, was formerly a school teachers' dormitory and was in desperate need of repair and upgrading. Thus began over a year long renovation project. Acting as general contractor, I did the redesign and some of the work myself, subbing out the more difficult wiring and heavy construction to others. I made many forty-six-mile round trips from West Point to the nearest Home Depot to purchase most of the materials: kitchen cabinets and appliances, lighting and bathroom fixtures, wiring, plumbing, hot water tanks, paint, lumber, shutters, windows, and roofing.

One day I had filled my van and, while returning to the apartments, calculated the cost of what I had just purchased. It should have totaled about $2,000. I was puzzled because the bill had only been for $1,563. When I unloaded and checked the list, I found that they had undercharged me almost $400. I immediately left to go back and pay them the difference. When I arrived at the store, I told the same clerk that had checked me out that I had been there about three hours earlier. She smiled and said, "Yes, I remember you!"

"I'm sorry, but you didn't charge me accurately and I would like to

508 Apartments, LLC, West Point, Georgia, across the street from Point University office.

correct my bill. I wrote everything here on this list and there is a $400 error," I explained.

"Have you left the parking lot? Do you have everything in your truck, so I can send someone out and check it?" she asked.

"Well, no, you see, I unloaded everything in West Point and my van is empty."

"I'm sorry but we can't give a refund if you have left the premises," she responded.

"I apologize. I wasn't very clear. You don't owe me anything. You see, I owe you about $400. You didn't charge me enough," I answered.

Somewhat flustered, she called her supervisor over and told her the story.

The supervisor said, "Say what? You came all the way back up here from West Point to pay us $400?"

"Yes ma'am," I said.

The supervisor went to get the store manager and told him the situation. The manager came over and very nicely said, "It was our error, and you owe us nothing."

"Well, in a way it is my fault," I said. "You see, I was talking to the young lady when she was checking me out, and I'm sure I distracted her. I had three large pull-carts full. They were loaded down and I probably disrupted her attention. So it is my fault, not hers. When I unloaded, I noted on this list what I received and what I wasn't charged for, and I want to pay for it."

After declining payment once more, they reluctantly rang up the items, which totaled to $387. I paid the bill and left. The supervisor said, "I've worked here six years, and no one has ever come back to say they owed us money. I doubt this was the first mistake we ever made." When I left the store, the three of them were still standing there, talking and shaking their heads.

When all else fails, try honesty. At the end of the day, serving as a positive role model is the most meaningful thing one can do. Just remember: someone is always watching you, and you usually don't even know it. In all probability, they are the ones you love the most and want to influence above all others. During the drive back that afternoon, I remembered those three Dr. Peppers and the day my grandfather and I walked three miles to return a nickel. The least I could do was drive forty-six miles for $387. If he had been there, that's what he would have expected me to do. I guess that he was there, in my memory and heart. The surprising thing is that I slept better that night than I had in three or four months. That apartment building was one of the best investments I ever made. You see, I learned by someone else's example that there are a lot more important things in life than money. Too often truth and honesty are knocking on the door, wanting to be let in, and we just ignore their presence.

When I was fifteen years old, my dad went bankrupt. He lost his business, our home, everything he owned materially. Emotionally we were all pretty far down the list. I didn't have a clue how I would be able to go to college, and I told my grandfather that I had absolutely nothing to be thankful for. With a patient smile, he looked at me with eyes that had traveled a million miles, all uphill. He said, "Take your forefinger and middle finger on your right hand and place them together side-by-side, like the Scout's oath. Now reach over with them and place them on the inside of your left wrist. Do you feel anything?" I did as he said, and responded, "Yes sir, I feel my pulse, my heart beating." He said, "That means you have something to be thankful for, and don't ever forget it. You are alive. All you can do is appreciate what you have right now. What you had yesterday is gone, good or bad, and it doesn't matter. We cannot live in the past. Nor can we live in the future. Experience tells us that one can only live in the present. To be happy, you must learn to appreciate what you have, not what you had or may have tomorrow."

I have thought about his comments many times since that eventful day, when things were going against the grain. He taught me that Southern Reality can be elevated to art in the right hands. So when times are tough, I just reach over and feel my pulse, and if it's beating, I smile to myself knowing everything will be okay because Papa said so. Then I let that thought marinate for a moment in my prefrontal cortex.

26

The Beauty Contest

Life in a mill village is not so much overpriced as it is underappreciated. Not long ago I thought I had done and seen just about everything. How wrong I was. In the furthest ranges of my imagination, I would never consider myself a polymath or a man of many talents. At best, I perhaps possess one single talent—related to prolixity—that was perhaps applicable to many disciplines. I then discovered rather quickly that an emergency experience in Southern Reality can be a lot stranger than fiction.

As a little boy I could live inside my head and entertain myself with thoughts and ideas all day long, day after day. The fact is that intellective insight can flood any normal mind, while actuality is waiting to come along in ambush. One of the most transcendent moments I can recall came from an emergency and a partially inventive experience—a moment of truth coupled with a spark of possibility.

Superficially, fantasy resembles the actual world in a toned down way, primarily because it can never think of all the exclamatory things that might actually happen in everyday occurrences. Life often needs a little extra help with reality. As a small-town boy, I can boil shortsighted thought down to only four simple words: "No common sense." (Yes, I know. I was just seeing if you were still paying attention.)

For over forty years, in our spare time, both Claire and I have volunteered at various hospitals and nursing homes around the country. We enjoyed serving at EAMC-Lanier Memorial Hospital and Nursing Home, snuggled along the Chattahoochee River on the Alabama side of the Georgia and Alabama divide. I had served as chairman of the hospital board and

228

foundation, among other things, and Claire had merchandised the gift shop for many years.

Early one morning on the edge of summer, we received an emergency call from a friend—Diane Glenn—asking if we would be judges at the hospital and select the beauty queen of the year that very evening. We changed our plans and said yes! I could just visualize eighty-five to ninety-five-year-olds parading by in a bikini, singing, dancing, and doing stand-up comedy. In the real world, even with a vivid imagination, that's not the way such a contest works. Of course, an extrovert rarely stops to question or explain; he just agrees and forges ahead with his mouth wide open, even into unexplained and sometimes dangerous territory. Of course, no one wants to drown in shallow water because of their own poor taste.

When we arrived that evening, Diane Joyner, who was in charge, said the minister who was supposed to give the invocation had just been called away on an emergency. Could I also give the invocation? Of course, I was glad to fill the agenda. The program was to start at 7 p.m., but by 7:30 we were still waiting in the overly packed cafeteria with a large assortment of interesting and uneasy people and their families, half of whom were confined in uncomfortable wheelchairs.

Diane came over, concerned, and said, "There is a problem. The Master of Ceremonies just called and has run into difficulty getting here. Can you be the Master of Ceremonies for the evening, as well as do the invocation and also be a judge?" Without thought I said, "Of course, I'll be glad to," although I had never witnessed such an occasion. More comfortable than me, she sighed in relief and returned to her seat. Being born under the astrological sign of prolixity didn't impede my response, and they immediately gave me the floor—which can be dangerous. It offered me the great opportunity to review plans for the evening and tell a few Auburn/Alabama jokes, among other things. For some reason, the Auburn folks present seemed to enjoy them a little more.

After a few ad-lib audience introductions, the individual contestants were introduced to the group and publicly interviewed before the gathering. Some light commentary was presented—mostly unnecessary from the loquacious M.C.—and everyone was finally relaxing, laughing, and having a good time. There were seven beautiful ladies between eighty and ninety-six years old being evaluated for the title, all but one of them in a wheelchair and the other with a walker.

They were in various physical and mental states, some good, some bad, and some worse. Yet here they were, competing in one of the most difficult contests I have ever witnessed, even compared to the shark-infested waters of the corporate world. Everyone deserved first prize, but only one could receive it—a real shame. The sweet lady in the walker was physically challenged and could only speak slowly but was understandably selected as Miss Congeniality to the thunderous applause of the happy crowd. Then a worthy second runner-up and an equally praiseworthy first runner-up were selected.

Finally a beautiful, deserving lady in her ninety-fourth year was chosen as "Ms. East Alabama Medical Center, Lanier Memorial Hospital-Nursing Home 2015," and that's a mouth full. The banner was long enough to wrap around her body three times. She received a standing ovation from those that could stand. Her mind was good, and her glow encompassed the entire room. Unfortunately, her tired body could hardly move and had seen many better days, but perhaps not many happier ones. The tiara looked stunning in her attractively coiffured hair. All contestants received a bouquet of beautiful red roses that generated big smiles and set the world right in everyone's mind.

In so many ways it reminded me of when I was in charge of a critical hospital fundraising event many years earlier. The ladies in the nursing home back then had knitted, crocheted, and quilted items that they sold to raise money. The hospital's interim CEO asked me to come down at noon that particular day to receive a check for $1,632 that the ladies had proudly raised and wanted to present to the fund drive. It was a very emotional visit that I will never forget. I stood in the center of the large room, and circled around me were one hundred or so elderly ladies in wheelchairs. When the check was presented, they were very proud of what they had done. I told them that I could only accept the check under one condition. They were surprised and puzzled. I said, "I can only take this if you will let me come around the room, thank each of you personally, and give you a big neck hug." I received a rousing round of applause.

I was perhaps halfway through the gathering when I reached down to a tiny lady of about eighty-six. I asked her age and name, gave her a big neck hug, and said "Thank you!" She looked up with sad eyes and said, "You have made this a very special day for me, too." I said, "How's that?" She said, "My husband died fourteen years ago last Thursday, and you are the first man to give me a hug in fourteen years." My heart leaped into my throat. It was one of the few times in my entire life I had been at a loss for words. I finally recovered my composure and said out loud, "Let me have everyone's attention. How many of you are widows?" About 90 percent of the hands went up. I said, "Okay, ladies, today I'm running a special offer. All widows who are interested get two hugs. If you only got one, I'll be back." I believe I would have gotten a standing ovation if they could have stood up. It was the greatest applause of the day and one of the best ad-libs I have ever made. That very day I decided to become a professed hugger for the rest of my life. That was over twenty-five years ago, and I haven't regretted it a single day.

The 2015 EAMC-Lanier Hospital and Nursing Home Beauty Contest Winners.

As Claire and I left the cafeteria that evening, a well-dressed elderly lady of about five feet came up and caught Claire by the arm. She asked, "Are you the Mrs. Andrews that taught first grade and special education at Fairfax forty years ago?"

"That was me," Claire said.

"I was hoping I might meet you again one day. You see, I'm Fancy's mother."

Claire had held Fancy back, to a great deal of consternation, and didn't promote her to second grade. In Claire's opinion, she wasn't mature enough, couldn't read adequately, and wasn't ready to be advanced. Her mother had been very upset, came to see Claire and the principal, and loudly complained because she wanted Fancy to be promoted with her first grade friends.

Claire said, "Yes, I remember Fancy well, and especially that last day of class. How is she doing now?" The little lady smiled and said, "She is an award-winning elementary school teacher, and I am very proud of her. If she had been promoted, like I wanted, she would probably have never made it. Your decision inspired and better prepared her to improve and do her best, and even inspired me. Education became her passion. I was wrong and you were right. I was just hoping that I would see you again someday. For years I have wanted to say that I'm sorry for what I said and for the way I acted that day. I just wanted to thank you for all you did for my daughter. I'm embarrassed and thankful." They said a few more words then smiled and hugged.

We walked out of the nursing home, through the hospital, and into the parking lot. I don't believe Claire's feet touched the ground as we made our way to the car. You just never know when you get up in the morning how your day will end. If you are honest with yourself and try to put other people first, even to your personal detriment, somehow it always seems to turn out okay. Life can be an inspiring lesson in retrospect, if for no other reason than the art of surviving one's own honest decisions. Truth has always been there to hold our hand if we will only reach out for it. There is no point where care and callous meet. They are at opposite ends of life's spectrum. Surprisingly, at times the real world is much stranger than fiction. Just be careful. Everything you take out does not always go back in the same box.

It's funny how life is not so much overpriced as it is undervalued. Yet it takes most of us a long time to finally realize that it will go on with or without us. There is always tempered hope, but it's in short supply. I guess if we could reinterpret who we are today, we would probably choose to remain the same. In a strictly neutral sense of the word, it sweeps us up into thoughts and possibilities that sound reasonable, right before it drops you down a rabbit hole.

27

Old People

"**O**ld people" just happen to reside in history, including calendar events, facts, and things of the past weighed heavily by community. They are important for many reasons, the primary one being that they are the gate-keepers to our future because they experienced our yesterday and witness our present. If there was one thing we had an abundance of in our little hamlets, it was older people, and it was also good pasture for the tired and weary. Age had a way of embracing not only one's extended mill-village family but many painterly portraits with different brush strokes for diverse individuals. Elderly people have learned that history is not necessarily what really happened but the memory that remains after the real past is forgotten. Like duct tape, we are held together by words, and when the mind that creates them loses its velocity, nothing is left. Yet elderly happiness is its own reward, because life is simply a lot of pulp with a loose purpose, waiting to be formed. Regardless of age, living is always relegated to the "Department of Speculation," pausing to be sorted out by bespoke beholders of goodness. Yet it's so hard to say goodbye to the past.

We mortals have a way of residing in a weak bargain with chronology. In advancing years, the self-conscious mind reaches for the sky, fighting against reduction and distillation, hoping to find its purpose for existence. Sometimes I think elderly is just a nice soft pastel word of acceptance im-plying thought without having to think. The "rub of seasons" always leaves its mark, because life rarely wastes its benevolence on the old. Time is like a river and has a special way of carrying you along in its current, whether you want to go or not. Often, as we aged, it seemed as if each passing day was in league against humans. For all of us, there are isolated moments and occurrences that are forever fixed in the narrative, at least what we profess, want to know, and remember. That is especially true with the elderly. I could never come close to a passable facsimile of their prodigious and profuse examples. They admired truth and honesty four times over and just seemed to have a monopoly on character and mordant wit. They learned early on that "self" is the weak underlying condition and the epic substance of reality.

As we age, we have two significant remembrances: those aspirations that never come to pass and the reminiscences that you wish hadn't happened. As encroaching years arrive at our front door, we gradually bend to the gravitational summons of Father Time. There was often a kind of caved-in sadness in the elderly, dangling off, caught in the tightening grip of advancing years, a hold impossible to escape. Some fell short of their goals, and perhaps even more never passed through their own preset thresholds. But few were ever bitter. Old age is nature's charity in a benevolent mode, part of creation's delicious surplus in a kind of free-will offering to mankind. Yet one cannot ignore reality or the physics of time. I can't believe how ancient the people my age are. I never knew it would happen so fast. Based on the past couple of years, I think caducity and senility are going to be a fairly easy transition for me.

I've tried to pick the lock on some of the earlier memories of my youthful days, as remembrances become the main bridge back across the years. It seemed to start the very moment I began to think about my dreams on the other side of the mountain. Like most kids, I was taught to grow up with an open mind, thankful for what I had, not regretful for what I didn't have, always with a song in my heart and book in my hand. As I got older, I didn't change much, I just became an exaggerated version of my earlier self. Youth never completely leaves; it stays hiding within us. However, as we get older, love goes deeper and we are not still looking for someone to stir our heart to conflagration.

Often the minds of timeworn folks seemed to go unused for days. I guess they just pray that, with the strong undertow of time and the weight of years, they will still be able to escape each moment with dignity intact. They waited with open arms for the future they helped usher in, and when they paused to catch their breath and enjoy it, it was gone. Perhaps their greatest concern was that no one wants to become referred to in the past tense when they are still here. Yet it helps to be a gifted observer, because history is always a tale in retrospect. Even with its elucidation, the conscience guards its secrets well, knowing to always tell the truth, because no one wants to go through life with their fingers crossed.

When I was a teen in the mid-1950s, Fairfax was a small unincorporated Alabama town of 3,500 people with a textile mill of 1,800 employees. At the time, it was the largest plant in the West Point Manufacturing Company. It was actually two mills—the greige spinning and weaving plant and the finishing plant—under one manager. We were somewhat isolated from the world (except for Highway 29, which went through the middle of town). Of course, there were the six other mill villages in the Chattahoochee Valley that adjoined it. The historically friendly Southern culture had persevered over many decades. There were five Protestant churches on the huge circular boulevard surrounding Fairfax Mill and a number of smaller ones on the outskirts of town. The only thing missing was a Catholic church and Jewish synagogue, where miracles were mainstream. A strong Protestant belief had given the people who lived there an awareness of faith and the trust in someone or something stronger than themselves. As kids, we all had dreams of walking in the giants' footsteps, in their shadows, or hand in hand. We learned as we got older and wiser that those giants would become our grandparents, parents, and elderly neighbors. I think when someone dies, they dissolve into the ones that loved them and are still here in a different form. Fairfax imprinted on me in an indelible way through its people in a virtuous loop. They didn't just tell us what to do; they also modeled the behavior.

As a kid, our family couldn't keep up with the Joneses, but I was just happy they lived next door so I could see what I was missing. However, conspicuous consumption and extravagance were not the mill village way. Compared to today, there were no serious crimes committed (or crime of any type that I recall) because everybody thought it was wrong. In our little town, and throughout the entire Chattahoochee Valley, we loved and admired older folks. Fortunately, they lived on every street. Some still worked in the mill, others had retired, and some just were. Today the typical Social Security check in Chambers County, where the mill villages were located, is $967 per month. That's the primary income for most recipients. We didn't admire and respect them because they were old, or for their wealth, but because of the positive example they set for the rest of us, kids and adults alike.

If someone had a problem, the first to volunteer to help was an elderly person, even though they were probably less able. Over the years, I was afraid that most of the older people I knew would have their hearts wear out before their souls. Too many did. Perhaps what preserved their sanity, like the rest of us, was that they had their own private rabbit holes, and people have a way of misremembering a lot of what they want to forget. Yet, in their deep wisdom, they knew it was hard to be both a true three-dimensional human and a two-dimensional mirage. If a situation with an older person ever requires you to bend the truth a little bit to make them feel better, don't worry—the truth will forgive you. I have always respected my elders, but at my age it's getting harder and harder to find one. It's kind of surprising, though; growing old didn't take nearly as long as I thought it would.

I noticed at village sporting events that old people were easy to spot when they played the national anthem. They were the first to proudly respond. Many times I saw them being assisted from wheelchairs by someone so they could stand unsteadily, remove their caps, and cover their hearts. I did the same. I have seen tears roll down their cheeks as they emotionally sang the anthem. They knew every word, believed in them, and remembered those that gave their lives for their country and flag, some in their own extended family. When I was a teenager, they earned at best only $5,000 a year working six hard days a week, not $6 or $7 million a year like today's athletes or the privileged 1 percent in some large corporation that have never served their country. Neither did I ever see a single one take a knee to their flag or their national anthem. That was not Southern Reality or their way of doing things.

Older people are not necessarily out of date; they just grew up in different times. They remember when Black Friday Eve was better known as Thanksgiving. They were here before the word Christmas went out of fashion and "Happy Holidays" took over. They lived before there were hashtags. It was a time when you could invent reaching aspirations in your own vivid imagination. Most were born prior to frozen food, polio shots, penicillin, the pill, and Viagra. And would you believe it, even before the Kardashians and Donald. Those were the days when there were no credit cards, very little credit, no ballpoint pens, almost no college scholarships, no air conditioners, dishwashers (other than manual), clothes dryers, calculators, or a man on the moon. They never heard FM radio. They had never seen an electric typewriter, a CD, an Xbox, girls with tattoos and piercings, guys wearing their pants down around their knees, or men wearing girl's earrings. Thank goodness!

Back when they were young, there was no Pizza Hut, McDonald's, or instant coffee. "Fast food" just meant it was quick off the dining room table and was a compliment to the cook. There eventually became generational gaps in the understanding of certain words and their meaning. "Pot" was something you cooked chicken and grits in. "Grass" was always mowed by kids. "Coke" was a cold soft drink. A "chip" was a piece of wood, and "hardware" was found in a store that sold tools. It was a different era.

Older mill villagers had character and took pride in who they were. Wherever you found them, there were usually courteous, gracious families growing in their shade. Being old was a special way to enter history by assisting their children and grandchildren, helping create a better shot at the future than they had. They wanted to help them copyright their lives and they loved to say, "Bless your heart!" Life was about education and college, in the most conventional tableaux that had not been available to them. There were parents and grandparents still reaching for their comfort zones, fully strapped by their own defeats, which were usually related to growing up in the Great Depression. Those were fractious times and people were just trying to survive. They were caught short on their own formal learning, but now they could finally see opportunity for their family. They knew education had strong value. It encouraged their every day and personal outlook on the remaining time they had left. Old people also have a gift for "deep listening." Of course, no one is perfect; even Albert Einstein and Bo Jackson had some bad Monday mornings and Saturday afternoons.

Like a diamond, there were many facets to their lives, some brighter than others. There were aspects swallowed up by the lack of hope and the excesses that rapidly poured into their every day when they didn't have time to pay attention. They were just trying to get by. They had learned through heartbreak that we Homo sapiens can become complex characters, caught between human nature and inhumane consistencies. They didn't want family, friends, and children to make the same mistakes they did. There was a painful clarity when probing the personal wounds and scars endured and created. At the same time, I think they liked their path on the road to herohood, because they understood from experience that you never miss the taste of water until the well runs dry.

Seniors also had a special perspective. They could remember World War II, Pearl Harbor, Iwo Jima, Normandy, Adolf Hitler, Mussolini, Tojo, and Stalin. They were also there at the beginning of the Atomic Age, Korean War, Vietnam, Apollo 11, Cold War, and the multitude of police actions and peacekeeping missions around the world where thousands of Americans died in foreign lands. Most of those I knew—like my Dad, uncles, and neighbors in mill villages—volunteered to fight for their country and didn't wait to be drafted or claim bone spurs in their heels. If you are honest and have a clear conscience, close scrutiny should never bring on insolence or self-disrespect. One day I asked my Dad why he had volunteered for service

The Andrews sisters. Left to right, Great Aunts Carrie, Thelma, and Dempsey Ruth.

at the beginning of World War II and didn't wait to be drafted. I will never forget his answer. "Son, we would not be Americans if there was no America."

When accidentally bumping into an elderly person at church, the grocery store, movies, on the street, at a restaurant, or on the sidewalk—even if it was your fault—they are always the first to crack a smile and apologize. If you passed one somewhere, they would break into a big grin, look you in the eyes, and nod hello. I've also found that old people trust strangers, are courteous to women, love little children, never harm animals, and treat all with thoughtful consideration and respect. Every one I ever knew aspired to doing what was right, to plausibility and acceptance. At my age, I don't mind filling out all those tax forms, but for the life of me I have trouble remembering my maiden name.

In our little hamlets, recognizing everybody made you feel comfortable, connected, and safe. You knew when there were problems that family, neighbors, and old people always had your back. As kids we felt secure, recognized, known, and loved. They liked us—in spite of ourselves—even though we tried to define who we were through our individual terms and personal brand. There were always high community standards to live by that were established by wise mature citizens, who we looked up to, cherished, and didn't want to disappoint. Not one that I knew, regardless of age, set a goal to grow up to be a person of no importance; it's just not part of the graying human nature. Neither did they want to be left all alone in a tiny room in a nursing home, as lonely as an empty desert, becoming an alien in their own world. Every person over seventy that I can recall had an extraordinary gift: they freely gave to others without remembering and graciously accepted without ever forgetting. They liked the noon hour each day best of all, when the clock hands join together in prayer, reminding us of our better nature.

For oldsters, scars are actually treasured as a badge of courage and most have quite a few of them. Scars mean the hurt is finally gone, the wound is closed, the healing is done, and you survived and are still around to testify. Scars are positive proof that life exists beyond the state of survival. I saw so many elderly men and women hold open the door of life for the next generation to pass through, as they did for me. When a gentleman walked down the street with a lady, he always made certain she was on the inside, under his protection and away from the crowd and traffic. Every mature person in the mill village I knew, which was just about everyone, had strong morals and exhibited high personal integrity. Growing up I don't ever recall one saying curse words in front of a woman or child, even in the barber-shop. I'm sure I cleaned up many a conversation as a little boy when I was listening to the gossip. Neither did they accept filth, vulgar words, or dirty language in books, TV, movies, or elsewhere. We all try to transcend our own self-appointed cleverness, but if the truth be known, it rarely works. As I've gotten older, I find I still do stupid things; I just do them a lot slower.

Yesterday, wise senior citizens knew accountability was always a moving target that travels from generation to generation. They also knew that truth maintains reality in a way that fiction can't touch. Yet reality and truth do not always hang out together. The discerning sagacity of the elderly knew that the moving finger, after writing on the wall, turns and points back at us.

You know, it's interesting how old people seemed to understand many things long before the rest of us. They knew that our wonderful country (with all its faults) is protected not by puffed-up politicians, high-paid lawyers, the 1 percent, or large corporations but young men and women between eighteen and twenty-five years old in the military who risk their lives every single second. Permit the youth a dream and they will offer you their lives.

Older people living along the Chattahoochee River understood the futile hope of finding something better and just embraced the ordinariness of what they already had. Few had anywhere better to go and felt they were lucky living and working where they did, so they stayed until the mills were finally closed. Moving to a new place was not always an option or the best way to make a new self and there weren't many choices. Wise, mature individuals know from experience that your problems don't always leave of their own accord, and you can't walk or run away from them. The tone in our little backwaters was more ephemeral, but the problems were just as hurtful as in the real world. I wish if we didn't like the results of each day we could pretend it was like an Etch-A-Sketch and just shake it and start over, but that's not the way the world works.

Experienced senior citizens taught us that sometimes our finest hour only lasts five minutes, but we should try to make the most of it. Perhaps that's because human weaknesses are as maddening as past mistakes and can be as painful as the truth. Today, if there were any around, a skilled weaver working in one of the mills would probably say, "America has low thread count leadership in a high thread count world." I would have to agree. One thing is for sure: they were authentic and fully at home in themselves. Some experiences were so rich and intense that they never forgot them, and they left behind an indelible signature. As hard as they might try, it was still difficult for them to be in the moment, because it was changing too fast.

Now, don't get me wrong. Everything in our little towns in the Chattahoochee Valley was not perfect for the timeworn. They were also human and fallible like everyone else, carrying around their hurts, scars, and heartbreaks. Yet they had a special mature way of handling the painful, undeserved punishment that goes along with life. Few of them were ever hamstrung by success, and they had a method of internalizing the shadows and disappointments that tugged at their thoughts and better nature. Somehow they always kept smiling. They were not even fearful of their mortality, because they knew it came as a by-product of living. They were perpetually presentable but weren't overly concerned about being flawlessly coiffured, stylishly coutured, or medically contoured.

Growing old was not for sissies. As one ages, you watch time and light shorten in the shadows, diminishing by the moment. Life comes offering smaller and smaller handfuls of flowers each day until finally the greenery disappears at the end of the season. The deeds that came out of their tumbling minds disappear. They may have been innovative, even lyrical, but perhaps not quite erudite enough to earn public recognition or their long overdue applause. But they were always trying.

Now, I never feel sad about timeworn people the way I use to. One day I figured that a Southern man of eighty had spent twenty-six years in bed—mostly sleeping—over seven years eating, and thirty-two years playing, watching, talking, or thinking about football. That's not a bad ratio. Rarely were the elderly drained by disenchantments or waning expectations. It was just part of their learned persona and vitality. Somehow they learned to live with the reality that knocked at their front door while plumbing the sadness left by such visits. I frequently saw hard and exhausting things, often placed there by family, friends, neighbors, health, and life in general. But I never recall any unconscious or self-conscious renderings of inhospitable thoughts or animosity toward anyone. I think by and large the older people in our little towns believed in the command to love your neighbor. Maybe I'm a little bit melodramatic, but I think all good relationships begin with an overloaded amount of rationalization.

Most seniors in the Chattahoochee Valley were too polite to show hostility and were very traditional in their actions. You could have their cake and eat it too. They knew truth was primarily to comfort the afflicted and afflict the comfortable. They still had pride in their age and experiences, which encouraged us to believe in the eternal value of everything. Signposts and hallmarks were left all along the way for us to follow, but few of us did. Seniors stood fast, had a strong resistance to flinching or blinking, and knew from their encounters that dawn arrived just about every morning like clockwork when the first shift whistle blew. Life always suffers from retrospective wisdom, because we must weather one bad storm after another, and it's difficult to imagine an era where doubting reality was the norm. Yet at my age I am beginning to wonder if I will ever be old enough to know better. Seniors also knew we could easily get lost in the familiarity of comfort, laziness, and routine.

Today old people still hate "fake news" and "alternative facts" that try to inoculate us against proven truths. They also want to look their best, and to them being in style means wearing clothes that fit. The wrong things happening in our little hamlet often got under their skin, and they took it personally. Anything negative said something about the town and by extension something detrimental about you. We had learned, sometimes in an abrasive way, that it was easy to deceive the self if you became engrossed, self-absorbed, and overly inflated by your own accomplishments, and ego tripping is not a good way to travel. As a kid and adult, hurting or disappointing someone older whom you loved and respected was much worse, so we stayed on our best behavior.

At the end of their enigmatic journey, the aged in our mill towns accepted the fact that our short visit here in the real world was not actually about money, power, career, or even prestige, although we may have thought so many times along the way. We learned from them that relationships are the true purpose of life's rhythm. Some learn it sooner, others later. It shouldn't be surprising, because we eventually discovered that the single most important thing we all had was simply one another. We always knew that someday, if we were lucky, we would get old. I am just amazed at how fast it happened.

As we grow older and change, the mind keeps a running critique about what happens as it tries to bargain with the real world, often grasping for words to fill the gaps in our thinking. Perhaps that's the reason we spend most of our existence trying to see the world through fog and mist. We only want to be remembered and loved, because we have learned that happiness is not a destination but the path we travel to get there. In spite of the high cost of living, it still remains our most popular pastime. The truth of the matter is that we tend to overcomplicate history when it's simply about a lot of old people and the successes and failures they once had.

Life does have a way of showing favoritism in its uneven contest, but it offers no quarter to anyone toward the end of the race and only Heaven knows the concluding score. At the close of the day, love should always have the final word, regardless of the conversation. If you don't believe me, just ask an old person.

28

Auburn

College is one of the most significant, life-changing obstacle courses faced by many young adults, and there are more to come. I guess the closest I ever felt to being mill-village perfect was that special moment when, at graduation, I prepared a résumé for my first management job with the Company, sat down, and carefully read over it. It has been all downhill since that day. In my first job interview, I was a little naive. The interviewer asked if I would be interested in participating in a 401k. I said, "No, I don't think so. I don't think I could run that far." It was a long while before I punched any holes in my Nerd Club card, which tells you something about my ordinariness. Any fool can learn to read, write, and think, but it takes a wise man to sell those skills to someone else. One of the great challenges for young adults is that you never know where you are going to end up until you get there, and it's best to travel with an education. Life is always under siege, but a truly honest country boy doesn't have to worry about the reality of intentions. Each step along the right path will keep you off the wrong one, and curiosity just makes us a better observer of life.

December is always a big month for our extended family, with birthdays, anniversaries, dinners, parties, trips to New York City, traveling, and (of course) Christmas. It was also Claire's and my fifty-ninth wedding anniversary. A couple of weeks prior, I was in my tiny, junk-laden office between naps. I keep telling her that clutter is the evidence of a productive life. I had been studiously pondering how to take her out to a four-star restaurant with one-star prices to celebrate. About that time, the front doorbell rang. It was the postman with a few packages and the mail. One letter was an invitation from Auburn University President Jay Gogue and his lovely

Auburn University, Samford Hall, 1994.

wife Susie to be their dinner guests (with one hundred other Auburnites) on December 15th. You guessed it; that is our anniversary. So it became a five-star, dressed-up dinner at no-star prices—the best kind. But I'm sure it will cost me much more in time and money during the months ahead; it always does. For years I have heard "there is no such thing as free lunch." For some reason that message was never adequately conveyed to many Americans, or if it was, it didn't sink in. Someone always has to pick up the check. If it's not me, it's you.

At dinner with the Gogues, we were seated at a table with some interesting couples, all Auburn graduates: an MD, a cattle rancher, a Ph.D., an agri-science researcher, their spouses, and one of Claire's friends, an interior designer whose fame was on the rise. She was telling us about helping to design and build a new home in Auburn for the great Atlanta Braves professional baseball player Tim Hudson and his family. Tim is from the Phenix City area, a good ole Southern boy who played at Auburn as a star outfielder and pitcher and has been recognized as one of the better pitchers in professional baseball. He is mentioned in the same breath as other Auburn Hall of Famers, such as "The Big Hurt" Frank Thomas, Bo "Knows" Jackson, Pat Sullivan, Cam Newton, and the one and only Charles Barkley. They were some of the more famous straws that stirred the Auburn sports drink.

Claire's friend had helped design a new home in Auburn for Tim, his lovely wife, and family. Tim's talented partner Kim is very pretty, a bright lawyer, looks after their children, handles several foundations they have established (primarily for children), and was still able to oversee the day-to-day construction of their new home. She was kind enough to take a number of us through their fabulous residence on a tour after they moved in. Tim led me to figure out that though not all men marry way over their heads, all the Auburn men I've ever known do. It wasn't an epiphany or a miraculous vision that revealed this, and it didn't take me fifty-nine years to come to that conclusion. Claire is so smart, because she told me that a long time ago. Who am I to question her? If it wasn't for Gilmore, she would have been the valedictorian! When I was in school, I didn't even know what that big v-word meant, and I still have a hard time spelling it. However, I was well respected by the smart students in my class for helping hold the grade point average down.

Many of my friends and family, and even my very closest enemies, think I'm a rabid Auburn fan, but I'm really not. I was a freshman there at sixteen years old, when it was still API. I'm also proud of the fact that I finished in just four terms: Harry S. Truman's, Dwight D. Eisenhower's, John F. Kennedy's, and Lyndon B. Johnson's. My parents were truly elated. They thought it would take me much longer. It usually did for Valley students, especially Lila Jo. Now, Billy Lane was the smartest of all; he graduated in only three terms. In recollection, my fourth freshman year was probably my best, but that third junior year was also pretty good. But I would like to clarify one point. Some people think that I'm a corybantic Auburn man and that I hate the Crimson Tide. That is not true. I have many wonderful Alabama people in my family, and I love them very much. They will always be in my family, but I don't send them a birthday card or Christmas present and I do not invite them home for dinner.

Ever since that eventful Auburn (API) graduation in 1959, I wear my Auburn pin on my suit or sport coat lapel with pride every single day. The fellows I used to work with in New York, Maine, New Jersey, Texas, North Carolina, Georgia, California, Michigan, Florida, and Arizona didn't have the same Southern respect for their university that I did. They rarely wore a college pin. They were from Princeton, Boston College, Southern Cal, Syracuse, Harvard, Notre Dame, Dartmouth, Williams, Slippery Rock— you get the picture. I don't know if they even knew what football was all about at those schools. In spite of this shortfall, they would kid me about my lapel pin all the time.

They changed their tune after we had lunch in New York City with one of our largest customers. That particular day, Sam Walton asked me if I was wearing an Auburn pin. Sam, who was a good ole Arkansas boy and super salesman, said, "Auburn is one of the finest schools in the country. I wish I could have gone there." At that time he was one of our biggest customers and perhaps the richest man in America. We were doing several hundred million dollars a year in sales with Wal-Mart. The following week, I was in a hurry one morning and left the Auburn pin off my jacket. One of the fellows kiddingly wondered where it was. I said, "Well, Sam Walton asked me if he could have it, and I gave it to him. I also gave him my signed Auburn football from Coach Pat Dye, autographed by Bo Jackson and Pat Sullivan. He wanted to place them in a prominent place in his office in Bentonville to impress his visitors. I'll get me another football, and I still have nineteen Auburn pins at home, if you would like one." No one ever mentioned it again. However, in recent decades, and even more frequently in my November years, I find that I forget to put it on my jacket from time to time. Many mornings when I get up I'm in such a hurry to tackle the tasks at hand that I forget and leave my Auburn pin on my pajamas.

Riding the American merry-go-round for more than fifty years, through four careers, I received far more honors, awards, and public recognition than I deserved. Because of that, I have been asked to speak to a lot of business and civic organizations and to numerous diverse groups on high school and college campuses. After speaking to a large contingent of students, faculty, and deans at Auburn University one day, I was asked to become executive-in-residence and visiting professor in a special two-year teaching program at the university. It was an itch I always wanted to scratch, so I developed a course called Creative Analysis, teaching seniors and graduate students how to be creative in the new world they would face. I was always inspired and energized by the interaction of teaching innovation in industry and the classroom. It has a way of loosening up the tightness that comes from reality, because creativity resides far above the timberline of normal thought and curiosity. Perhaps our greatest challenge is not to have power over others, but over ourselves. There is just something about the conscience in motion that strengthens resolve.

When each day comes knocking on your door—and it will, usually before you are up, dressed, and ready—nothing is ever seen concisely or in the whole. It is viewed through a thin veil of words, events, and problems and we have to make choices. I always made a great effort to avoid trouble and trips down Wikipedian rabbit holes because it takes up too much time and headspace. I developed several syntheses of myself over the decades, and I'm still trying to figure out which one was really me. So don't wait for a productive future; it's past time for you to figure out who you really are. Just remember, there are not too many world-class practitioners of self-examination, and reality may not always be sitting on the surface for everyone to see. When we decide not to make decisions, and spare ourselves the torture of choices, that in itself is a decision.

This was my quandary just a few days ago. I played sports growing up and then later coached baseball for several years in youth leagues when my boys, Andy and Benjy, played. Andy, playing for the Pepperell Dragons, led the Opelika Little League in home runs the year I coached the Opelika All-Stars to winning the state championship. Benjy, a left-handed pitcher, set a high school playoff record in strikeouts at Springwood School. Against better parental judgment, he pitched a double-header one day in the state championship playoffs and struck out thirty-four of the forty-two outs as his team won both games. So being a baseball and Auburn fan placed me in a quandary when Auburn University faced Troy University at Auburn's

Billy Hitchcock Plainsman Park. I had never before pulled against Auburn in any competitive activity, but one should learn that it is wise to "never say never," even if in a low voice.

My nephew Max Newton, a phenomenal left-handed pitcher and hitter, helped lead Smith Station to an Alabama High School State 7A Championship, and there were several colleges expressing interest in his skill set. Auburn was strongly intrigued, and we had our fingers crossed until the head coach was replaced at the end of the season and interest from the new Auburn coach didn't materialize. Troy University offered Max a scholarship and he accepted. Now Troy was headed to Auburn, the number five ranked college team in the nation, for a conceivable mismatch. The day before the game we learned that Max, a freshman reliever, was to start on the mound for Troy. Shaded feelings were rampant as twenty-two family members loaded up—all Auburn fans—and headed for the night game, afraid we were going to see Max get "killed" that eventful evening. Instead, he was superb, flawless on the mound with his change-ups, sliders, and curves. The final score was Troy 5 and Auburn 2, a huge college upset as mixed emotions abounded because we were so proud of Max. It was kind of like learning after the election that Clinton received three million more popular votes but Trump had won the Presidency. With Max being a freshman, I'm sure there will be many more confrontations in the years ahead. But it's so hard to go against Auburn. I just hope my heart and head can handle the stress. After seventy-plus years as an Auburn fan, my favorite game is always the next one.

You can believe it or not, but, as a mill village kid, I once thought about pulling for the University of Alabama in a football game. My Dad figured my problem was an anomaly on a chromosome and took me in for genetic testing. Fortunately, they found it. Since then, for years, I take a special neurological medication for the illness and am doing just fine now. During that rehabilitation I repeated an open mantra in my thoughts so I wouldn't stumble over the obvious or do too much conservative moralizing. The brain, in its linguistic exuberance, creates its own adventure. I'm just thankful many indelible convictions, personal mistakes, and mental deficits kept me from becoming a legend in my own mind. Neither am I prejudiced against the University of Alabama. A friend in Tuscaloosa recently told me some very positive info about Alabama football. Word is, Coach Nick Saban will only have to dress thirty-two football players this season. All the rest have finally learned to dress themselves, including several of his fourth-year, five-star freshmen.

A view from the top for a mill-village boy can be exhilarating but also cold and lonely, especially when one tries to cut and paste along our path's leaky seams. Yet the life at Auburn was rarely less than good. Truth is always an interesting, exciting game to play unless it's about you. I have learned to have complete confidence in man's better nature, because we all have a beating heart. It just takes a little longer for some to warm up and start working. At the close of the day, whether you end up living in a one thousand or ten thousand square foot home, the happiness or loneliness is the same. It's pretty much up to you which it will be. All you've got to do to improve the situation is yell "War Eagle" every morning when you get up.

29

6th Avenue and 48th Street

New York is the city that never sleeps, buoyed by its overabundance of distinctive, kaleidoscopic personalities and venues. It's a place where the South has tried to blend into the North over the years, with little effect. It loves to pursue a life of iconic wanderlust that knows no bounds. Everyone goes about their everyday trying to find those special moments of enjoyment, rare little pockets of simple grace that one needs to survive the nonstop assault of the day. Of course, we would all like to be the predominate figure in our own premeditated light. The idealized corporate executives and their economic corridors of the 1 percent have already acknowledged its personal sense of self-importance. It is unique in many ways. For one, more people live there than in forty of the fifty states. Everyone makes a living selling something—even if it's just a smile. Back when the days were fair and nights generous, I adored the iconic city and enjoyed being in those places where words, egos, and cocktail glasses competed for attention. It is simply millions of busy people enjoying themselves and being lonely together.

Business is like football: you either attack or defend, but you must clearly define both positions. Life is the same way. We have the choice of attacking reality or defending it. New York has a culture and persona dissected by its own uncategorizing mythology while never admitting to its own failures and bad publicity. But in spite of that, it still stands at the top of the ladder of the world's greatest cities. In our superficially enlightened world, lifestyle has become a tool of marketing, telling us that their way—whatever it is—is better than everything else.

I worked as hard as I could to get out of the mill village and to New York City, and when I made it I worked even harder to get back. There is great intercourse between the three broad functional business areas: creative design, manufacturing, and marketing. They are inescapably connected. One could not survive without the others. It is a garden variety of codependency. So the health of the New York office and the many branch offices around the country and in foreign venues was critical to the ultimate survival and success of the manufacturing environment. Of course, before I made my first trip to New York City many years earlier, no one had told me it was twenty years from the mill village by telephone. Even so, the city still has a special way of attracting the adventuresome and inspiring the young. If it ever loses that, it will greatly diminish its domain. The real world has a way of fooling you into believing that life is simply for the taking; it's not.

I attended Harvard Business School AMP in two well-stuffed summers in 1978–1979 and after graduating relocated to New York City in the consumer products division, the branded flagship image of the Company. The lifeblood of the mill villages flowed swiftly downhill from marketing, merchandising, and design to the broad manufacturing facilities, with communications and relationships between the two areas critical to the success of the whole organization. There were completely different mindsets that had to be bridged to find common ground. One could not make it without the other. I loved everything about New York. Psychologically and viscerally, it could get an iron grip on the imagination, as Yankees placed a high value on cleverness, sophistication, ambiguity, and resonant words. By our nature we learn to see clouds from both sides but always dream upwards.

Yankees also talk a little funny. Being from Alabama, I initially needed an interpreter, but they were easy to find and not too expensive. Ambiguity and language were arresting features of working in that hyperactive environment, and big words were important for utility. People liked to hedge their bets. It became a suspension between two distinct states of mind: equivocation and clarity. You just had to learn to sort it out. Quite different from our little mill villages, where people were more straightforward. It seemed that in marketing, as opposed to manufacturing, rarely were one's reasons identical with your motives. I had to quickly grasp a wide variety of new skill sets while imagining and adjusting to people with different codes and customs. Integrity was essential and as present in our little towns as a permanent watermark. It was reflected in feelings and had a way of grabbing you by the heart and mind. NYC was completely different.

Even though I lived uptown, there were times I still felt like the poor kid from the basement in Alabama, but that feeling quickly passed. I stayed in New York City almost eight years, the longest of the thirty-five or so management jobs I had in a pivoting career. The surprising thing was that by the time I returned to the South, my grandmother's vision of thirty years earlier was on target. I had become a true Yankee at heart, a peddler. Untruthful reality is rarely an Instagram photo you like to show others and brag about. In fact, it is often heavily weighed by specificity that imposes certain truthful constraints we like to avoid. During those engaging years, there were few unmeaningful throwaway vignettes; they each seemed to coalesce into their own place in the whole. Each experience was a new point along a changing arc, not the real arc itself.

Life has a funny way of intruding on our routine and teaching us something new when we least expect it. This is especially true where creativity and innovation are concerned, and the value presented is not only in the idea but also in the packaging. It can be a simple thought, with incisive product accoutrements, interspersed with an inventive presentation and a polished patina. So it is with a bright mind in need, thinking out of the ordinary. Of course, it's much easier to recognize an original idea, an innovative event, or unique thought than it is to actually create one. Where crisis of confidence is concerned, we are usually guilty of our own indiscretions, or maybe it's just a reality estrangement and an expedient embrace of the impractical.

While in the city, I was only a few blocks from the office. It was pretty clear that I wasn't working in a mill village anymore. The economy was in terrible shape. Jobs were as scarce as hen's teeth. I was senior vice president of the consumer products division, with perhaps 25,000 employees in the Company at the time. We hadn't employed anyone in New York City in several months, and neither had our competitors. We had over two hundred employees working out of our New York office. There were literally tens of thousands of college graduates and experienced people walking the streets of the financial capital of the world, desperately looking for a job. The business cycle was in a deep ditch.

In the Big Apple, everyone is always in a hurry. But on one particular day, some distance ahead of me, standing on the corner of 6th Avenue and 48th Street was a well-dressed young man. He wasn't moving or walking fast like everyone else, but just simply standing there on the busy corner. As I got closer, I noticed that he was dressed in a nicely pressed dark gray suit with a white button-down and a striped repp tie, an American flag pin in his lapel. It was the IBM dress exemplar for that time. He was cleanly shaven, his hair combed and his shoes shining. He presented a stiff dose of good taste and thoughtful practicality.

When he saw me walking toward him, he turned and faced me with a pleasant smile. Then I saw it. He had a neatly printed white sign with black letters tied around his neck. It said, and I paraphrase, "My mind is not empty. It is full of creative ideas and potential. I have a college education. I just need a job. If you will take a chance on me, I promise I won't disappoint you." It was signed "Bruce." I remember it well, because that's also my name, my son's name, and my grandson's name. I was very impressed, smiled, and said "Good luck" as I passed him. He smiled back. I thought about him several times that busy morning, and I wished we could have brought him aboard. It dawned on me that perhaps we all search too much for the tried and true, the normal, easy version of the answer. Yet everyone is looking for the same thing—innovation, which helps bring our dreams to fruition. A change of life doesn't have to be monumental. It can also be just a simple conversion of attitude and way of thinking. However, creative change coupled with improvement is not taking a red door and repainting it red. Neither is it turning on the air conditioning to make it cold enough to build a fire to get warm.

We human beings are awakened each day to a fresh influx of *everything* as it waits, pausing for our attention and erudite decisions—or not. Innovation is very powerful and an important part of success's equation, especially when it reaches out to engage the more impressionable of all spaces: the mind. It can be strongly transitional, which is why we usually learn so much more from the before and after stories. Inventiveness becomes a wellspring of inspiration and reflects one's personal aesthetic, as it begins to bring out the best in problems when it presents itself in the transformative process. No thoughts ever arrive in the mind without some kind of weight and substance. Like freshly ground coffee, our thinking just heats up and percolates what's waiting there for action. If there is nothing of value present, it becomes a weak and tasteless brew. This young man was on target. Thinking is always the delivery system for innovation, but it helps if one has imaginative determination. The wise person knows there is futility in that which has little value and doesn't really count. I guess as Americans we all work the same side of the philosophical street; we just walk in different directions.

When I went to lunch that day, I was going to stop and speak to him, but he was gone. I never saw him again. I liked his candor, his initiative. He used his creative thinking to set himself apart from the thousands of others looking for the same job. You see, his approach was simple but creative, far outside ordinary thinking regarding positive self-promotion. I'm sure someone liked his unique, inspiring overture and hired him that particular morning. In a very small difference, he set himself apart and above all the rest. The others were just thinking about their own personal, desperate need for employment. That unique young man was rationalizing beyond that level. He was trying to think of what would motivate someone else to employ him. Where creativity is concerned, it's usually the little things that set us apart from all the rest and gives one the advantage over another. The same is true for character.

Years ago, I read that artificial intelligence will never offset natural stupidity, and I find that reinforced every single day. We have come to let Twitter, Facebook, blogs, and social media become the dirty bathroom wall of the 21st century. Cruelty and bullying are written on walls with lipstick and felt tip pens from behind anonymous small screens, exuding crass, hurtful tirades. Sometimes in our naïve innocence we still don't want to accept, as Dorothy discovered, that the Wizard of Oz is just a middle-aged man from Hoboken nervously living out his fantasy.

We want to believe that magic and wizardly solutions will come along to solve our problems, but that's just not the way life works. It's still pretty much up to you and me. Plain common sense better equips you to maneuver through the rough bumps in the road. As a pinched kid, I came to understand that wisdom begins when one recognizes what a precondition to reality is. That's when we fully comprehend our vulnerability. Perhaps it's simply Mother Nature's way of enhancing her children's survival skills in the real world.

The future, in its many manifestations, will not fit smoothly into the grooves of yesterday. We have to plow and plant seeds that will sprout and grow into crops of learning and performance. The crop is called creativity. The well-worn competitive territory has been rerouted on a different road that has a much higher speed limit. The wise man knows that we are far from perfect, but his greatest deception is that he won't suffer from his own shortcomings. Like Narcissus of mythic infamy, our human philosophy falls in love with its own distorted image, and it usually drowns in the shallow end of the pool. That young man standing on the corner of 6th Avenue and 48th Street can swim in deep water and had already read the book on creative success. He is now probably writing a revised edition for his lucky new employer. In the real world, we must individually learn to think strategically. Yet we still exist in our ordinary thoughts and language, which is part of our universal instinct, determining how we process Southern Reality. Behind every degree of wonder there is a sense of possibility. Why, a good writer can travel long distances in a single sentence and explore decades in a simple paragraph.

New York is deeply engaged in one's own personal marketing, and in that environment, if we are not careful, we can become affected by our own mythology. Too often we ignore the important things in life and meticulously autopsy the minutia. This young man knew we were in an answer-hungry moment in time, and he had broken the creative code of the real world. He understood that innovation is nothing but a slow curve ball, over the outside corner of the plate when the batter is least expecting it. We should just remember that actuality has been around a long time, and I don't think it's going away any time soon. In the innovative planning process, the main thing is to keep the main thing. He recognized that.

30

The Mama Bird

Along the way, I determined that we should be very careful about what we say or do, especially in front of children. If not, we could become chaos magnets, pinballing around, taking off down Google rabbit holes, and looking for unfounded substance and empty sustenance in our lives. Don't fool yourself; children are very perceptive and don't miss much. One day my five-year-old granddaughter Annie—who was an early book-looker and is now a psychiatrist—and I were driving very slowly by the corporate office in West Point. She said, "Papa, why are you driving so slow?" I responded, "Because we are in a residential area, honey, and that's the law!" She added, "And you don't want to break all your wine bottles!" "And that too," I said. I was proud this sharp little dude called me Papa. Yet it's still a delicious deceit to say I was Southern born, Alabama bred, and mill-village raised, which makes me sound like a Chattahoochee River catfish. Maybe it's just a humblebrag on my part.

Growing up in the South, one learns that values and character are a community kind of thing and one's authenticity is an invitation to be a part of the equation. We can only blame ourselves for our predicament. There is no excuse, but I have discovered that if I don't stay busy, my Philistine mind begins to wander to places it has no business being. In the real world, few of us could teach master classes in character, morality, or good taste. I am still puzzled as to why we spend so much money trying to find intelligent life in our galaxy, or the far reaches of the universe, when we can't even find it in Washington, D.C. In travels over the years, I have noticed that not a single microwave dish or telescope searching for rational life in the cosmos is pointed toward our capital. Southern discernment, where are you when so desperately needed?

When we lived in Kennebunkport, Maine, in 1969–1970, it was literally on the seashore. You could throw a stone from the front porch and hit the Atlantic Ocean. We frequently took the kids walking on the rough pebbled beach in summer and winter because it was unique compared to sandy Southern beaches and so appealing to the eye. The shore was covered in beautiful striated and rounded granite pebbles, ocean smoothed over eons, ranging from the size of small pinheads to marbles, stunning stones up to the dimension of your fist, and much larger. One day I looked down and by chance spotted an exquisite, perfectly heart-shaped stone. I had never seen one before from our many walks. It was beautiful.

I guessed that out of the untold trillions of stones on the beach, luck, and the abrasion of the sea by random selection, at least one would be shaped like a heart. Then, as I started to look closely for more intriguing choices, I found several hearts, gradually accumulating a small collection

West Point Pepperell, Inc., Biddeford Mills, Biddeford, Maine.

in random sizes. It seemed that the more hearts I looked for, the more I found, just like with people. I then came to realize that whatever it is you are searching for will usually be found if you try hard enough. I believe if you truly look with an open mind, whatever you beckon will soon be beckoning you. The best memories are usually made with forethought from inside the head and heart.

After completing that multi-mill project in Biddeford, Maine, we returned to the South and I became head of corporate industrial engineering for a time. I have always had a soft spot and special place in my heart for children of all ages, so I gave my unique rock collection to a little seven-year-old girl named Hannah, a neighbor lobsterman's daughter. I said, "Hannah is such a pretty name. How did you get it?" She said, "Mother named me Hannah because it's special. You can spell it backwards and forward and it always spells and means the same." She was as cute as a butterfly, extremely diplomatic, and was very happy. She said, "This collection is the most beautiful thing that anyone has ever given me." That really did make me feel good and helped make up for the loss of my prized gathering. She said, "I have never seen stones like this before, and I have lived on the seashore all my life." I told her it was because she hadn't been looking for hearts, just like I had done in the beginning. She said, "I'm going to start looking for hearts everywhere I go, from this very day." I hope she did.

I always admired the Mama Bird sitting quietly and patiently on her brood of nest eggs each spring. She is a vision of responsibility, dedication, and warmth, often ignoring personal safety to protect her family. There used to be one that every year had her nest and brood of babies at the top of the same post on our front porch in Fairfax. Then when the eggs hatch, she tirelessly brings back food for the nestlings to eat, nurturing and teaching them how to fly. She teaches them everything they need to know until they are strong and wise enough to leave the nest and go out into the world, flapping their wings on their own. This familial dedication and affectionate expression of love and care puts humans to shame. Shouldn't common sense tell us to be as thoughtful, and set as positive an example, with the same integrity for our own progeny? The Mama Bird is profoundly dedicated. Even with such a small brain to guide her, she knows the difference between right and wrong. In turn, she has set an example for her offspring to follow.

Perhaps we have taken the enormous capacity of the human mind and filled it with too much personal greed and selfishness, leaving little for our children or anything else that's meaningful. We humans are creative people, although weighed mightily by our own twisted expectations and shortcomings. The primary functions of a family are to provide each of its members a place of security, peace, love, belonging, learning, and mental comfort. Compared to the tiny Mama Bird, we are not even close to our human potential. One of our weaker traits is that we don't like to analyze ourselves too closely. When we do, we may not like what we see. We know that such a truthful insight will diminish the self and our falsely embellished personhood. The deeds where our family are concerned will either tabulate our faults or foreshadow the waiting blessings of what's ahead; they rarely do both. We litter the margins of life with broken promises to ourselves, forgetting that introspection is always the beginning of wisdom. Yet it's easy to get into the habit of dishonest self-examination, because our

Three wild birds in a nest in 1992—granddaughters—l to r—Annie, Hannah, and Molly.

thoughts patiently sit in the mind, anchored by facts and well-established truths clamoring to be used.

Children are an expensive impermanence, because like clockwork they quickly grow up. We may sometimes feel disappointed in our kids, but how do you think they feel about us? Have you even thought about it? It matters! Have we been positive examples, paragons of virtue for them to follow? Like it or not, we become the choral leaders of our families and mill-village choirs, and the choir usually follows the music director's lead. We should never leave children grasping in isolation and loneliness, looking for direction, without love and affection or the ability to connect to a family with this substance. The examples set by parents are the symbols of a child's loftiest dreams and ambitions. They are simply baby birds in waiting, not yet fully grown and able to fly on their own. Yet we have an increasing tendency to abdicate our familial responsibilities as though they were insignificant, usually because we embrace too much self. Life is not automatically prognostic. It just lives out the personal decisions we make—positive and negative—one by one.

I sometimes think we humans have finally arrived and don't have a clue where we are because we didn't know where we were going in the first place. So never ask a woman eating ice cream directly out of the carton with a tablespoon how her love life is going. It also dawned on me one day that women who are substantially overweight live longer than the men who tell them.

Looking back, as a Papa Bird, there are few things other than select memories and some choice people that I want to bundle in tissue paper or bubble wrap for safekeeping. If we are not careful in our arc and purpose, we will be weighed heavily by our personal counterfeit. We face a perennial challenge with the truth and don't want facts to get in the way. Perhaps our most common prayer should be, "May God protect me from myself."

Curiosity has been the driving force in mill villages and humanity's evolution since day one, and hopefully this will never change. Curiosity let loose in a child can be like an eighty-foot oak tree: impossible to jam back into the acorn. Growing up I was not preternaturally mature or unusually precocious; I was just a small town boy blessed with equanimity in a problem-saturated age. I discovered that inventiveness is like keys turning in old rusty locks as progressive change caroms around in a loose ramble, hopefully touching all relevant bases. I don't pretend to have all the answers, yet village wisdom hasn't completely abandoned me, and I try not to get it too mixed up with fantasy. But recently I have been thinking too much about the many contradictions and complexities of our lives. Wouldn't it be great if Monday was actually the fun day of the week? If cheeseburgers, milkshakes, and junk food didn't make you fat? Why couldn't we be lucky enough for sweatpants to be sexy as well as comfortable? Wouldn't life be so much simpler and more fun if guys were just a little more comprehendible? Wouldn't we all be happier if girls weren't so self-conscious? Why couldn't a smile always be sincere and a hug mean I love you? What if goodbye only meant until I see you tomorrow? We all swim through dark waters, but there is absolutely no reason to swim alone. I'm still trying to figure out why the taste of sour cream pound cake blinds you to all its caloric flaws. Sometimes I am disappointed with myself when I think about what other people think about, when they are thinking about what other people think they are thinking. Glad I could get that off my chest.

What it's all about in 2002—grandchildren: front, Bruce III and Sarah Beth; back, from left, Claire, Georgia, Gerald, Annie, Hannah, and Molly.

I've found through extensive experience that life in so many ways is all about corners, like going around the block time and again. You round a corner and face the unknown, but by the time you get your act back together, there is another corner looming ahead. You just keep turning, running into the unexpected. You never seem to arrive at your appointed destination; it's always somewhere ahead. So we spend our life turning corners. Yet I have never known a single person that became exceptional by accident while standing still. There are always a few times in life where everyone needs to exceed expectations.

Truth is also becoming harder to define. It behaves like a long string of ones and zeros in a binary code that keeps changing, jumping back and forth at will. It has become taxing to just be a plain and simple human being. Frequently I think we wear the character equivalent of an oversized nightshirt and become very loose in its confinements. We have a way of purposefully distorting the facts, trying to give ourselves a little boost. I'm still waiting for the post-veracity era to depart so that all comments and proclamations can once again be based on truth and not alternative facts. For me, upholding Southern sagacity simply means mill village honesty. Responsibility and wisdom have always been cut from the same cloth. If you don't believe me, just ask a Mama Bird. Maybe we all need to go with little Hannah and look for some more hearts. There are plenty out there, looking for us.

I have come to believe that the best measure of a father and mother, twenty-five years down the road, is if your children and grandchildren still enjoy hanging out with you. The Mama Bird knows that life is really quite simple: it's all about making wise choices. Why, if I had to choose between drinking wine every day or being thin and sexy, I'm not sure whether I would choose red or white.

31

The Hostile Takeover

Dreamweavers have a way of conniving our nature and nurture, bringing back yesterday's thoughts along with culinary aromas and the kitchen's savory whiffs. The real world also carries a certain infectious seductiveness in its sensory immersion while life is busy with simple existence, fraught with harsh competiveness. There is an unending inventory of echoes rebounding in my head. They rest on the lintel of possibility about yesterday's values that are missing today, and the memory is not gender perfect. But there is one intellection that stands out above all, one particular "hostile takeover." It can become the most rapacious capitalism one can imagine, as the world transitions into a very slippery place, as if coated in WD-40. Each day is an audition, and it is designed to make us remember what we don't have and cause us to want things we really don't need. It's okay to look back in the rear-view mirror; just don't look too long or stare. Remember what happened to Lot's wife! That's why truth is much like the Holy Bible: you can misinterpret it, doubt it, or ignore it, but you can't change it.

I clearly remember sitting around the big kitchen table hand-in-hand, in laughter and genial conversation. Public school was challenging, and growing up in a boarding house—among many other places—was a unique experience. This was especially true of a stretch during World War II when husbands and fathers were away and mothers were working in the factories. The danger and concern for the future was close at hand and many times in doubt. Yet, in over two hundred years, no one ever made a dime betting against America. Now that era seems like the Cretaceous Period. This may not be scintillating stuff where pain and heartbreak are concerned, but in this country, the ground has been especially well-plowed with discontent in recent years, as leaders have come to accept a more flexible notion of ethics and character. I'm not sure we would do much better if our performance was graded on a curve.

The South has always been in the deep mental grip of the past. In the late 1980s, other parts of the country joined the Southern contingent in a painful transition to an uncertain economy. There was once a certain small town isolation that wasn't all bad. In fact, it sometimes bled into the big city. It gave everyone a certain comfort as it separated ordinary people from a fast-changing economic and technological conversion. It became a head-on confrontation with a knowledge economy, weighed by increasing world technology, free trade, and global ultra low-wage competition. This pending transmutation could be clearly understood by the Southern mind. Most could see the high-speed train of change coming down the tracks but just hoped it would pass on through their little towns and villages and go away with minimum effect. It didn't. The political seeds of dire transformation and disruption had been planted and would grow out of control like weeds. It was a path the powers that be had decided to pursue, whether it was advantageous to the U.S. and middle-income Americans or not. It was all in the eye of the beholder, and politicians generally were lawyers, had astigmatism, didn't live in small towns, and had never worked in industry. How wrong the decision makers were. . .

Unknowingly, we resided in little backwaters of timeworn papier-mâché. Few days passed by without misgivings or a weak flutter of doubt. Perhaps we were spoiled, even too trusting. Then, in a transitioning world, the dependable and historic West Point Company changed ownership in a hostile corporate takeover. The new owners quickly dropped a line verifying the plumb. It was nothing unordinary for that time, nothing unknown. We were just preparing for Cicero's famed Sword of Damocles to fall. When it did a short while later, it left a hefty cloud of dust containing tomorrow's dreams. We all love excitement when it's in our favor, but this was not the case. So many people, including production employees and managers of all ages, were gradually unemployed in a crumbling world, left behind with nowhere to go and so much of their future hollowed out. It was like a runaway train speeding down the tracks: you knew it was going to wreck, but didn't know exactly when. We were certain that when it did, it would be devastating, and it was. It brought a darkness that thrummed like a deep bass line being struck, one that would never rise back up to tenor. The hurt had a gestation period like none other in memory.

The "historically" robust West Point (Pepperell) Stevens Company was being pulled down a fast-moving river by a try-anything current that quickly prevailed. The fat lady hadn't started to sing, but she was in the proscenium with the microphone in hand and was clearing her throat. Adverse periods, when cotton was king, were finally brought into many mill-village group portraits. In one corner, there was a huge corporate debt accumulated in the buyout that had to be paid back. In the other corner, an emerging flat world with high-tech machinery, free trade, changing competitive winds, and low-wage imports squeezed profits, jobs, and life out of manufacturing corporations and families across the land. These were the same families that had helped generate prosperity, strengthen the American middle class, and build our dreams. Now there were problematic years encompassing intellectual, emotional, and spiritual exhaustion. Instead of receiving encouragement, everyone fell through the open trapdoor. The day the plants finally began to close was the same day the center of a classically self-contained world disappeared for good. In a free-trade philosophy, you are either an invited guest with a favored seat at the table or part of the menu, which changes daily.

The voicelessness of those affected—management, employees, and the community—was irrelevant. There was little creative triage for the injury at hand, and no need for an Oxford English Dictionary to interpret words for the outcome. After 120 years, the shareholders had decided the Company's fate was only in the value of the shares, and corporate hostile takeovers were a new way of life. There were economics as well as elements of spiritual calling—even a frisson of fear—but no amusement by accident or design. Reality had begun to tear the sentimental veneer off village life. There were days in which we felt we were drowning on dry land. It seemed as if limitless quivers full of sharp arrows were waiting for their targets to appear. We humans have an inherited trait of carrying our experiences around in our heads like an open conscience, remembering what we want and leaving the rest behind, often ignoring the most hurtful threads woven into the fabric we design. The hostile takeover is one experience we would like to forget but can't.

The world behaves more in emotional dysfunction than as a safe harbor to anchor a seriously listing ship. It was impossible to destigmatize the inimitable Company capture, because it was foolhardy to try to escape the staged melodrama bubbling up in the process. Everyone was perplexed, faced with a stacked deck and looking for an escape hatch that didn't exist. At the end of the day, all that was left was the painful curiosity of the unknown challenge, with the eventual value of its history, in the transformative second guesses and think pieces that followed. Even the self-possessed alpha male, with a tendency to free associate truths for extra inspiration, was at wits end. Everyone was trying not to press all the hurt they were feeling into the moment, but it was hard to rest or sleep with a broken spirit. There was airlessness in uncertainty that needed a firmer foundation. It's not necessarily the initial explosion from a combative unfriendly takeover that gets you, but more often the mental secondary and tertiary flying shrapnel.

There were many capable, exceedingly talented managers in the West Point Manufacturing Company that grew up in these mill towns. A college co-op scholarship program was initiated at Auburn in the mid-1950s by Joseph L. Lanier Sr., a farsighted West Point CEO visionary. Almost every participant was born in our mill villages and were second, third, or fourth-generation employees. William Lane, Richmond Terry, Charles Crowder, and Lanny Bledsoe were exceptions, just to name four of many. This extended group had a major stake in growing the Company to become the largest, most diversified in the textile industry.

In 1988 West Point Pepperell acquired J.P. Stevens in a white knight merger, a rescue mission that ultimately resulted in the Company becoming the largest, most diversified publicly owned textile company in North America (if not the world). We integrated J.P. Stevens manufacturing, marketing, products, and retail stores into our new organization: West Point (Pepperell) Stevens, Inc. This corporate merger was one of the many triggers in the rapidly evolving trend in corporate American history known as "hostile takeovers." These were outside acquisitions opposed by incumbent management. It quickly became clear that the overspill of what was ahead would not be protected by little bubble wraps of white space, and the ranging decisions to be made would be cold to the touch. It was the experience of a pending nightmare from which one will never wake up, even more difficult than Pythagoras trying to explain his theorem. To minimize the hurt, one is told to rip the Band-Aid off quickly, but fast or slow, the pain defied description.

In 1989, one year after the WPP-Stevens merger, a major battle ensued in a New York Stock Exchange bidding war between Farley Industries of Chicago and WPS CEO Joseph L. Lanier Jr., a very competent executive in West Point. Joe Lanier was well liked and highly respected by Company employees and management. Eventually CEO William (Bill) Farley of Farley Industries—which also controlled Fruit of the Loom and other companies—won the public stock battle. After an acrimonious bidding and public relations war, Farley Industries purchased 95 percent of WPS stock at $58/share for a total of $1.7 billion, 20 times earnings and 2.2 times book value. Considering the precarious nature of the American textile industry, the acquisition was substantially overpriced by knowledgeable opinions. Yet there were even more painfully damaging management transitions to come before the mills, property, and other assets began to be sold off and facilities closed. There was a perilous river to navigate (or not). To help pay down the huge new corporate debt, extensive assets had to be sold. I was asked to sell some of the retail properties. Then, when I retired from West Point Stevens in 1992 to become president and CEO of Johnston Industries, we bought the iconic Wellington Sears Company Industrial Division from West Point. I had been production controller of the division a number of years earlier.

In the hostile takeover, reality was stacked against everyone—even the winners. It brought mental, physical, and economic discomfort with a straight-up hurt to thousands of people in the shadow of open capitalism and free enterprise. The dynamic was completely destabilizing to the mill village communities and had highly damaging elliptical side glances on the broader stratum of local society. One of the key things missing from the past was trust in others, which is a lofty certainty that denotes action without thought. Life takes on a slight sepia tint if we don't fully embrace it, when without confidence or hopefulness we seem to fall off the page between the cracks. Either way it brought on an alienation and reaching estrangement with actuality. Under the circumstances, it was hard to walk down emptying mill-village streets with a smile on your face. The next few years were like a three-ring circus without any of the fun. We were trying to flip the script, like unchoreographed whirling dervishes dancing in an elusive atmosphere of possibility as confounding as a square circle, a round square, or a rectangular triangle.

Bill Farley was a demanding executive, clearly under great financial pressure and frequently rather harsh where his Farley Industries and WPS executives were concerned. He was not once acerbic or rude to me in any way, and we had what I would consider a civil relationship, as I reported to him for almost three years. However, you learn that you can't comfortably carry around your sensibilities in a sealed Mason jar for long without dropping and breaking it.

Farley Industries didn't make it, and in December 1993, in another ownership change, the West Point acquisition obtained the balance of Farley bankruptcy stock and merged with several subsidiaries to restructure. Over the next seven to ten years, as cheap imports began to precipitously rise from low-wage countries, plants demanding greater capital investments—with diminishing profit margins—began to close. Gradually the Chattahoochee Valley plants and other manufacturing locations discontinued their operations. From a peak of ten thousand employees in the local area, mill village employment dropped to zero. Life for the wonderful mill villages across the land just became too toxic. Reality was a timely central thesis, shaking everyone left fully awake in the middle of the day. It was unbelievable this could happen. No one ever thought that with such a deep lauded Company history something would come along and blow everything up, but here we were. In the competitive world we never dispense with subjectivity. So, when is a mill village no longer a mill village? When there are no longer any mills. Without a paternal corporation on the scene, it was time for everyone to worry about the "daily me."

Perhaps the handwriting was on the wall that very first day. At the time of the Farley takeover, there were several top Company executives in a special corporate compensation program. I was one of them, having been in over thirty different management positions and at the time president of one of the five operating divisions. A new slate of Farley officers was brought in the first day. Then most of the top West Point (Pepperell) Stevens management were marched into the board room one by one and interviewed by the new Farley team, which had generally never met them.

Each approached the closed board room door at the pace of a New Orleans funeral dirge without the music, uncomfortable in the rhythm of the moment. It was a paradigm of indirection down a deep rabbit hole, probably never to return. For those strangers waiting around the table for the interrogation, they ran the whole gamut of management emotions from A to B. I looked around the room for a smile, camaraderie, even empathy, but there was nothing there, no faces around the table without an edge. It was a flamboyant example—in an overstated imitation—of what new leadership should never do. It was strange entering the adversarial room, alone in a solemn procession of one, where so many historic decisions had been made over the years. It was the kind of meeting where you clear your voice twice before speaking and then grudgingly decide to say little, if anything. In two days, most of the corporate management that I had worked with for many years had been terminated. This rapid transition left the few remaining in a surprisingly frosty draft downhill from cold power.

It was a time of heavy disquiet, a season of the greatest transition in the history of the Company. As each of us entered the board room that eventful day, the future was unknowable. The climate had a dramatic change, and a new storm was breaking in every thought. It was impossible to find pleasure in the moment or even anticipate it in the future. There was a distinct lack of empathy and sensibility in the new group. Paying down the new heavy debt was the only objective. Life was starting to take shape in fast forward, with a lot of half-court rim-shot gestures that missed. A corporate world is always fed by a culture of performance.

I stayed for almost three years, reporting directly to Bill Farley. There were excellent job offers to leave during that time. After thirty-nine years, I was in a difficult position, because I was so attached to individuals I had mentored, those who had worked under my supervision, and the many that

I had enticed to join our organization during my tenure. To leave them in a hostile and questionable environment was difficult. So, I stayed much longer than originally intended, until I couldn't take the continuing demise and demeanor of the new Company any longer. I had started when there were only about nine thousand employees in the organization and served in many management positions as it grew to its eventual size of over forty-two thousand. At the time, I had been promoted back to New York City as corporate executive vice president of Merchandising. I finally left to become president and chief operating officer (later CEO) of another corporation in New York City. The rapidly deteriorating health of the West Point organization presented very sad days on Combs Street in Fairfax, where I was born, and in every single mill village in the Company.

The Chattahoochee River seemed to barely move the particular day I left, as if it was in mourning with me and all the people in the mill villages who would eventually lose their jobs. A few years later, with a heavy hand, the lights were turned off for the last time. Life is the fabric we weave, but traditions that emerge from experiences are the threads we use and are clearly in the real patterns we design. So it was! It's hard for the head to float without judgment as it looks for a comforting anchor. Yet wisdom is realizing we are the only somebody we will ever be. So, thinking deeply, I subconsciously just bit my lip a little harder. Truth was no longer relational; it became transitional, and we would have been so much better off if its original lifespan had lasted longer. But truth is always near at hand. It simply depends on whether we want to know it or not. Honesty is a palate cleanser, freeing the mind from dangerous frustrations but placing one in the precarious crosshairs of reality.

Years later I walked down Combs Street in Fairfax looking for the ghosts of my past, but they had long departed. In my revisit, the mill village seemed sad, lonesome, and glad to see me, as if it knew that I would come back one day. I could feel the past grasping me in a warm grip, trying to pull me back to better days that had lost their promise. There had never been "Don't Walk on the Grass" signs around the expansive mill. Now they would be unnecessary, because there is no longer any grass, or even a mill. I stood there on a lonely sidewalk on Boulevard, looking at the huge rubble-strewn acreage engulfing the entire block that was once the center of my life and where many dreamspinners like me had lived. Where for ninety years a massive four-story manufacturing plant had resided, there was only a forlorn vacant lot. A place where more than two thousand people had once worked was now covered in tall weeds and debris. Not a single person was in sight. Once there were living, breathing, animated buildings of over two million square feet, which I walked many, many times. I can now only see them in my mind.

This same view could probably be multiplied over forty times, reflecting the demise of the once robust West Point Companies. Five miles north in Lanett, the same scene occurred, as Lanett Mill and Lanett Bleachery and Dye Works (three thousand employees) were coming down. I had heard that the Guinness Book of World Records stated in the 1940s that Lanett Mill was the largest manufacturing plant in the world under one roof.

Closing mills not only affected jobs and personal economics of the people and the broader community, but inflicted considerable family, civic, and collateral hardships and damage. It was the aggressive affront that you would

Lanett Mill in 1968.

expect. After all those years, when the mills were silenced, the ensuing scene made your jaw drop. The pathological almost became ordinary. Losing one's job without personal cause harshened a dependable Southern trademark once mellow and amiable. It was not like a big city where there were other job options. It was so disheartening that it made you crazy miserable, but it was not quite bad enough to put you out of your misery. Since caveman days, humans by their very nature used identity with something bigger as a progressive upward, comforting mental advancement but also serving as a defensive weapon. Now that was all gone. Reality and self have a way of yanking one to a whole new lower level of uncertainty.

Today, in every town, faded houses meander down numerous streets from which the many closed and demolished manufacturing plants once stood like the stretching legs of a dead octopus. Realism is what's left when people lose their jobs and have to leave their future and self-interest at home. All across the nation, we have now witnessed a storyline of pain and lack of progressive leadership for this very reason. Leaders are always in search of a bottom line with the lowest economic denominator. Now jobs have departed, leaving the salt of the earth that built this nation—the condiment of blue-collar flavor—behind. Trust became a much plundered treasure, an improvisational stage for all of us bit actors, making the world go 'round and human nature churn.

Final corporate decisions across the country were pursued with empty coffers and thin pasteboard hearts, reflecting economics in a rapidly changing free-trade world. In hundreds of mill villages across America, everyone sat and waited for a miracle. But it didn't show up, and reality completely voided boundless families and good manufacturing jobs across the land. West Point was only a small part of the over one million textile and apparel jobs that disappeared in small and large towns across the reaching horizon. There were many gestures, but with little substance or weight, promises were an empty offering at a distant altar. This was reflection of the devastating demise of manufacturing of all kinds in this country, which put a crimp in middle-class, blue-collar neighborhoods and millions of good people out of work, reduced to lower paying jobs.

I can clearly remember as a little boy in a mill village that there were only three times: daytime, nighttime, and when the whistle blew at shifttime. Now there was no time, unless it was one of those times you feel like getting back in bed and pulling the covers up over your head. But you can't; you have to go out and look for a new job. After the hostile takeover, everyone was just waiting for the next shoe to drop from that many-footed centipede. Everyone in the mill villages was shell-shocked, just simple people living in a tightly knit world trying to survive and keep up appearances. So much of life is in a hurry, defined by time and circumscribed in the hands of a clock in constant motion, with or without you.

No one ever wants to go through a phase—good or bad—that asserts its true meaning by completely undoing itself. Such was the case on those eventful days when all machines in the Greater Valley gradually went silent, gates were locked, and whistles blew their last welcoming call. All job vacancies were filled, because now there were no jobs. It's extremely difficult to clear the mind of external distractions and painful obstacles when it requires one's full targeted attention to find a new living-wage job. Especially when they don't exist! It's also impossible to have a calmness and sense of purpose when those feelings are wed in a long-lasting partnership with stress and anxiety. The river of pain and suffering is always the same no matter where you step in.

We would all prefer a providential ending like in the movies, but not everyone is lucky enough to ride off into the sunset like Clint Eastwood. In retrospect, creativity and invention have always been renewable resources that rode in to rescue us in American history. Maybe we are beginning to find that's not true in every movie, though.

Think with me for a minute. In the real economic world, jobs are not a fantasy of residence. Anything man-made can be done better and cheaper somewhere else, and it may not be in your hometown or even your nation. It's just simply the cadence of a flat Earth economic system and increasing education and technology coming home to roost. When you are on flat ground and have nowhere else to go, you realize that whatever your personal mountain is, you've got to start climbing. Everyone in the world wants their share of equality and fairness. Yet all one can do is tighten one's belt with determination, stand up straight, and start over. I have thought many times

Above: Fairfax Mill in 1968 before closing. Below: Fairfax Mill in 2018 after closing and demolition.

that that's exactly what my grandfather and father had to do. Why should fate smooth the way for me? In the capitalistic system, the imagination is a counterweight to reality, promising triumph over low expectations. We are all waiting with stool in hand looking for cash cows that need milking, but there weren't any left in the mill-village pasture.

An opinion without knowledge is simply loose supposition. We like to pull back the curtain to see what's there because we know that every culture has its own straw men onto which we can pass along the blame for our own shortcomings. Now Bobby Jones clearly understood that. He was the greatest amateur golfer in the world in the 1920s and '30s. Later on, he suffered from a tragic and debilitating disease. One day a friend asked him, "Bobby, what do you think about your illness, your infirmity?" Bobby replied, "In golf, we play the ball where it lies." So it is with each of us. We can't fully control our circumstances, but we have to move on the best we can from where we are presently located in life's continuum. We only realize and fully appreciate the importance of warmth and light when we are standing all alone in the harsh, cold darkness.

Looking back on when the mills were closed, I searched high and low for a happy man, but I couldn't find one. I just gave up and went out looking for a discontinued ink cartridge for my home printer.

32

Mill Village Reality

A mill village, with all its interesting personalities, was a little dull at times, but it refused to be backward. You can guess how intriguing it was when my favorite excitement was vanilla ice cream. It was closely peopled and tightly knit, with a matter-of-factness and a zigzagged line of communal adherence stitching everyone together—a leftover historical artifact in contemporary times. One could always find comfort in the familiar, and fathers and mothers were never exempt from the expectation that they would also be exemplary. It wasn't hard to tease one out of their small town introversion, because people were bountifully friendly and accommodating. Yesterday just becomes a diaristic presence. Yet it had a strong community bond, mutual interest in cooperative decency, goodwill, and moral character with a grip on reciprocal obligations. There was also a shared identity between the Company, management, and production employees, providing working class families a comforting measure of livelihood, security, paternalistic stability, and promising futures for their children. Ordinary life just happened, in a new unexplored tier of possibility, as we appreciated how much we needed one another. It was clear that happiness had to be shared to be enjoyed.

Each of us is born poor, rich, or some place in-between, and money has nothing to do with it. One's real value is what resides in the head and heart. As a small town boy, I remember warm lazy afternoons quietly sitting on the front porch, reading, thinking, watching the grass grow, listening to my heart beat, and slapping at the buzz of Southern mosquitoes. I never could figure out what was so great about putting a man on the Moon when a cow had already jumped over it, and I couldn't wait for my new cousin to be born to see if I was going to be an aunt or an uncle. I was just pausing on the far side of time in breathless silence, waiting in its depths and shallows. For what, I was not sure. Yet I knew in my head I would recognize it when I saw it. So today there is at least one university teaching experience, two major universities attended, three corporations, twenty-five different homes, twenty-six blue-collar jobs, thirty-five-plus management positions, over eighty honors and recognitions, at least one hundred civic engagements, boxes of personal mill-village archives filled with experiences, and 'a partridge in a pear tree' all stored in my mind waiting to be forensically reconstructed. They lead to an inspirational story of uplift, because on the margins, there is always a certain amount of friction, pushback, and collision built into life's equation. How we handle challenges will reflect our success or failure. I doubt we would have done any better if we had taken a shredder to history and who we were and started over.

We were simply "mustard-seed Protestants," and some gifted people were much more equal than others, shaping self-confidence. Each day, as I looked out the window past the front porch to the sidewalk, I saw many less fortunate people pass by. However, most of us would have probably suffered from an inferiority complex if we had known what it was. Perhaps it just reflected the small-town version of our Darwinian inheritance in an ominous transition. Today's Democrats and Republicans are nearly crossing the threshold of the time-honored inheritance of Cain and Abel. Now I'm not certain karma exists, but I do believe that those who express warmth, compassion, love, and affection toward others are also more likely to receive it.

Friendships were all about the front porch. Every conventional little mill house had one, and it was a simple architectural fixture that played a major role in shaping our Southern hospitality and culture similar to the effect of New England's front parlors. A place to gather day and night, to talk, reminisce, enjoy, plan, and honor, from one generation to the next. Porches were outsized in their significance to small homes, social life, fellowship, and friendship. They were where the community lived most of the year. A place where neighbors and strangers became friends, memories were made and reborn, and stories evolved—some true, some not. It was all in the spirit of honoring civility, where people could laugh and cry while exchanging their narratives of the moment. It just seemed to a little boy and girl that each day was like a big group hug.

The warmth and congeniality present was sometimes hard to see from the sidewalk but was easy to feel when you opened the screen door to smiling faces. There seemed to be little worry about the precision of verbal delivery. Concentration was more on the validity of the thought. In its own way, it was where the life story of the mill village was written, embracing an eclectic theme of so many similar but different tales. Where everyone in town learned your business and personal foibles, but was lenient with the truth and embraced forgiveness. I remember reading somewhere long ago that, "It's not life that's so important, but those people you meet along the way that makes the difference." They were right, and in retrospect, it's amazing how many of them I met on the front porch. Life is both prologue and epilogue, covering all the bases, and no one wants to be considered ambivalent in their own light and shade.

In our little hamlets, we never felt entitled to anything. Our thoughts seemed to cluster in strong ambitions that floated down the swift Chatta-hoochee, waiting for their moment to dock. In a special way, we collectively had our own mill-village style, which didn't include too many cluttered verbs, buttered nouns, ranging adjectives, or elongated prepositions. Even love was more a noun than a verb. We were just plain, ordinary, ambitious folks in an unordinary world, struggling to get by. Everyone in their individual way wanted to carve out their personal niche, a place that was truly one's own, to feel meaningful and not expendable. So we went about painting self-portraits of who we thought we wanted to be, but we learned that if we were going to reach for a star not to choose one too far away. Perhaps somewhere light years distant on another Earth-like planet, in a less petulant and absorbed world, there is less ego driving decisions. Ego arithmetic never adds up; it only subtracts.

Truth is always the first chapter in the book of knowledge, and everyday problems have a way of getting lost inside our head, so we have to learn to curate them. Our little hamlets proved time and again that one out of every three people was just as confused as the other two. It became evident that alternative truths would tear right through the strong fabric of honesty. Reality has a kicker that's hard for one to accept and that is that there is no exit. Part of it is due to hypocrisy, which is tough, thick, hard to chew, and impossible to digest. We humans have been wrestling for eons with our conscience and losing. Yet fact and fiction still exist, even when they are ignored. We should have learned by now to never bungee jump off a high bridge until you are sure the ankle knots are tight.

We never believed that spoons make people fat; that pens and keyboards misspell words; that cars make drivers drunk; that words lie; that report cards give you easy grades; that pens write bad checks; or even that guns kill people. Neither were we naïve and believed the politician who promised everything. His motive is simple: to get elected the first time, or the next. All else is secondary or tertiary. Language has become an expedient subterfuge for integrity and what we don't want to be known. I don't think the fever that was diagnosed has been broken. Mill villagers recognized that we were in various stages of the short-running American experiment, but it had started to deviate off course and was not going according to the original plan devised back in 1776.

Wholeheartedly, we believed in peaceful democratic protest. It's the mill village way, but we should deplore unemployed masked gangs that destroy property, riot, loot, trash police cars, injure people, and torch buildings while demeaning and burning the American flag. Those are the ones that need to be deported, and that action would not be acceptable in our old neighborhood.

Somewhere in our lineage we are all immigrants to this blessed land—to the Native Americans' consternation. It is just a matter of when we arrived. If we go back far enough, we all have an "elsewhere" in our bloodstream, and breaking the law has nothing to do with your origins but with your actions. But for me, Alabama has always been my center of gravity. I well remember Montgomery, and Rosa Parks refusing to give up her seat on a public bus. I wish I had been there with her. She, like the peaceful sit-ins at soda fountain counters, didn't trash the bus and try to burn it. Rosa did it the right way, and it worked. I much prefer that someone tell me

"Well done" than "Well said." Yet no longer do we color the facts staying within the lines, like most of us learned in kindergarten.

Self-interest has made us incurious about the world outside our own, and in turn without sagacity has confined our identities. We have become organized not by political party affiliation as in the past but by group characteristics such as income, education, status, race, gender, religion, sexuality, and geography. We are weighed by identity politics, but most of us don't recognize what it is. We need to constantly and shrewdly rebalance our priorities without paralyzing the capacity to understand and reason, encouraging different people to sit down together and simply talk to one another. Too often when it occurs, it's with individuals who look like us, act like us, talk like us, and think like us. We need different people at the table. We must never forget the one thing we all have in common is citizenship and one another. Democracy is always about compromise.

Personally, I have great confidence in the American people and their eventual judgment. Americans voted for Jimmy Carter for president, even when he might not have been elected governor of Georgia again. His Christian ideals and perceived honesty resonated. They voted for the Bushes because they were recognized as the good guys that wore white hats and loved America. They voted for Barack Obama (at least in part) because he was a talented minority, and they figured that it was time to prove that we had rounded that curve. We voted for Trump in spite of his penurious character, narcissism, low morals, untruthfulness, and depleted values because he was for change, and the good Lord knows we needed that. It seems that we try to find fault with presidents and other leaders just so we don't have to look too closely at ourselves. Political power or authority of any kind, unconstrained by facts, the truth, and wisdom, is not constrained by anything.

Now, as a mill village graduate I'm not sure we get any smarter as we get older—only a little braver. Money and power are staples as well as elastic commodities. They are also the primary way that our society has come to measure success and keep score. But it's not necessarily the best measurement. Giving back is probably the better value for the greater good. That's why mill-town people have always subscribed to the notion that tomorrow will be a brighter day. Although, I'm still trying to figure out what makes one truly happy, because poverty and wealth have both failed. We are uncomfortable composing a full-body portrait of who we are or think we are, because an open mind wanders like a teenager on a first date seeking unexplored territory. Yet it was very clear in our village neighborhood that the American system was designed to float all boats, not just yachts. As time progressed, we became decidedly predictable in our unpredictability.

A Mill Village Story presents a never-ending series of multiple-choice questions. Some pull us into the paths of opportunity, and others point us in the direction of problems. We tend to select those challenges that are relatively easy and make us feel good, all the while trying to avoid those that are hard or with a potential downside. When younger, we trusted our learning head more. As we get older, we tend to make better choices based on experience, but also because we begin to rely more on our intuition or gut feelings, weighed by our hearts. There is a lot of heavy computing power between our ears, and when we learn to couple it with education and wisdom, we make better decisions. Yet we have learned that over the long term veracity and integrity pay the best dividends. Frank Trentmann said, "In 2010, in the thirty-four richest countries in the world, each person consumed over 220 pounds of 'stuff' every day, while in the other 165 countries, children, adults, and the elderly die of starvation each hour." Nothing like that would have ever been acceptable in our mill villages.

One must adjust to becoming more responsive to our discontents. Just don't try to hide your ignorance in plain sight. I've discovered a few bits of village wisdom along the way. Perhaps the most important is that life is completely unfair. If your team comes in second in the World Series in baseball, all the fans call you a loser. At the same time, if you are in medical school and come in dead last out of 212 in your graduating class, they still call you a doctor. It's just not fair. I also learned to never, ever tell other people your problems. For one thing, everyone has a list of their own, and 95 percent don't care about your issues. The other five percent are glad you have them. Another bit of mill village sagacity that I couldn't always follow was that one should never let the demands of your career peep into your private life—although it's much easier said than done.

From the time I was a little boy, until I got older and wiser, I looked out from my sheltered boarding house environment to a new reality that was waiting. Being stretched and living week-to-week was relative in a small town. It wasn't just a condition or statistic; it was also a context in which one simply tried to survive, as longing expectations became one of life's most constant companions. One learns it doesn't help if we continue to do stupid things in intelligent ways. I tried hard to counterbalance the real world with self-deprecating wit. It didn't always work. However, one thing I did discover was that a smile and laughter are the two best ways to improve your looks. I also found there was a discrepancy in the world about what the truth really is. Was it just a loose accumulation of facts, or was it emotionally based, empathetic, motivational, meritorious, and political? Does it just change to meet our personal perspective? Actually, the truth never changes, regardless of our view and whether with a smile or frown. We just need to avoid the idiocracy that can spring up when closed minds are present. Just remember, the wise man never believes everything he thinks or thinks everything he believes. This enlightenment is called common sense. Perhaps we just need to publicize that the brain is an app and maybe people would use it more. Mama would always say, "Just be sure your cornbread is done in the middle before you take it out of the oven."

At the height of the voting season, I was driving through a mill village where I had worked many years ago. The plants are now closed and the machinery is on the scrap heap or on an extended vacation in China or Timbuktu. There were the same red, white, and blue political signs in the front yards everywhere I looked. Each house seemed to be supporting the same candidate—or so I thought—which was a little surprising. I couldn't read them very well at a distance, so I slowed down to see a sign near the street. It said, "Vote for Jesus. He's the only one we can trust." It is a triste day when we come to this. Sadly, where politics are involved, I think President Teddy Roosevelt may have had it right years ago. He said, "When Congress calls the roll, they don't know whether to answer 'Present' or 'Not Guilty.'" I think more corporate leaders and the one percent are starting to read from Teddy's playbook. Trust only exists when grounded in proven experiences and relationships. With so much leadership uncertainty, we must embrace the future the same way amorous hedgehogs do: slowly and carefully.

Now for me, as a mill-village product, where America is presently concerned, I am an eternal optimist. For those that don't fully understand what that means, let me explain. It's like going after Moby Dick in a rubber raft and taking a knife and fork, catsup, and tartar sauce with you.

33

Summing-Up

Don't fool yourself: everything to do with the South is complicated. The people, history, culture, language, politics, religion, relationships, and even food are complex. Looking back at the remembered mill-village account, without all the dust and debris, it's nearly impossible to recall all the multitude of circumstances left in its wake, good and bad. Even facing each day with a smile strikes me as a blessing of nerve. My recollections are usually best early in the morning when it's quiet, coffee in hand, my mind rested and clear, and the heavy clouds of the day haven't yet taken up residence in my head. In this mindset, it has always amazed me that hatred and prejudice could come from the same universe that produces love and compassion—but it does. We become the arbiters of our future as we draw tight concentric circles within which we try to live, whether big or small.

From this environment, the individual tales that have been presented stand on their own, not only as the coming of age of a little boy, but as a brief ambitious detail of small-town living, with each story a collective part of the whole. At the same moment, the white space left between the words and thoughts conveys very little except emptiness best left unspoken. Unfortunately (or fortunately), we are not given the full privilege of refereeing one's own life. Even so, every person confronts things that undercut and erode our idea of the beauty and benevolence of human nature. We also engage things that embrace and enhance it. The mill village was the latter: the voice of reason, and never peripheral. I always felt part of the imaginative whole. Fortunately, coming of age, I didn't have to worry about the anxiety of privilege. The first time we moved into a plant manager's house, the living room was as big as most of the previous ten homes I had lived in. I never remember having a bank account with a comma in it until I was out of college for four or five years.

We spend most of our lives trying to rebrand ourselves to look better and appeal to the eyes of other people because the world—in its increasing technology and diminishing wisdom—has become an expansive open stage in a play that has been cautiously written by man and terribly cast by fate. After 240 years as a republic called the United States of America, we have finally reached a point where everyone is concerned about their rights, but fewer and fewer people are worried about their neighbors, responsibilities toward others, and where we are headed. We seem to be walking into deeper shadows, unguided by points of light. It's hard to hold reality in one's head because we deny the imagination a chance to wander down long streets in search of who we really are. It wasn't that way in the salad days of the 1950s and '60s. As kids, we learned we could mess up and still be liked and loved, giving us a strong sense of self and the courage to take risks for rewards. Creativity has a way of prefiguring the value of open possibility, because living is simply an existential reminder of the real world in which we become a layered portrait anchored somewhere in mental space between the obvious and the obscure. Existence is neither here nor there; we are simply standing in its midst, trying to decide what to do next.

Integrity is a rare morsel of truth and authenticity. Yesterday's parents were more concerned about character, morality, and personal values than a good portrait painter was about accuracy of shading, contrast, and color. Without such anchoring ballast, we drift off into a stratospheric layer of pure caprice and whimsy. Now don't get me wrong. We were not the most sophisticated connoisseurs of high culture or haute cuisine in our little hamlets, because there was the street level accounting of the real world, and of course simple Southern fried fame. Affluence, elegance, and sophistication had never been a big part of our life. I didn't know the difference between sobriquet and aperitif and couldn't spell either one. Yet we were far from country bumpkins. Our opinion of a fine wine was one that was not homemade, was packaged in a pretty bottle, cost less than ten dollars, wouldn't gag you when you drank it, and didn't strip the enamel off your teeth.

Every story, just like every day, eventually comes to an end, and so it is with mine. However, as a good, honest small-town boy and a facile storyteller, I can assure you with full confidence that every single thing I have written in these pages is true, except for the parts that aren't. It was a privilege to carry forth the spirit of Southern Reality as a simple organic creature of the commonplace, a slave to the real world in mosaic, and a captive of the mind. Over all these years, I was never once accused of conspicuous consumption, and there are few experiences noted that never happened. They can easily be verified in my imagination. In all honesty, I can't complain, because I have traveled a long way and met some of the most powerful, interesting, and odd people that our Homo species has to offer. I doubt my fluency in thinking has as deep a source as Wikipedia, but sometimes even the real gives the feel of make-believe. Maybe, if I haven't entertained or changed your mind, I broadened or deepened it a little more with a smile.

I'm not sure our ordinary existence has been adequately studied with enough seriousness or refined in our many years of inaccurate curation. In life's ambience, truth is the only antidote for delusion, and it is easy to find without bloodhounds. In contrast to today, we would have been completely alone, far out in left field, if we had thought "the truth, the whole truth, and nothing but the truth" were three different things. Honesty has become extremely valuable because it's in such short supply. Waiting patiently in our conscience, integrity has a way of interacting seamlessly as a force multiplier. If I could only learn how to cultivate it's essence in a distilled pill form, I would make a fortune, and it would be a much better world. No writer's slight-of-hand or worldly words will ever suffice or replace the truth.

As a scrutinized and tested kid, I knew that waiting out there somewhere was a lifetime of obstacles, challenges, opportunities, and all the exciting, unexplored worlds they bring along. I kept patiently waiting in line to be invited to life's grand cotillion, but while lingering in the queue, I discovered the secret to success was avoiding the shadows and pitch-darkness hiding in the sunshine. Life is perpetually incomplete, and our challenge is to keep trying to fill the gaps. Boys and girls— in their little worlds of hopes, desires, and curiosity—are always on an excursion between boredom and exploration, weighing their demons and longings. It was the mill village way.

Of course, each day is relative to the person, parsed in degrees and tailored to personal interests in their own universe. My job was to untangle mine and define it. I finally decided that the human condition in our town, in all its manifestations, was simply an artifact of living out each moment. What so encouraged one as a kid was believing the best days of our life were still ahead. Of course, along our extensive journey, we recreated ourselves time and again. In that effort, one's self-acceptance should be high and personal standards even higher. The real world is always longitudinal, offering cheap and unwholesome calories, so we must be careful what we eat at its buffet. If we are not honest and open-minded, it's easy to get caught up in the echo-chamber of personal interest. Actuality rarely appears in exaggerated form, but we have a human tendency to use truth alternatives as our thumb on the scale to make the weight come out where we want it to be.

The penultimate question for everyone, regardless of where we live, is "Do we have a sense of purpose?" That's our ultimate challenge and quest, mine and yours: finding out what it is and doing something about it. The mill village was the perfect setting for me and my life's play. All the props were there, as well as the actors, characters, costumes, directors, challenges, and drama. All that was needed was the script, and we each could write our own.

Whether we want to or not, we eventually become the author of our biography and the actuality that comes along with it. All writers and thinkers, in their pensive reflections, strip-mine their families and the past for insightful material. It may have a simple or complex plot, but regardless it's still our personal story. We get a daily rehearsal and all the rewrites we want. The curtain goes up and the play is performed, then the curtain falls until the next act. We are in the proscenium for only a limited amount of time, then the end, when the final words of dialogue are read. It's our tale and we become the author and main character. We also have to write the script and be on stage every moment before a live audience. So we become very good at protecting self-interest by self-editing. The play is your legacy, all written in your name, so you don't want to screw it up. Regardless of background, we are usually self-educated in one way or another, and end up with holes in our curriculum vitae. Notwithstanding our personal situation in life, each day just gets "curiouser and curiouser," as Alice said.

Now I don't want to give the wrong impression about mill villages.

Everyone in town wasn't good-looking, perfect, nor had air-brushed complexions, genius IQs, sartorial splendor, or clean thoughts, but they weren't bad either. They were normal, friendly, honest, and supportive, with casseroles passed around from home to home as the need arose. I grew up in that mise-en-scene, with an open mind and sense of humor connected to an intellectual curiosity and weighed by blue-collar microgravity. As a teenaged extrovert in training, I enjoyed participating in plays, and those that saw me perform and heard me sing were very encouraging. People would say, "Just stick with performing on stage and you will have a great future—working in the mill." I did. Just saying! Our future becomes an open history book without a cover, nothing to confine us except ourselves.

During my over sixty years as a Problem Doctor engaged in numerous diverse venues—related to various businesses, mill villages, large cities, and civic affairs—I had to saddle up many a lightning bolt and ride off into the future, not always understanding where I was going but knowing I couldn't let go 'til it landed. After each new management challenge, you wait in high anticipation for life to come up with your next personal draft and once again redefine who you are. Many experiences were just unrecorded footnotes on the pages of time, some offstage and others center spotlight. The mental adaptation was always hovering over the narrative, waiting for the written words, challenge, and new job description to appear and usually confound. I think the only thing plain and normal about it was me. At the end of the day, I guess I turned out to be just a simple common denominator.

In fact, I found that a creative mind is the only way to run away from home without leaving. We learned long ago in little manufacturing hamlets around the country that work provided the means to survive, but family and those we love give us the true purpose of living, its reasons and pleasures. Neither has someone made their mark each day until one has done something for someone else who will never be able to repay you.

I have never ceased to be amazed by young people. Maybe there is hope after all. In speaking to a high school class one day, I asked several students at random to give me one of the weirdest experiences they had ever had. A young girl said, "Last year my dad built us a house all by himself, way out in the edge of town, and we had to move in several weeks before it was

Mentoring is always about giving back to that which nurtured you.

completed. The electricity had not even been turned on. So we had no lights, TV, computer, Internet, and my cell phone was too far out for reception. Every afternoon, night, and weekend I had to spend a lot of time with my parents, my brother, and two sisters. We did a lot of interesting fun things we had never done together before. You know, after four weeks I was absolutely astonished. I discovered my family was filled with really wonderful people. I didn't realize how special and important to me they were. It was also amazing how much more homework I got done and how my grades improved. Sometimes I wish Dad had never turned the power on." This is truth, out of the mouth of babes.

Working parents that spend quality time with their children discover it is a lot more important to them than money, and they will also remember and value it much longer. This is one of the most significant lessons we will ever learn or teach others, regardless of where we live. Most of us have more time than money anyway, so it just plays into wise hands and the practical rhythm of life. It certainly did in textile villages. But I learned there are many things you can do to improve relationships that cost very little. For example: smiles, hugs, love, encouragement, friendliness, kind words, and offering to help are contagious and cost absolutely nothing. Although sometimes in friendships and families, love has to be constantly applied like Gorilla Glue to hold everything together. It's hard for the mind to exceed the eloquence of the heart. There are even times when the right words just won't reach far enough and only a hug will do.

Mahayley Lancaster frequently comes to mind. Like her, you can't always prove certain things exist, but you just know they do. Things like affection, respect, honor, integrity, authenticity, truth, compassion, and (fill in the blank) _______. Neither are the facts what you always see, or what people tell you they are. There are usually a few daydreams, some fairy dust, curtains to be parted, and curvilinear mirrors in the equation. The face of conventional wisdom bears plenty of accepted and meaningful truths that are hard to prove. Even so, life without some fantasy, humor, and imagination wouldn't be an interesting existence at all. The bottom line is that it is faith and trust that gets us through each day, bringing joy and promise as it affirms reality. I have sat in more cheap seats than I can count, but to my knowledge, none were subsidized—unless through prayer.

Driving down Fairfax's Oak Street one day, it dawned on me that I'm nothing special. Just a plain, simple, normal breed of the elderly white guy from a little mill village. Neither am I un-ordinary, just the common-variety male that has become a rapidly diminishing category of American humanity. A species that is reminded daily that he is responsible for all the problems, injustices, prejudices, wars, inequality, illegal immigration, crime, hatred, inordinately high CEO pay, political misfires, corruption, Internet hacking, high sugar in colas, exorbitant pharmaceutical prices for Viagra, high college tuition, global warming, fracking, and every one of our other worldly ills. After all that, I'm still not even in the elite 1 percent. Instead, without all the benefits, I'm just a commonplace Southern boy accused of ozone depletion, ocean pollution, fresh water diminishment, and climatic changes that are destroying the world. We humans practice life imperfectly and have an inherent predilection for discovering things that have great value, after they are gone.

Life is not as complicated as we try to make it sound. It's just the progressive journey of our experiences and decisions from birth to death. There are no exceptions, and through all of our existence only one man got a free pass, but it wasn't painless. If we thought worry would cure our sickness or increase one's life span, then we should worry more. If worry were to improve our job prospects or income, then we should worry more. If we thought worry would change life's disappointments to happiness, then we should worry more. But it doesn't. Life and happiness begin when you stop worrying and start caring and loving others. Your mind will always place you in the neighborhood where your heart wants to live, ready or not.

It's like the night I was alone in Cambridge, Massachusetts. I was a little lonely walking back to the dorm that particular evening when I passed this bar with a sign out front. It said, "Sorry, but we do not serve women. You must bring your own." Now that really made me smile and feel more comfortable and right at home, because that's exactly the way it was in the little town where I grew up—but we had no bars. In fact, it was a very safe hamlet where there was no place to go where you shouldn't be.

I have tried in these rambling thoughts to give you a few poor red-dirt country boy's experiences and philosophy and the best of the little towns that rubbed off on me. There are bits and pieces of these stories that have found their way into my everyday temperamental nature, helping mold and make me who I am. Yet there are so many more encounters not covered, not even scratching the surface: a catalogue of mill town intrigue, corporate challenges, and the numerous times being set adrift in a never-never land of problems to solve. Even trials and errors that became metaphorical in reach. I look in my rearview mirror as a Problem Doctor and remember how many of the situations I had to tackle that were like trying to rake leaves in a hurricane. Yet true self-knowledge is hard to come by, because we are usually too close to the subject to have an objective view. I truly enjoy writing and expressing myself. I have tried to avoid lengthy recursive sentences, winding themselves around a thought until it is strangled or lost in the moment. I guess by nature an author, each in his/her own way, tends to unravel their personal identity for all to see.

It is not easy to dance in a storm, especially if you don't know all the steps. Thomas Freidman of the *New York Times* notes that today's technology is becoming obsolete every five to seven years. It is also quickly distinguishing and extinguishing everything we are using and have used as hallmarks and road signs to guide the way on our journey. That means life's benchmarks will be different about three or four times before we reach full adulthood and will continue from there. This includes not only education, science, community, and career, but character, morals, authenticity, and faith for individuals, families, and those institutions that determine society's measurable parameters. The world in its benevolence tries to enlist the heart as well as the mind, but it's a challenge, because there is always increasing competition.

Experiences are available for the purpose of learning, and mistakes seem to come along for the ride. Then there are some days that just bring major angst and leave it at our door. It's too late to ask Mayhayley for advice, because she's gone . . . I think. At the same time, often the unexpected detours we take are where we find the best music, and if we are fortunate, even some of the words to go along with it. I did. In fact, it became quite clear to me that God does not reside far away in Heaven. I think he lives close by: in our hearts. Victor Hugo said, "Most of us are not loved for ourselves, but in spite of ourselves." I think he was right! Man with his creative genius can do miraculous things, but God will always be the greatest miracle worker of all because only he can make saints out of sinners.

If aliens from another world were to land on Earth tomorrow, somewhere in North America, they would encounter a great surprise. They would think we had been bountifully blessed compared to the rest of the world and the barren universe they had been able to observe. We have so many things to enjoy that we have come to take for granted. Things like an unbelievably ultra-thin atmosphere, clean air to breathe. Our life sustaining atmosphere is only about four miles thick, and the Earth is 7,926 miles in diameter at the equator. Visualize that for a minute. Have you ever realized how thin "life" really is? You can call it a miracle or not. I've already decided. We have fresh water to drink, food to eat, a comfortable place to live, flowers to smell, trees, mountains and oceans to enjoy, freedom, love, family, friends, resources to embrace, and most of it is gratis. How spoiled and privileged we free humans have become, because the world as a whole has not been that fortunate. Looking back, I may have been rich and didn't realize it, because as a little boy all I ever wanted was vanilla ice cream. Yet I never met a single impoverished or hungry soul whose top priority was ice cream.

Somewhere I once read that at the end of writing a book, you regret the things you didn't say, not the things you did. By that logic I feel content, although a lot was left unspoken in the white spaces. The little unincorporated town of Fairfax that I called home, and hundreds of other similar hamlets, doesn't have to be canonized. They are only a special memory I keep trying to hold in my head. I'm sorry they didn't fit on Norman Rockwell's artistic easel; they should have. I came to even visualize along the way that the most compelling love affair could be at the DNA level in the elusive attracting chemistry between a small boy and a little town. Yet, in all my years, I never remember a single day when reality was subtle. In fact, life seemed to always be under siege—and still does. Even back in the 1950s, college was writ large for mill village kids like me. Now, at this final juncture, all that remains is the happy wisdom of sad remembrances, which includes the many thoughts I wish I could unthink and deeds I wish I could undo. Honesty works well at so many levels, and there is no advantage to try to jump the queue. Growing up a fortunate but fortuneless kid, I was taught that love and compassion for others were truly indescribable gifts that even the poor and destitute can give away.

In retrospect, the clarity of one's lens is essential to what we see. Over the years, the Greater Chattahoochee Valley became known for many things, other than its friendly, warm, hospitable, and industrious people: home of the Creek Indians, before the white man came; Fort Tyler and the last fort battle of the Civil War; the West Point companies establishing a national textile manufacturing center; Cusseta's Pat Garrett, who relentlessly tracked down Billy the Kid; Lafayette's world-champion boxer Joe Louis; Lanett, family home of Fob James Jr., governor of Alabama; Langdale's Rod Bramblett, voice of Auburn Tiger Sports; Cam Lanier III, William Scott III, and their management teams, establishing an incubator environment, birthing more new national entrepreneurial companies than perhaps any similar sized city in America; the home of Batson Cook Company, a national construction giant; five hundred miles of shore line on Lake West Point to camp, fish, hunt, canoe, and explore; and much, much more.

Point University, Administration Building, in 2016, in the previous West Point (Pepperell) Stevens, Corporate Office in West Point, Georgia.

The historic West Point Manufacturing Company's facilities are now gone, yet the broader community hierarchy didn't despair. Civic, city, county, and state leadership stepped up to the plate and hit the ball out of the park. Almost ten thousand textile and related jobs had been lost, but perhaps more have since been added. In 2006, KIA built a huge automotive assembly plant on a 2,200 acre site in West Point, bringing fifteen or more support facilities to the area along with thousands of jobs. Point University moved (ironically like the A&WP Railroad) from East Point to West Point in 2012, with educators and over two thousand students. Perhaps it's fate that the Point University administration building is the old West Point Manufacturing Company corporate office. Other smaller non-automotive manufacturing facilities have joined the parade to the area. Interestingly, the largest solar energy facility in Alabama was built in Chambers County in 2016–2018. George H. Lanier Memorial Hospital and Nursing Home merged with East Alabama Medical Center-Opelika, providing a strong foundation for healthcare in the area.

Added university and residential apartments in the vicinity, along with a boomlet in new restaurants like Pokey's, Johnny's, Ash, and Coach's, has brought life back to a wonderful, easygoing mill-village environment. We have also gravitated to the higher echelons of sophisticated Southern society with our own winery—River's Bend Winery and Vineyard—and the "Chattabrewchee," our own Southern brewery. What more could we ask for?

One might concede that the intriguing and heartening thing about this dramatic transformation is that, against all odds, the leadership initiating these progressive changes came from men and women that grew up in those small villages of Riverview, Langdale, Fairfax, Shawmut, Lanett, Huguley, West Point, and surrounding communities. Survival requires curative effort and lucky coincidences to change fate's direction. In this case it was insight, planning, creative thinking, and strong initiative on the part of a lot of good people. So today there is promise for tomorrow. Life is always seamless from beginning to end, but sometimes it needs the heartfelt affection of people to hold everything together. Every day I wondered, "Where have all the Joe DiMaggios and Stan Musials gone?" Now we know. They

Beautiful downtown West Point in 2018.

haven't gone; they are still here. Our little enclaves in the Chattahoochee Valley ultimately defined us, as they became acutely personal and now belong to our fading memory.

History has proven there is no second act in life, as we only get one ride on the merry-go-round. The conscience has a difficult time in the real world and barely produces enough antibodies to fight off the germs of politics and alternative reality. So it's a blessing to look back and recall a few stories that shaped us during a time when the unexpected and unexplainable resided in territory beyond reason. At the same moment, words, like electrical currents, let us transmit our recollections, ideas, opinions, and persuasions. They become an excursion into cerebral debate, in search of sincere understanding. Growing up, I always wanted to go to Auburn University and Harvard Business School because they were the best in the world, not fully realizing it was completely out of reach for challenged mill-village kids with my background. Such a dream was also financial insanity. Then one day, fate and a benevolent Company smiled down and paid my way to both.

Now, glancing back, the universe of human experience is wide and deep. I'm pretty sure I wasn't the worst manager in the Company, because I never had to talk a single person down off the ledge. Neither was I born into privilege. Yet when I hear the word Fairfax, it's a pleasant sound, like hearing my own name. I guess I always had a valedictory crush on my hometown and the people. After eighty-plus years, millions of miles, and uncountable experiences, I finally figured out that everyone else in the world is different, just like me. As a kid and adult, I was never subdued by wild tendencies. So maybe in a final tribute of generosity, when my season comes to a close, the city fathers will let my ashes be scattered somewhere inside the city limits.

At the end of each day, it's hard to redact the ordinariness in our lives, because that's what makes us human. Each moment just seems to be a suspended enigma like the mythical Phoenix, born again from the ashes, waiting to rise up and change into something new and exciting. Now, I'm not certain I have adequately explained exactly how I became myself, but I have tried. "I guess it's finally time to send in the clowns! Wait, don't bother. I think they're already here!"

Grandchildren at 2008 Christmas Party at Callaway Gardens, Pine Mountain, Georgia: from left, Annie, Molly, Hannah, Georgia, Sarah Beth, Claire, Gerald, front—William and Bruce III.

The Last Mill Village

Memory copiously returns, generously cached in a treasure trove
Of ruminations, augmented in a fresh landscape comfortably and
Cognitively familiar. I'm always in that place, and that place will
Always be in me. In homage I treasure childhood remembrances,
While a solemn melancholy arrives unbidden in the irretrievable

Chattahoochee Valley. Without consultation, and conventional
Indelicacy, mills were finally closed, scavenged for their material
Substance after a whistle blew its last call. Houses stand vacant
In disrepair. The jobs have now departed to who knows where.
Days long, clouds dark, hanging, foreboding, pregnant, lethargic.

We silently awaited an equitable undersong of rescue; it held back
And never appeared. Life became too much tyranny of the urgent.
In that abode I was many people. Now I'm not certain any of them
Were really me. There will never be a right time to turn one's back
And walk away, unless now. It was as a surreal voice in articulate

Thinking, from a dormant memory pool, telling that villages never
Wanted to be known for not being knowable. There were thoughts
Of blind certainty, mirroring the lost imaginings of yesterday in rest.
Introspection and veracity were eternally cautious, being right with
One's soul, while wisdom ignores people, who also neglect wisdom.

A decision was made, sucking all oxygen and spontaneity from life.

It was like a giant vacuum, starting in corner of the heart, stomach.
It moved to upper regions of confidence, reality, doubt of the tired
And depressed mind. In retrospect, a long day stretching into night.
On fateful morning, the last whistle blew in our little mill villages.

Hearts were heavy, too weary to say goodbye, too sad even to cry.
The mills were our reason for living, sustenance and promise of life.
Finally came the pain, heartbreak, disappointment heavy with strife.
But this time they gave us a huge mountain, dangerous and unkind,
Because this time they gave us a mountain, too high for one to climb.

— GBA

Acknowledgments

Writing is a pleasurable journey into the realm of words and expressions, explaining the real and fictive experiences of the mind. I'm grateful to those contributing to this effort, enabling me to participate. I especially want to thank Dr. Jim Buford—a teacher, experienced author, and good friend—for his guidance. Without Jim, this book wouldn't have been possible. Editing is removing excess words and meaningless thoughts, enabling it to be both readable and make sense. George Littleton is an editing wizard, keeping me on the straight and narrow. My gratitude for George's expertise, creative focus, and friendship.

I want to thank Fairfax and its many wonderful people, where it all began, in the Chattahoochee Valley and the mill villages that birthed me. Special thanks to New York City, for its legacy of life, literature, creativity, and culture that stimulated my thinking. The *New York Times*, the *New York Review of Books*, *The New Yorker*, and their plethora of inspiring writers as well. Neither would these stories exist without the many interesting people noted in the book, real and unimaginable. Thank you to the gracious family members, friends, and mentors that helped smooth off the rough edges, bend and mold a little boy into a man, especially Grady Webb Jr., Clarence "Kjor" Kjorlein, and Bill Addison, who helped educate me. I am grateful to my exceptional children—Andy, Suzanne and Benjy—and grandchildren—Hannah, Molly, Annie, Georgia, Sarah Beth, Bruce, William, great-grandson Micah, and those to come—for listening to my endless tales, songs, dances, and attempts at being humorous over the years. I'm always trying to make them laugh, or at least smile.

Most important of all, thanks to my patient and sustaining wife Claire, who put up with me, my peripatetic life as a Problem Doctor, living in seventeen homes, and as a volunteer giving back to that which nurtured us over the years. The time expended on writing this book and four others drove her up the wall. Hopefully my family and others will now have a better understanding of me and the valiant little mill villages like the one I grew up in, which no longer exist. They are the disappearing places in the South and across America where the sky was the limit and you could copyright your life in Southern Reality.

I would also like to thank the H. Grady Bradshaw Library, Cobb Memorial Archives, and Robin Brown, archivist, for assistance and many of the photos used. A special thanks to my grandson Bruce Andrews for all his computer expertise.

Last, but certainly not least, I want to thank God for explaining everything to me, for letting me in on life's secrets, and for permitting me to be born in America. And, most of all, for always being there when I needed him, which was every day.

About the Author

Gerald Bruce Andrews Sr. was born in Fairfax, a small unincorporated mill village now part of Valley, Alabama. He has lived in twenty-five different places, started to kindergarten and grammar school a year early, then was double-promoted, skipping a grade. He graduated from Valley High School in 1954, entering Auburn University's College of Engineering when he was 16. When in high school and college, he worked 40+ hours a week in the local textile mill for six years, while commuting to school 78 miles round trip five days a week. He received a two year diploma in Textile Manufacturing from Auburn University (1954–1957); BS degree (TM) from Auburn University, College of Engineering (1954–1959), with enough hours today for a minor in Industrial Engineering. He was a member of PHI PSI and PI SIGMA EPISLON, honorary and service fraternities. He completed a two year business course from Alexander Hamilton Institute (1968–1969); graduated from Harvard Business School AMP (1978–1979); and completed numerous post-graduate courses from various Universities in the U.S. In recognition of his service to the International Textile Community, in 1998 he became a Senior Fellow of The Textile Institute in Manchester, England.

Gerald was continuously employed 39 years (1954–1992) by the continuum of West Point Companies—West Point Manufacturing Company; West Point Pepperell, Inc; and West Point (Pepperell) Stevens, Inc.—in more than thirty different management positions. Most of this time is best described as being a Problem Doctor, responsible for helping resolve major company management problems and challenges. The West Point Companies grew to become the largest (NYSE), most diversified, publicly owned textile corporation in North America, with more than 40 plant/facility locations,

42,000 employees and Retail Outlet Stores in 23 states. For two years he was Chairman of the Corporation Political Action Committee. He retired from West Point in June 1992, while serving as Corporate Executive Vice-President, Merchandising, in New York City.

Later in 1992, he became President and COO, and then President and CEO, of Johnston Industries, Inc, with corporate offices in NYC, which he relocated to Columbus, Georgia. He was with Johnston Industries five years before retiring a second time. To scratch a long-time itch, he taught for two years as executive-in-residence and visiting professor at his alma mater, Auburn University. The course that he wrote—*Creative Analysis*—taught senior, master's, and PhD students how to be creative, innovative and inventive. At the time, no similar course was taught at any university in the U.S. He later helped establish and became CEO and chairman of the board of Accelegrow Technologies—an international agri-science company—producing a patented product for increasing yield of food crops, plants, trees and bio-fuels, with marketing programs in North America, South America, Europe and Africa.

During his kaleidoscopic 50-year career, he held more than twenty-six hourly blue-collar jobs and thirty-four management positions, not including many executive civic responsibilities outside the corporate hierarchy. He has received more than eighty-five honors, awards and special recognitions for management, leadership, creativity and extensive civic involvement. Just a few of these recognitions include distinctive honors and special citations by four State Governors, the Alabama House of Representatives and Georgia Senate. In addition, he was made an honorary Alabama Colonel by the governor for his many contributions to the state. In 1998, by special invitation, he was asked to speak to a National Science Foundation symposium on "Creative Cooperation between Industry and Government." He has been listed in five different "Who's Who" in America and the world.

While he was president and CEO of Johnston Industries, it was selected the industry company of the year in America (TW) (1994), and in 1994 the Opp & Micolas Division was chosen the Model Mill in America, an example for others to emulate. The next year he was selected the Industry Executive Leader of the Year in America (TW), and the following year (1996)

Johnston Industries was recognized as the Most Innovative Company in the Textile Industry (ATI).

In 1979 he was selected the Boy Scout Council President of the Year in Georgia, and Boy Scout Council President of the Year in the Southeastern United States, and the Boy Scout Council President of the Year in America, for leading his Council to #1 out of 334 councils in the U.S. and its territories. He has also received the second highest volunteer honor in Scouting, the Silver Beaver Award.

He has served in many civic leadership capacities, including as chairman of the board of Point University (ACC), retiring after 18 years as the first honorary board trustee-emeritus. He was also graduation speaker at Point University (ACC). He was chairman of the board of George H. Lanier Memorial Hospital and Nursing Home; president of the Chattahoochee Valley Hospital Society and founding chairman of the Lanier Health Services Foundation; He was a founding trustee and board member establishing Springwood School (K–12, college preparatory) in 1968, and came back as co-chairman in a major capital campaign to serve as trustee a second time and still serves on the Legacy Board. He was chairman of Mid-Town Realty (2006–2014), and president/owner of 508 apartments (1998–2008). He was on the board of American Red Cross and a member of its Five-Gallon Club, vice president of the Chambers County Mental Health Association, and a founding member of the Fort Tyler Association. He was chairman of the committee to develop and build new a Fairfax community center and basketball court. In 1992 he was selected as Citizen of the Year by the Greater Chattahoochee Valley Chamber of Commerce for his extensive leadership in healthcare and the greater community.

In 1993 he was selected Auburn University's Outstanding Alumnus, and in 1997 he was chosen as its Distinguished Engineer. He has been a Dunston Circle Scholar and a member of the Eagle, Samford, George Petrie, and Foy (Cater Circle) societies, and in 2009 he was an Auburn Golden Eagle. In 1995, he served as co-chairman of Auburn University, Alumni Engineering Committee, to help develop a long range plan for College of Engineering to meet needs of 21St Century. In 1994 he was recognized with the Chandler Award of Excellence for corporate management and leadership, and 2014 he was chosen Distinguished Citizen of the Year. He is or has been a member of Harvard Business School Association, Harvard Alumni Association, Harvard Club of Atlanta, and Harvard Club of New York City. He has also served on the board of the National Textile Center. In the 1980s, as president of West Point Pepperell Stores Division, he was one of the industry leaders who helped build, develop, and establish retail factory store outlet centers in 23 states across the U.S. Mayors have given him the "Keys" to six cities.

He is given credit for helping develop and implement the electronic vendor marking system used today on all home furnishings, apparel and soft goods sold in the U.S. This is one of several reasons why in 1995 he was selected as a member of the Alabama Engineering Hall of Fame. He serves or has served on various boards of five colleges and universities and eight corporations. In 1968 he was selected the Little League Coach of the Year in Alabama for leading the Opelika All-Stars to the State Baseball Championship. He was chosen president of the West Point Rotary Club, president-elect of West Point Lions Club, and president of Pepperell School PTA. He was twice selected Junior Achievement Advisor of the Year of a National Award Company. For years he was a featured speaker at the Auburn University MBA program, Point University, and many other universities, business, and civic enterprises. He is also a member of the Alabama Writer's Forum.

Gerald has been a leader in numerous industry organizations, including as president of the Alabama Textile Manufacturing Association, as chairman and director of the Alabama Textile Education Foundation, and as a director of the executive committee of the American Textile Manufacturers Institute (ATMI), representing the American textile industry. He has served as president of the Southern Association of Textile Industrial Engineers. He is a certified manufacturing engineer in manufacturing systems (1975). In 1997, while serving as chairman of the environmental committee, for ATMI, he was asked to accept the only award ever given by the federal government, specifically the Environmental Protection Agency (EPA), to the industry for environmental improvements. He was a senior member of the American Institute of Industrial Engineers. He was selected as speaker for the home furnishings industry in America for a special program on CBS's *Today Show*.

He has served on more than thirty civic and nonprofit boards.

Gerald is an experienced family genealogist and a member of the Jamestowne Society. In various churches he has attended, he has been active as elder, trustee, chairman of the board, choir and Sunday school teacher.

He and his wife and favorite cheerleader, Claire, have been married 62 years; they have three children and seven grandchildren—most are Auburn graduates, two are physicians. Having lived and worked all across the U.S., they now live in West Point, Georgia, in their 17th home. He has also written a second book entitled *The Problem Doctor,* reflecting many years of experience in creative problem solving based on an original 10-Step Creative Analysis Process (CAP) that he innovated and taught at Auburn University.